Over $30 billion a year!

How much does alcohol abuse cost the United States each year? Who bears the cost? How is it measured? These are some of the questions examined in this book, the first in-depth investigation of the economic cost of alcohol abuse and alcoholism. It is based on a study sponsored by the National Institute on Alcohol Abuse and Alcoholism which the authors directed.

The authors identify six major sources of economic cost and systematically analyze each: reduced productivity, medical and health services, motor vehicle accidents, fire, crime, and the social responses to alcohol abuse — the social welfare system, alcohol treatment programs, highway safety and fire protection expenditures, and the criminal justice system. In evaluating the economic cost of alcohol abuse and alcoholism, the authors cite numerous studies.

The authors' estimate of the economic cost of alcohol abuse indicates the areas of appropriate policy concern, but, as they emphasize, further research is needed to determine the specific direction of sound social policy. For example, they recommend research into the

abuse and cer-
reduce driving
xtent to which
iolent crime.

most significant
try today. The
ost of Alcohol
sights into the
the elimination
f programs de-
ntrol, and treat-

ofessor of Eco-
blic Health at

enior Associate

THE ECONOMIC COST
OF ALCOHOL ABUSE

THE ECONOMIC COST
OF ALCOHOL ABUSE,

Ralph E. Berry, Jr.
James P. Boland

THE FREE PRESS
A Division of Macmillan Publishing Co., Inc.

NEW YORK

Collier Macmillan Publishers

LONDON

The Free Press
A Division of Macmillan Publishing Co., Inc.
866 Third Avenue, New York, N.Y. 10022

Collier Macmillan Canada, Ltd.

Library of Congress Catalog Card Number: 76–19642

Printed in the United States of America

printing number

1 2 3 4 5 6 7 8 9 10

Library of Congress Cataloging in Publication Data

Berry, Ralph E
   The economic cost of alcohol abuse.

   Includes bibliographical references and index.
   1. Liquor problem--Economic aspects--United States.
I. Boland, James P., joint author. II. Title.
HV5105.B47   362.2'92   76-19642
ISBN 0-02-903080-3

CONTENTS

LIST OF TABLES

PREFACE

This book is based on a study undertaken to determine the economic cost of alcohol abuse and alcoholism in the United States. That study was sponsored by the National Institute on Alcohol Abuse and Alcoholism (NIAAA) in May 1973, and was directed by the authors. The original study generated a first approximation of the economic cost of alcohol abuse in 1971 of some $25 billion. This first approximation was included in the Secretary of Health, Education, and Welfare's Second Special Report to Congress on Alcohol and Health in June 1974. In the interim, the authors have had the time and the opportunity to rethink many of the problems, reflect further on several issues, and refine the analysis. The result, we think, is a better approximation of the economic cost of alcohol abuse.

Economics is an appropriate perspective from which to assess the problem of alcohol abuse, but it is not the only relevant one. The economic cost of alcohol abuse is but a part, albeit a significant part, of the total social cost. This book was written in large part because the authors felt that the whole field of alcoholism research would benefit from the insight provided by an economic analysis of the problem. In fact, we expect that many more noneconomists than economists will read this book. As a consequence, we have tried to organize and present the material in such a way that it will be intelligible to anyone interested in the problem. Still, it is cast in the framework of economic analysis; hence, we have added, as a postscript to chapter 1, a brief review of economic concepts that someone unfamiliar with economics and its jargon may find useful. It can be skipped, however, with no loss of continuity.

This study involved significant efforts on the part of many, and the authors owe a debt of gratitude to all. Foremost were those who contributed significantly to the original research effort—Donald Hayler, Joan Laxson, Claudia Sanders, and Margery Sillman. The staff of NIAAA provided consistent aid and made our task easier; John Deering, David Promisel, Nathan Rosenberg, and Irving Wolf were particularly helpful throughout the project.

We owe a special debt to the Social Research Group of the School of Public Health, University of California at Berkeley, for providing us with necessary unpublished data, and especially to Robin Room, who was a constant source of help. In addition, several persons in the alcoholism field contributed in a variety of ways, not the least of which was in tolerating the inquiries of relative novices. There were more than could possibly be thanked individually, but we would be remiss if we did not thank Mark Keller, James Richards, and Richard Zylman. We should thank collectively the twenty-nine persons in the alcohol treatment field who participated in a special survey designed to provide us with insight relative to the utilization of health services by alcoholics, along with Laurel Hayler, who assisted in conducting that survey.

We also benefited considerably from the extensive review and helpful suggestions of several colleagues, including Paul Feldstein, Rashi Fein, Carl Schramm, and Florence Wilson.

Special thanks are extended to Mary Louise Fisher, who labored long and well over several drafts of the original report and the final manuscript. Sheila Salamone filled that inevitable last-minute gap in completing the final manuscript.

Finally, to an even greater extent than usual, the authors owe a special debt to their families, who allowed them the inordinate luxury of time necessary to complete the task.

ACKNOWLEDGMENT

The work upon which this publication is based was performed in part pursuant to Contract No. HSM 42-73-114 with the National Institute on Alcohol Abuse and Alcoholism, Health Services and Mental Health Administration, Department of Health, Education, and Welfare.

CHAPTER ONE

INTRODUCTION

THE COSTS OF ALCOHOL ABUSE

A general awareness has long existed in our society that the problem of alcohol abuse is both pervasive and significant. In fact, alcohol abuse is one of the most important public health problems facing our nation at the present time. Nearly everyone could recall an adverse social or personal event that could be linked to alcohol abuse. Such unpleasant or unwanted events as broken families, accidents, acts of violence, mental anguish, physical suffering, work not done, and personal degradation are representative of the negative implications of alcoholism and alcohol abuse. This book is intended to look at the phenomenon of alcohol abuse from an economic perspective, and is specifically concerned with those adverse social consequences that are manifested in such a form that they lend themselves to being quantified. As such, it is offered in part as an indication of the relative scope and magnitude of the problem of alcohol abuse in our society.

Until rather recently, our society's general attitudes and attendant policy toward alcoholism were dominated by the view that alcoholism reflected an individual moral weakness or failing. Although many still subscribe to this view, alcoholism has increasingly come to be viewed within our society as a disease. Social policy has evolved to the point where Congress created the National Institute on Alcohol Abuse and Alcoholism (NIAAA) in 1970 with the responsibility of formulating and recommending national policy and goals regarding the prevention, control, and treatment of alcohol abuse and alcoholism.

During the first few years of its existence, as the NIAAA engaged in program development designed to achieve its specific objectives, it perceived a need for a reliable estimate of the economic costs of alcohol abuse. The NIAAA had estimated the annual cost of alcoholism to the United States in 1971 at $15 billion; other estimates ranged as high as $75 billion. Clearly, the range of existing estimates of the cost of alcohol abuse and alcoholism was too wide to be operationally useful. And the agency perceived that information as pertinent to its area of responsibility. In a benefit/cost context, the elimination of specific economic costs of alcoholism would clearly be among the primary potential benefits of programs designed for the prevention, control, and treatment of alcohol abuse and alcoholism.

In May 1973, the NIAAA sponsored a study to determine the economic cost of alcohol abuse and alcoholism in the United States. The authors directed this study, and this book is essentially based on it.

Conceptually, the problem of determining the cost of alcohol abuse and alcoholism is straightforward. First, a reliable estimate of the number of individuals who are alcoholics or alcohol abusers must be determined. Second, the costs of alcohol abuse need to be identified. To what extent does a person's affliction affect his own health and well-being? What effects does his affliction have upon other members of society? Finally, there is the issue of quantifying and measuring the costs of alcoholism and alcohol abuse. What is the cost to the problem drinker of his affliction? What is the cost to others of the effects imposed upon them by the problem drinker?

THE AGGREGATION OF SOCIAL AND ECONOMIC EVENTS

Although the problem of determining the cost of alcohol abuse is conceptually straightforward, it is empirically very difficult. Suppose that research into alcohol, alcohol consumption, and the behavior of alcohol abusers could conclusively establish that alcohol consumption was a causal factor in a certain number or proportion of unwanted social and personal events. Would it then be possible to add up these events and thereby obtain a total measure of alcohol's adverse social consequences? Given the current state of the art of social accounting, the answer is clearly no. There is no general unit of account to which such diverse social consequences as, say, illness induced or intensified by alcohol, family anguish occasioned by an alcoholic parent, days of work missed by an alcohol-troubled worker, and alcohol-induced suicide can be reduced.

Many of the adverse social consequences of alcohol, however, have specific economic consequences which prompts a second question. Is it possible to aggregate the adverse economic effects that may be related to alcohol and thereby derive a more limited but socially significant measure of the economic consequences of alcohol abuse and alcoholism? With reservations, the answer to this second question is yes.

A completely general economic approach to the analysis of social behavior such as the consumption of alcohol would involve the identification and measurement of the economic benefits and costs of such behavior. Our concern here is with the latter. The economic costs of alcohol include the costs of producing the alcohol in the first place, plus the additional costs borne by society as a result of alcohol abuse and alcoholism. It is the existence of these additional or *external* costs that distinguishes alcohol from most other consumer goods. These external costs, not considered in the private calculations of the individual consumer, make alcohol a legitimate concern of society. Identifying and measuring these costs is the purpose of this volume.

It is important to identify as many costs as possible. Often it is somewhat easier to identify particular costs than it is to esimate their specific magnitude. Thus, for example, an incomplete list of the costs associated with alcoholism and alcohol abuse would include: medical expenditures associated with alcohol-related illness, loss of productivity resulting from alcoholism, anxiety and mental anguish suffered by the individuals afflicted and their families and friends, anxiety sustained by the general public, and increased social expenditures for public safety and law enforcement.

This list is far from exhaustive, but it is intended to be representative not only of the costs of alcoholism and alcohol abuse but also of the difficulties inherent in seeking to quantify and measure these costs. Some costs can be quantified and estimated in a rather straightforward manner; medical expenditures for alcohol-related illness would seem to be in this category. Other costs have been estimated in traditionally acceptable ways. Loss of productivity, for example, is generally quantified in terms of discounted earnings, on the assumption that average wages are a reasonable approximation of the value of the lost output. Still other costs, however, virtually defy quantification. How does one quantify the anxiety of a family, for example? What is the cost to society of the nagging fear of highway disaster?

We can attempt to delineate the specific adverse economic consequences of alcohol abuse and alcoholism and to aggregate the effects in terms of economic costs. It must be remembered, however, that albeit the final result is socially significant, it is but an approximation of the social cost of alcohol.

Since the framework of economic analysis will be the frame of reference used throughout this book, it may be appropriate and useful to the noneconomist to digress briefly and consider the concern of economics and the concept of economic cost.

THE CONCERN OF ECONOMICS

Economics is the science of scarcity. The relevance of economics derives from the fact that while productive resources are exceedingly scarce, the wants of individuals and society are virtually unlimited.

Even the most affluent society is faced with the basic economic problem of how to allocate scarce resources. What goods and services should be produced? Which members of society should receive what goods and services? The choices involved are real and significant. A society can choose from among alternative allocations of resources, so that more of certain goods and services and less of other goods and services are produced. And a society can choose to alter the pattern of distribution among its members of the goods and services produced. These choices are relevant at virtually all levels of aggregation; the magnitude of the problem is different at different levels, but the nature of the problem is the same.

In any context, resources are limited. We have to be concerned with which and how many of the wants of individuals and society are satisfied as a result of a particular allocation of resources. In the last analysis, the objective is to use resources in such a way that we get the most out of them in terms of the satisfaction of wants.

Each time a particular good or service is produced, some of the scarce resources are used up. The production of more of one good implies that less of some other good can be produced, since the resources used for the one cannot also be available for the other. Hence, the cost of any good or service is appropriately described as the foregone opportunity of using the resources employed to produce something else—which is its *opportunity cost.*

Hence, when we ask what is the economic cost of alcohol abuse, we are asking what opportunity costs society incurs as a consequence of alcohol abuse and alcoholism. In fact, the economic cost of alcohol abuse may be manifested in either of two forms. On the one hand, society may actually lose some potential production as a result of alcohol abuse. On the other hand, it may be necessary to produce certain goods and services to cope with the consequences of alcohol abuse; and society must forego the alternative goods and services that could have been produced if alcohol abuse had not generated such consequences.

The task at hand is to identify those consequences of alcohol abuse that result in lost production and foregone alternatives. If we can identify and quantify the opportunity costs associated with the adverse consequences of alcohol abuse, we can estimate the economic cost of alcoholism and alcohol abuse. (For those who might prefer a somewhat lengthier digression on the concern of economics and the concept of economic cost, we have added a postscript at the end of this chapter.)

BENEFIT/COST ANALYSIS AND THE ECONOMICS OF ALCOHOL ABUSE

In a fundamental sense, the function of the market is to balance the value in consumption with the opportunity cost of scarce resources. (See postscript.) When the market is functioning well, this balance is struck, and the resulting equilibrium is characterized by economic efficiency (see note 7). When the market is not functioning well, for whatever reason, there is a need for an alternative mechanism to assess and affect the market outcome. Benefit/cost analysis is such a mechanism and can be applied to some advantage in assessing the net impact of alcohol and of social decisions respecting programs designed to affect alcoholism and alcohol abuse.

In the most elementary sense, there is a profound similarity between the private decision-making process and the public decision-making process. No consumer would choose to purchase a product that had a higher private cost than private benefit. Similarly, society should avoid those products whose social costs exceed their social benefits. Furthermore, since the consumer's resources (i.e., income) are limited, he usually consumes only those goods whose benefits exceed their costs by some margin. Society's resources are likewise scarce, so its choices ought to be made on the some basis. Certainly no program or project is worth doing if its benefits do not at least equal its costs, and, given limited resources, choices among programs and projects should favor those with the greatest excess of benefits over costs.

Conceptually, benefit/cost analysis is straightforward. Benefit/cost analysis in the social arena is analogous to the private decision-making process. The essential elements involved are a summation of the relevant benefits and costs and a comparison of those sums. In practice, however, the identification of all the pertinent benefits and costs is extremely difficult, and their exact quantification is often infeasible if not impossible. This should not be surprising, however, since the very need for social evaluation is usually a consequence of market malfunction, and the data necessary for exact quantification are often the very data that would be provided by the market if it were functioning appropriately.

It was stated at the outset that the purpose of this discussion was to outline a frame of reference in which to consider alcoholism and alcohol abuse. Is alcohol abuse an appropriate subject for economic analysis? The answer would seem to be a resounding yes. There is certainly ample evidence that alcohol abusers are not capable of accurately assessing their own private benefits and costs. But even apart from that consideration, there are unquestioned *externalities* (see postscript) associated with the excess consumption of alcohol in many contexts.

To the degree that it can be accurately measured, the economic cost of alcohol abuse and alcoholism will be a measure of scarcity value or opportunity cost. It is a meausre of the foregone output that results from the consequences of the problem. Foregone output of goods and services resulting from alcohol abuse and alcoholism can take two basic forms. First, people may be less productive because of alcohol abuse than they might otherwise be. That is, the economic value of their production is diminished (it may even fall to zero); the value of reduced production that can be attributed to alcoholism is foregone output and is thereby an economic cost. A second form of foregone output attributable to alcohol abuse and alcoholism can result from the diversion of resources into the production of goods and services required because of the various consequences of the problem. Thus, one might note the economic value of resources devoted to treating alcoholics; or the resources utilized to produce additional health care related to the exacerbating effects of alcoholism on other diseases; or the resources used to produce such goods and services, made necessary by the consequences of alcohol abuse and alcoholism, as augmented police and fire departments. In these cases, the notion of economic or opportunity cost is again relevant. For, as noted, the market value of these resources is an estimate of their economic value in alternative production opportunities. Because of alcoholism's consequences, this alternative production must be foregone; this foregone output is therefore an economic cost of alcohol abuse.

In concluding this discussion, two final remarks are in order. First, while the concept of economic cost can be stated and examples can be given of how it might be applied relative to alcoholism, economic analysis alone cannot determine the cost of alcoholism. Rather, it is what is known about the changes in behavior of persons directly and indirectly affected by alcohol and about the subsequent consequences of their altered behavior on actual resource utilization that will provide the basis for estimating the economic cost of alcohol abuse and alcoholism. Second, once estimates of economic cost have been made, it is important to stress what such dollar estimates mean and do not mean in a social context. Economic cost as outlined above would mean that as a result of alcoholism and alcohol abuse, the economic value of a society's output would be both smaller and different—and that is all. Economic cost is not a measure of human or social value. Money values do not measure human values; they only approximately measure scarcity or economic values.

THE BURDEN OF THE ECONOMIC COST OF ALCOHOL ABUSE AND ALCOHOLISM

Given that alcohol abuse and alcoholism are responsible for some magnitude of economic cost in the form of foregone output, it is reasonable to ask, "Who bears the cost?" In the aggregate, of course, society bears the cost. But society is made up of individuals and groups. Which elements within society bear the economic cost of alcoholism? In other words, who within society is going without?

The answer depends on the particular form of the economic cost involved and the effects of the existence of social institutions and programs that serve to transfer burdens among the members of society.

The economic cost of alcoholism can take either of two basic forms. On the one hand, it may be manifested simply as a reduction in total output due to diminished productivity. In effect, the total output of goods and services is less than it otherwise would have been because alcohol abuse has had an adverse effect on the productivity of resources. The most obvious example of this type of loss would be an alcoholic who is unable to work because of his affliction. In this case, the alcoholic and his family might suffer the loss in the form of lost income.

On the other hand, the economic cost may be manifested in the need to produce certain goods and services to cope with the consequences of alcohol abuse and alcoholism and thereby forego the alternative goods and services that might have been produced if alcohol abuse and alcoholism had not generated those consequences. This type of economic cost is borne by those who pay for the production of these goods and services. The most obvious example of this type of loss would be the extra health care that must be produced to treat alcoholism or the diseases exacerbated by alcohol abuse. To the extent that medical resources are used to treat alcoholism, the output of other medical care services will necessarily be less. In this case, the economic cost may be borne by the alcoholic or his family if they must pay for the services, but it may be borne by others if the services produced are paid for by health insurance or by public medical care programs.

Economic losses in the form of lost production usually result in lost income; the cost is borne by those that suffer the loss in income. The alcohol abuser and his family often suffer loss of income, but in many instances there are nonalcoholic victims of an alcohol-related incident such as a motor vehicle accident who also suffer loss in income as a result of diminished productivity. If family income falls because of alcohol abuse or alcoholism, the family's ability to purchase goods and services is reduced; they must forego some consumption because of their reduced income. Thus, the economic cost of alcohol abuse and alcoholism takes a tangible form for particular individuals within society.

In assessing the burden, however, it is important to recognize that society in general is usually unwilling to allow family or individual incomes to fall to zero or even to very low levels. To compensate for part of the drop in income, cash payments are often made to those whose incomes have fallen. Such payments are often made through a variety of unemployment, welfare, or public assistance programs. These payments are referred to by economists as *transfer* payments, to indicate that they do not signify additional economic cost but represent only a shifting or transfer of part of the cost of lost production from the individual or family to the taxpayer. Thus, in cases where transfer payments are involved, the burden is in effect shared by the family and the taxpayer.[1] The burden of the taxpayer takes tangible form in his reduced after-tax purchasing power.

A simple example may be helpful in understanding the social significance of transfer or income-maintenance payments. Suppose that, because of alcoholism, a husband with a wife and children loses his job, which formerly paid him $10,000 per year. The lost production sustained by the society is approximated by the $10,000 loss in earned income by the alcoholic. The unemployed husband, who now has no income with which to support his family, applies for public assistance, and it is determined that the family is eligible to receive $4,800 per year in public-assistance funds. The $4,800 which is obtained from general taxes represents a transfer of funds to the alcoholic's family to help maintain a standard of living that is some $5,200 lower than their standard when the husband was employed. Thus, the family's share of the $10,000 loss burden is $5,200, and the taxpayers' share is $4,800. The total, $10,000, is equal to the economic cost or the value of the lost production.

Economic losses in the form of alternatives foregone because of production made necessary to cope with the consequences of alcohol abuse and alcoholism are borne by those who must pay for the production. In some instances the burden is borne by the alcoholic, in other instances by the nonalcoholic victim of an alcohol-related event. In many instances, however, the cost is borne by other members of society—in their roles, for example, as taxpayers or insureds.

A number of examples of the need to produce goods and services to cope with the consequences of alcohol abuse and alcoholism can be cited. The extra health care that must be produced to treat alcoholism or the diseases exacerbated by alcohol abuse has already been mentioned. It was noted that part or all the burden in that instance might be shifted from the alcoholic to others if the services consumed are paid for by health insurance or by public medical care programs.

A similar example might be adduced in the case of any property damage resulting from an alcohol-caused accident, such as a motor vehicle accident. To the extent that the alcohol abuser causes property damage, the repair or replacement of the property is an economic cost, since the resources used to repair or replace the property cannot be used for alternative production. The cost may be borne by the alcoholic (if the property damaged is his) or by other individuals whose property has been damaged. Often, however, property, damage is covered to some extent by insurance, and this burden is thereby shifted in large part to those who have paid insurance premiums.[2]

A significant part of the production of goods and services needed to cope with the consequences of alcohol abuse and alcoholism occurs in the public sector. To the extent that alcohol abuse increases the risk of motor vehicle accidents, for example, additional resources must be assigned to traffic safety and enforcement. Some part of the activity of the criminal justice system—police, courts, and correctional institutions—is undoubtedly necessitated by violent or antisocial behavior that can be linked to alcohol abuse and alcoholism. Public property is often damaged by alcohol-induced vandalism. On a more positive note, governmental agencies operate several specific programs directed towards alcoholism diagnosis, treatment, rehabilitation, prevention, and education, which are necessary because of alcohol abuse and alcoholism. In each of these cases, the economic cost is borne by the taxpayer; the burden may take the form of higher taxes, lower levels of other public services, or both.

THE ECONOMICS OF ALCOHOL VERSUS THE ECONOMICS OF ALCOHOL ABUSE

To this point, attention has been focused on the notion of the economic cost of alcohol abuse and alcoholism. But although alcohol abuse *may* result from alcohol consumption, most of those who consume alcohol are not alcohol abusers. Indeed, the vast majority of drinkers derive a variety of personal benefits from alcohol consumption and generate few, if any, additional costs for themselves or others. There is a difference between alcohol consumption and alcohol abuse, and perhaps making a distinction between the economics of alcohol and the economics of alcohol abuse would have some heuristic value.

Suppose that there were no real significant alcohol abuse. What would be the benefits and costs of alcohol consumption in moderation? In effect, what would be the economic calculus if alcohol were treated simply as a consumer good with only minor externalities in consumption?

Alcohol is consumed for a variety of personal, social, and even religious purposes. The proper use of alcohol can be socially, psychologically, and even physically beneficial. When nonabusing alcohol consumers purchase alcohol they are, in effect, indicating the value of alcohol in consumption. Hence, in the absence of externalities, the market price of alcohol is a reasonable approximation of its value in consumption—its economic benefit. In 1971, personal consumption expenditures on alcoholic beverages in the United States were reported at approximately $19 billion.[3] Additional amounts were undoubtedly spent on illegally produced alcohol. Thus, for the purpose of this discussion, $19 billion can be taken as a minimum estimate of the economic benefits that accrued to consumers from alcohol consumption.[4] Certainly that part of the $19 billion which is expended by nonabusers is a reasonable (and conservative) approximation of the economic benefits of alcohol to nonabusers.

On the cost side, the producers of alcohol must purchase resources in order to produce the alcohol. The pertinent cost in this context is our old friend, the opportunity cost. In effect, the resources used to produce the alcohol in the first instance are not available to produce other goods and services and thus represent the economic cost of the alcohol. The $19 billion figure is clearly a maximum estimate of the private costs incurred by alcohol producers. How can we draw this conclusion? Certainly it follows that if alcohol producers were willing to sell their output for $19 billion, that amount must have covered their expenditures on resources. In fact, since the total expenditure figure includes taxes, and assuming that alcohol producers earned any profits—which they certainly did—then the actual cost of resources must have been considerably less than $19 billion.

Hence, on balance, if we look at the economics of alcohol from the perspective of nonabusing consumers, the economic benefits of alcohol appear to be rather more than its economic costs. As a first approximation, the economic benefits of alcohol are somewhat more than $19 billion, while the economic costs of alcohol are considerably less than $19 billion. Indeed, since externalities in consumption are minor in the case of the nonabusing consumer, it seems reasonable to conclude that the net economic benefits of alcohol are positive.

So much for the economics of alcohol, what about the economics of alcohol abuse? What is the economic calculus when alcohol is a consumer good characterized by significant externalities in consumption? What are the benefits and costs of alcohol abuse?

On the benefit side, one would be hard-pressed to delineate any benefits of alcohol abuse. At most, one might count as a benefit the "value in consumption" to alcohol abusers; thus the expenditures on alcohol by alcohol abusers might be taken as an approximation of the economic benefits to abusers. Although this may seem to be an appropriate analog to considering the expenditures of nonabusers as a reasonable approximation of their economic benefits, it really is not. The problem is that the same deduction cannot be made with respect to alcohol abusers, since their affliction presumably inhibits their ability to accurately assess the true benefits of alcohol.

But suppose, for the sake of argument, that we ascribe to alcohol abuse economic benefits as approximated by the expenditures of alcohol abusers. Alcohol abusers probably account for something on the order of 10 to 12 percent of all alcohol consumers. But since alcohol abusers tend to be heavy drinkers, they undoubtedly account for a disproportionate share of the total expenditures on alcohol. It might not be unreasonable to approximate the expenditures of alcohol abusers at something on the order of 25 percent of total expenditures. Hence, for present purposes, we might take something under $5 billion (25 percent of $19 billion) as representative of the economic benefits of alcohol to alcohol abusers.

On the cost side, some 25 percent of the resources used to produce alcohol would represent the economic cost of the alcohol consumed by abusers. Before consideration of externalities in consumption, there is some net benefit to abusers of consuming alcohol. But this net benefit—clearly something considerably less than $5 billion—must be balanced against the extra costs that derive from the adverse consequences of alcohol abuse.

The economic costs of alcohol abuse include both lost production and alternative production foregone because of the need to produce goods and services to cope with the consequences of alcohol abuse and alcoholism. As we shall see, the estimated total economic cost of alcohol abuse and alcoholism in 1971 was approximately $30 billion. Hence, on balance, the economic costs of alcohol abuse are considerably more than the economic benefits that accrue to alcohol abusers.

At this point, the perceptive reader has undoubtedly inferred that society could well choose either of two perspectives toward alcohol consumption, with very different implications for social policy. On the one hand, society could well ask, What are the total benefits and total costs of alcohol consumption, including all the externalities? In effect, society could apply the economic calculus to approximate the real social benefits and social costs of alcohol consumption and all of its consequences. In this context, the economic cost of alcohol abuse might well more than balance out the net benefits of alcohol consumption. The sum of the economic cost of alcohol production (same proportion of $19 billion) and the economic cost of alcohol abuse (some $30 billion) is something on the order of twice the minimum estimate of the economic benefits that accrue to consumers from alcohol consumption. Consumer surplus would have to be significant indeed to strike a balance of positive net benefits. Such was the social perspective in the era of the Volstead Act and Prohibition.

On the other hand, society could well choose to distinguish between alcohol consumption by nonabusers and alcohol abuse; in effect, society could apply the economic calculus separately to alcohol consumption by nonabusers and alcohol abuse. This would seem to be the current social perspective. In this context, the economic benefits of alcohol consumption by nonabusers are somewhat greater than the economic cost of producing the alcohol they consume. Consumer surplus, if considered, would serve to increase the estimate of net benefits. By the same token, the economic cost of alcohol abuse is significant, to say the least—it is equivalent to something on the order of two percent of the nation's gross national product.[5] Clearly, if society views alcohol abuse as a separate problem, programs that serve to modify, control, retard, or eliminate the consequences of alcohol abuse have a significant potential in terms of reducing the economic cost of alcohol abuse. In the extreme, if a program could be designed that eliminated alcohol abuse entirely and cost less than $30 billion, the program would represent a social bargain.

As we noted at the beginning of this chapter, social policy concerning alcohol abuse had evolved to the point where Congress created the National Institute on Alcohol Abuse and Alcoholism in 1970 and gave it the responsibility of formulating and recommending national policy and goals regarding the prevention, control, and treatment of alcohol abuse and alcoholism. This act was consonant with the social view that the economic calculus should be applied separately to alcohol abuse. In a benefit/cost context, the elimination of specific economic costs of alcohol abuse would be the primary potential benefit of programs designed for the prevention, control, and treatment of alcohol abuse.

Given the current social perspective, it is important to apply the economic calculus to alcohol abuse. For purposes of social policy, however, it is not enough to generate a single estimate of the total economic cost of alcohol abuse. The adverse consequences of alcohol abuse occur in many and varied forms. Different programs will be needed to cope with different consequences. Certain consequences are more significant than others in terms of the magnitude of their economic costs. Given current knowledge, the potential for affecting certain consequences is greater than the potential for affecting others. The setting of program priorities obviously requires a careful, systematic analysis of the economic costs of the several adverse consequences of alcohol abuse.

We have attempted to do such an analysis. The general approach we followed is outlined in the next section.

OUR GENERAL APPROACH

A necessary condition for estimating the economic cost of alcohol abuse was knowledge of the social behavior of persons affected by alcohol, in order that the economic-cost implications of their behavior might be derived. A logical source of such knowledge was the diverse field of research into the multidimensional problem of alcohol abuse and alcoholism.

A first task was to review the literature and folklore of alcoholism to identify those areas of research which suggested that the economic cost resulting from social behavior might be significant. Within the identified areas, a second task was to determine the extent to which the research completed had been able to isolate the effect of alcohol on the behavior of people. If the "pure" effect of alcohol could be isolated, then the economic cost of behavior attributable to alcohol alone could be estimated.

The alcohol literature and a little analysis allowed us to identify six possible major sources of economic cost. A separate analysis was undertaken of each of these six sources. Unfortunately previous research within these areas did not, in general, succeed in isolating the social behavior that might reasonably be attributed to alcohol alone. As a result, the cost estimates in each case had to be based upon what the previous studies suggested might be a conservative estimate of the role of alcohol in inducing behavior that had economic-cost consequences.

Another difficulty in providing a coherent, integrated approach to cost estimation was the apparent lack of agreement among those in the field as to just what constitutes alcoholism or alcohol abuse. There is no single accepted definition of alcoholism or alcohol abuse; indeed, the latter term may well have evolved because of lack of agreement about the former. Related to the problem of defining alcoholism is the difficulty of determining its prevalence. The approach adopted in estimating economic cost within the six major categories was to rely on the definitions and estimates used and generally applied by experts in their respective fields of alcohol research.

Our reliance in this study upon varying interpretations of the nature and scope of the alcoholism problem does add some uncertainty as to the comparability of our several cost estimates. At the same time, the varying interpretations probably reflect the fact that alcoholism is an extremely complex social phenomenon which is just beginning to be understood by researchers from many disciplines. As the state of knowledge of the social consequences of alcoholism advances, it can be expected that the accuracy of economic cost estimates will also improve.

OUTLINE AND OVERVIEW

Six major sources of potentially significant economic cost were identified and then subjected to more intensive research and analysis in order to develop cost estimates for each. In chapter 2 the focus is on measuring the reduced productivity of workers that may be attributable to alcohol. It is estimated that society had to forego somewhat more than $11 billion in output in 1971 because workers were less productive than they might have been if it were not for the adverse effects of alcohol on their economic productivity. In addition, it is estimated that the excess mortality due to alcohol abuse resulted in a loss to society of future production with a present value in 1971 of over $3 billion.

In chapter 3 an analysis is presented of the cost of additional medical and health services that were required because of the effects of alcohol on the general health status of alcohol abusers. The emphasis in chapter 3 is on the less obvious and more difficult-to-identify costs of alcohol abuse rather than on overt medical expenditures for the treatment of alcoholism. It is estimated that society incurred extra health care costs of over $8 billion in 1971 to treat alcoholism and the diseases exacerbated by alcohol abuse.

In chapter 4 we have built upon prior research to first estimate the total economic cost of motor vehicle accidents at some $30 billion; we then estimated that part of the cost that is attributable to alcohol abuse. It is conservatively estimated that the economic cost of motor vehicle accidents attributable to alcohol abuse amounted to some $4.7 billion.

In chapter 5 we have estimated both the cost of fire in the aggregate, and that part of the cost that might be attributable to alcohol abuse. The latter figure is conservatively estimated at $377.7 million.

The somewhat controversial area of the role of alcohol in criminal and antisocial behavior is the subject matter of chapter 6. In fact, our research led us to conclude that available evidence and knowledge are insufficient to ascertain the extent to which alcohol abuse results in crime. Although there is ample evidence that alcohol and crime are associated, and the association is particularly significant in the case of violent crime, there is no empirical basis for estimating the cost of crime due to alcohol abuse. Instead, we had to settle for an estimate of some $1.5 billion for the cost of crime *associated* with alcohol.

In chapter 7 we have attempted to estimate the economic cost of *social responses* to alcohol abuse—the social welfare system, alcohol treatment programs, highway safety and fire protection expenditures, and the criminal justice system. In the aggregate, we estimate that the economic cost of such social responses to alcohol abuse amounted to some $1.9 billion.

Finally, in chapter 8 we have delineated the policy implications of what has been learned in this study. The application of the economic calculus to the problem of alcohol abuse does provide insight into the potential benefits of programs designed for the prevention, control, and treatment of alcohol abuse.

POSTSCRIPT: A BRIEF REVIEW OF ECONOMIC CONCEPTS

Productive resources, or factors of production, are usually classified as comprising *land, labor,* and *capital. Land* includes all those resources that are found in a natural state; *labor* includes any human effort expended; and *capital* is any produced means of production—that is, anything used in the production process that was itself produced at an earlier stage.

The United States is a relatively affluent society and is enviably endowed with resources. In rather rough orders of magnitude, the amount of land in the United States can be approximated at almost 3 million square miles. The labor force of the United States is approximately 90 million persons. The capital stock of this country—in machinery, buildings, equipment, and the like—is something on the order of 3 trillion dollars. But even this endowment of resources is scarce relative to the collective wants of the 210 million-plus members of the population of this country. The prevailing allocation of these resources in 1975 generated an output of goods and services with a market value of approximately $1,500 billion. This output represents the greatest absolute level of production attained in the history of the world; yet, consider the unsatisfied wants in this nation.

The above constitutes a rather simplistic overview of the economy of this nation, but it does serve to bring the concern of economics into perspective. The resources of the nation are limited. The nation is faced with a series of choices. The most obvious question is whether or not the existing allocation of resources is the appropriate one to produce the particular mix of goods and services being produced. If an alternative allocation of resources would allow for an increase in output, then the prevailing allocation is an inappropriate one.

A somewhat more complex question is whether or not the mix of goods and services being produced is the most desirable one. Would the society be better off in some sense if the mix of output was characterized by more of certain goods and services and less of other goods and services?

An even more complex question is whether the present pattern of distribution of goods and services among the members of the population is an appropriate one. Would the society as a whole be better off in some sense if a redistribution of goods and services took place?

The first two questions refer to the relative *efficiency* of the allocation of resources, while the last question refers to the *equity* of the distribution of the goods and services produced with those resources. In a basically market economy, the allocation of resources is generally left to be determined by the interaction of buyers and sellers in the marketplace. External intervention is allowed for when the allocation of resources proves inappropriate, or when society decides that the pattern of distribution is inappropriate.

Each time a particular good or service is produced, some of the scarce resources are used up. The production of more of one good implies that less of some other good can be produced, since the resources used for the one cannot be available for the other. Hence, the *cost* of any good or service is appropriately described as the foregone opportunity of using the resources to produce something else—the *opportunity cost*. This, in the jargon of economics, is the supply side of the problem of resource allocation.

On the demand side, consumers go into the market with purchasing power to express their preferences for certain goods and combinations of goods. In effect, the purchasing power of consumers represents their "command" over resources. By expressing their willingness to purchase a particular good, consumers indicate the *value* to them of the resources used in the production of that good.

This is the general framework of the market solution to the resource allocation problem. Since the basic objective is to utilize resources in such a way that we get the most out of them in terms of the satisfaction of wants, a reasonably well-working market can do a reasonably good job of allocating resources.

The profit motive implies that producers will try to maximize the difference between what consumers are willing to pay for their products and what they in turn have to pay to acquire the resources necessary to produce those products. It seems reasonable to expect that consumers, on the other hand, will purchase those products which serve to maximize their satisfaction. This interaction will tend to balance opportunity cost and value in consumption. Since opportunity cost reflects resource scarcity and value in consumption reflects want satisfaction, such a balance is appropriate.

A distinct advantage of a market system is that its operation generates data, in the form of prices, which tend to provide for the efficient production and distribution of goods and services. It is the prices of productive resources and of consumer goods and services that provide the necessary information to producers, on the one hand, and consumers, on the other, that enables the allocation and distribution functions to be carried out efficiently. Market prices tend to reflect scarcity values of both resources and consumer goods.

On the production side, the market prices of available resources enable producers to make efficient choices as to how to produce outputs at minimum cost. On the consumption side, the market prices of goods and services enable consumers to make efficient choices as to what to purchase and consume.

A simple graphical example of how the market serves to solve the allocation problem may be useful and illustrative. In fig. 1–1, we have depicted two consumer product markets and two input or

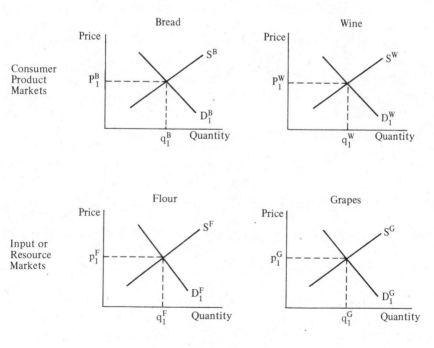

FIGURE 1–1

resource markets. The consumer products are bread and wine, and the inputs are flour and grapes. The demand by consumers for bread and wine is represented by D_1^B and D_1^W, respectively. The demand curves are downward-sloping, indicating that consumers, all other things being equal, will usually buy less of a good at higher prices and more of a good at lower prices. Producers' supply of bread and wine is represented by S^B and S^W, respectively. The supply curves are upward-sloping, indicating that producers, all other things being equal, will usually offer to sell more of a good at higher prices and less of a good at lower prices. The consumer product markets are in equilibrium, with a quantity of bread, q_1^B, being produced and purchased at a price of p_1^B, and a quantity of wine, q_1^W, being produced and purchased at a price of p_1^W.

The demand for flour in the input or resource market comes in large part from bread producers. Similarly, the demand for grapes derives in large part from wine producers. The supply of flour and grapes, of course, can be traced back eventually to the availability of grain fields and vineyards (illustrating that land is a resource with alternative uses).

Now suppose that for some reason consumer tastes changed such that consumers wanted more bread and less wine. Such a change is depicted in fig. 1–2. In the upper half of fig. 1–2, the changed preferences of consumers are represented by a higher demand for bread, D_2^B, and a lower demand for wine, D_2^W. The impact of the change in consumer tastes on the two consumer product markets results in both an increase in the price of bread and the quantity of bread produced, on the one hand, and a reduction in the price of wine and the quantity of wine produced, on the other. In effect, the market has provided a mechanism whereby consumers can signal producers concerning their changed preferences, and the producers can react by changing their production.

But, of course, the producers will accordingly change their demand for inputs or resources. Bread producers need more flour if they are to increase their production of bread, and wine producers need fewer grapes if they are to produce less wine. The lower half of fig. 1–2 reflects the impact of the initial change in consumer preferences for bread and wine on the input or resource markets of flour and grapes. The increased demand for bread on the part of consumers is translated into an increased demand for flour—D_2^F—on the part of bread producers, and the decreased demand for wine is translated into a decreased demand for grapes—D_2^G—by wine producers.

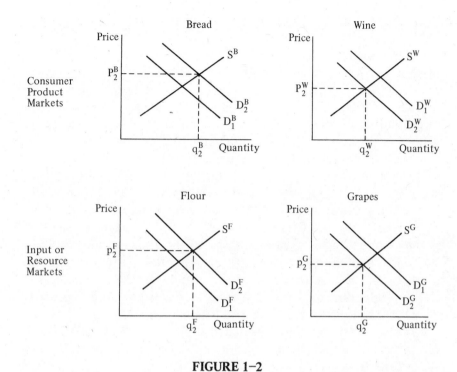

FIGURE 1–2

Indeed, both the price of flour and the quantity produced increase, while both the price of grapes and the quantity produced decline. The market has provided a mechanism for producers to signal that the relative scarcity value of resources has changed. In fact, the higher price of flour and the lower price of grapes will have a further impact on the relative values of land devoted to grain fields and vineyards. In the last analysis, the amount of land allocated to grain production will increase, and the amount of land allocated to grape production will decline. Thus does the market serve to solve the allocation problem.

The preceding example is of course oversimplified, but it does serve to outline the way in which the market tends to balance the value in consumption with the opportunity cost of scarce resources. When the market is functioning well, this balance is struck, and the resulting equilibrium is characterized by efficient production and distribution of goods and services.[6] The well-functioning market provides the necessary information to producers and consumers (in the form of prices) to enable them to allocate resources efficiently. In effect, market prices reflect the scarcity values of both resources and consumer goods—the real economic or opportunity costs of resources and the real economic benefits or value in consumption of consumer goods.

Unfortunately, the conditions that must prevail in order for market prices to reflect real costs and real benefits are rather restrictive and are rarely found in actual markets. Specifically: 1) the market for each good and service must be composed of a sufficiently large number of sellers and buyers that no single economic agent can influence the price of the good or service offered and purchased in the market; 2) the good or service (including the service of a factor of production) must be homogeneous, to the extent that each is a perfect substitute for any other; 3) there can be no barriers to the market—any buyer or seller must be completely free to enter or leave the market as he sees fit; and 4) all of the economic actors must have perfect knowledge—i.e., not only do all the above conditions hold, but each and every participant, or potential participant, in the market realizes that they hold. Furthermore, no external effects of either production or consumption can exist if market prices are to accurately reflect real costs and real benefits.

If any of these conditions fail to hold in a given market—if, in other words, *market failures* occur—inefficiency will result. If all of these conditions *were* to hold in a particular market economy, then that economy's production and exchange would result in an efficient equilibrium as long as each producer tried to maximize his profits and each consumer attempted to maximize the level of his satisfaction. In effect, this would be a world guided by the famous "invisible hand."

Of this world of the "invisible hand," three things of special interest are worth noting. In the first place, there are an infinite number of efficient solutions—there are as many solutions to the problem of resource allocation as there are possible original distributions of wealth. Hence efficient allocation of resources is entirely compatible with inequity of income distribution. In the second place, this model of perfect consumer sovereignty makes no allowance for the possibility of a complete lack of integrity on the part of some or all of the economic actors. The possibility of self-destruction is quite compatible with the competitive market model; thus an efficient solution might include drug addiction, for example, or any other combination of socially undesirable consumption goods. Finally, the model does not preclude the existence of government per se, even in the economic sphere; government is excluded only in the context of production and exchange. The political process exists side by side with the competitive market economy; in fact, it is presumed that the political process will provide the proper environment in which this economy can function. In effect, the role delegated to government in this world of the "invisible hand" is to codify and administer the rules of the market "game."

In fact, however, these conditions never obtain simultaneously in the real world—and hence the economic case for a role for government. An allocative role of government can arise when major imperfections in market structure prevail. Such imperfections are often referred to as *market failures*, and official policies relative to price discrimination, combinations in restraint of trade, and seller concentration amounting to monopoly control have often reflected a conscious attempt to improve the allocation of resources.

Public Goods

In many cases the market is unable to provide certain goods at all or unable to provide them in sufficient quantity. Public provision of certain goods is necessary if they are to be provided at all, and such goods are often referred to as *public goods*. National defense is a classic example of a public good, one that would not be forthcoming from the market.

Public goods have certain characteristics that are readily identifiable. *Joint consumption* is one characteristic. Consumption usually connotes the using up or exhausting of the usefulness of a given good or service by a particular consumer. In some cases, however, goods or services can be enjoyed simultaneously by a large number of persons, the consumption of these goods or services by one individual in no way reduces the satisfaction enjoyed by others. Concerts and sporting events are examples of goods that can be jointly consumed. No matter how much one individual enjoys a concert or sporting event he attends, the potential enjoyment of the other consumers in attendance is not diminished. Parks and police protection are other examples.

Some jointly consumed goods and services can be and are produced and distributed by private enterprise in the traditional market sense. Others cannot be provided through the market. The crucial characteristic that distinguishes goods which the market is able to provide from goods which the market is unable to provide is whether or not the *exclusion principle* can be applied. If nonbuyers can be excluded from consuming the good or service, then the market mechanism is capable of providing it. If there is no way to exclude nonbuyers, the good or service will not be produced by private enterprise. Admission may be charged for, and nonpayers excluded from, concerts and sporting events; the same is true for circuses, symphonies, and many other jointly consumed products, which are properly classified as private goods. In the case of some goods, however, nonbuyers cannot be excluded. If a system of national defense is established, all citizens will be defended whether or not they pay for the protection. The same is true with respect to police protection. If mosquitoes are eradicated in a particular area, all inhabitants of the area will benefit. Privately produced eradication could not be "sold," since the producer could not exclude nonpayers from consuming the benefits of the eradication program. Whenever there is no way of effectively excluding nonbuyers from consuming a particular good or service, that good or service will not be privately produced, regardless of its value. The market is unable to provide goods that are both jointly consumed and available to buyers and nonbuyers alike. If such goods are to be produced, public provision is necessary.

Externalities

In addition to *public goods* that the market can not provide, there are a number of goods and services that the market can provide, but only in an inappropriate quantity relative to some social optimum. In effect, whenever there is a divergence of private benefits and social benefits or of private costs and social costs, the market, which considers only private benefits and costs, will not provide the socially desirable quantities. What is involved, of course, is that certain goods are characterized by benefits and costs that are enjoyed or incurred by more than just the principal individuals involved in their consumption or production. These goods have benefits and costs—*externalities*—*external to* the individual consumer or producer.

Consider first an external benefit in consumption. Suppose Peter chooses to consume a vaccine which reduces his chance of contracting a communicable disease. He will benefit directly from this consumption, but so too will his neighbor Paul. This is a case of an external benefit associated with consumption. From society's point of view, the social benefit of Peter's consumption is the sum of the private benefits accruing to both Peter and Paul. But Peter's consumption decision will reflect only his own private benefit. In general, there will be too little of a good whenever the social benefits exceed the private benefits.

Alternatively, suppose Peter chooses to consume alcohol at his local bar to the point of intoxication and then drives home. Peter has chosen to run the risk of a motor vehicle accident that could cause personal injury and property damage. Peter may well incur costs as a result of his consumption, but so too might his neighbor Paul, if he happens to be an innocent victim of Peter's accident. This is a case of an external cost associated with consumption. From society's point of view, the social cost of Peter's consumption is the sum of the private costs incurred by both Peter and Paul. But Peter's consumption decision will reflect only his own private cost. In general, there will be too much of a good whenever the social costs exceed the private costs.

On the production side, consider the case of a private municipal transportation service. Such a producer can charge only a fraction of the total number of individuals who derive benefits from his production. Private benefits are enjoyed by the passengers, and they may indeed be charged. At the same time, however, the municipal transportation service benefits many *non*users by relieving traffic congestion, extending the markets of urban retail businesses, reducing the number of traffic accidents, and providing a variety of other indirect benefits. From society's point of view, the social benefit of the transportation service is the sum of all the benefits enjoyed by users and nonusers together. But there is no way that the private producer can charge the nonusers for the benefits they derive from the service he provides. His production decision will incorporate only the private benefits of users. Thus, such a service would generally be smaller than the socially optimal size, because the social benefits exceed the private benefits.

Alternatively, consider a factory incurring a variety of private costs for materials, labor, and rent. Suppose this factor tends to pollute the air by using coal as an energy agent. From society's point of view, the social cost of the factory's output includes not only the cost of materials, labor, and rent but also the cost of polluted air. But the factor's production decision only will reflect its private costs. Again, there will generally be too much of a good whenever the social costs exceed the private costs.

The point being made in these examples is that resources should be allocated on the basis of social benefits and social costs whenever there is a divergence of private and social benefits or costs.

NOTES

1. To count both the loss in earnings and the transfer payments as part of the cost of alcohol abuse and alcoholism would be to double-count. The loss of production, presumably reflected in the loss of earnings, is the extent of the economic cost; the transfer payment is merely a social mechanism for shifting part of the burden of that cost.

2. Indeed, insurance premiums in general are undoubtedly higher because of the increased risk of loss that derives from alcohol abuse and alcoholism.

3. U.S. Bureau of the Census, *Statistical Abstract of the United States: 1973* (Washington, D.C.: U.S. Government Printing Office, 1973), table 522, p. 322.

4. The estimate is a minimum for two reasons. The more obvious reason is that a significant amount of alcohol production and sales pass through illegal channels, primarily to avoid the tax on alcohol. A more subtle reason involves what economists call *consumer surplus*–the value in consumption in excess of market price. In effect, since all consumers pay the market price for alcohol (or any good), but some would be willing to pay more, the market price is a minimum estimate of the value of the good in consumption. The market price *is* the value in consumption for the marginal buyer, but it understates the value in consumption to all other buyers.

5. The total value, at market prices, of the nation's output of goods and services.

6. Technically, *efficient production* implies that the amount of any one good or service produced could not be increased without reducing the output of some other good or service; *efficient distribution* implies that no one individual could be made better off without worsening the position of at least one other individual.

CHAPTER TWO

THE ECONOMIC COST OF LOST PRODUCTION DUE TO ALCOHOL ABUSE AND ALCOHOLISM

LOST PRODUCTION AS AN ECONOMIC COST

The concept of lost production is synonymous with the notion of foregone output or opportunity cost that was discussed in chapter 1. The economic logic of lost production in the present context is simply that alcohol abuse and alcoholism may impair productivity, with the result that less will be produced. The unproduced output is irretrievably lost to society. With less output available for consumption, society's welfare is necessarily lower than it would have been if more output had been available.

Alcohol abuse and alcoholism can unfavorably affect productivity in a variety of ways and in several contexts. Perhaps the most obvious case of lost production occurs when alcohol abuse causes an individual to completely (and perhaps permanently) withdraw from the labor force. Less drastically, alcohol abuse leads to tardiness and absenteeism, and when the worker is missing or late, he obviously is not contributing to production. The worker with alcohol problems is often less productive *on* the job as well. He may be contributing to production, but his contribution is less than it would be if he were not afflicted. In addition, the alcohol abuser may well have an adverse impact on his fellow workers or on other factors of production. Certainly overall production suffers when alcohol abuse causes equipment to be misused or damaged.

In general, we tend to think of lost production in terms of goods and services that usually flow through the traditional market system. When alcohol abuse affects a person in his role as worker, the goods and services foregone as a consequence of lower productivity are those that we normally find in the marketplace. But individuals produce goods and services in other roles as well, and society suffers a real economic loss in the form of foregone goods and services to the extent that alcohol abuse lowers productivity in *non*market activities.

The family or household is the most important and obvious social system in which nonmarket production of goods and services takes place. Child care, housekeeping, meal preparation, and recreation are examples of family-produced goods and services. When a family member has a problem with alcohol, his or her productive capacity within the family may be adversely affected and the family will suffer the consequences in the form of lost family production. Goods and services produced by and within the household may not have market prices, but they are nonetheless valuable. A lower level of household production represents foregone output and reflects a real economic cost.

THE THEORY AND MEASUREMENT OF LOST PRODUCTION

The economic cost of lost production can be approximated by estimating the market value of what might have been produced by alcohol abusers if they had had no productivity problems associated with alcohol. It is usually easier, of course, to generate estimates of the market value of foregone goods and services that traditionally appear in the market place. It is much more difficult to estimate the value of nonmarket production, such as goods and services usually produced within the household.

In the most fundamental sense, lost production is output not produced and conceptually could be expressed in physical magnitudes. In the case of lost production due to alcohol abuse, for example, the question is how much of what goods and services were foregone because alcohol abuse resulted in lower productivity. Lost production attributable to alcohol abuse could be expressed in physical magnitudes such as loaves of bread, bottles of wine, numbers of automobiles, and tons of steel not produced. This lost output would then have to be valued at market prices in order to allow for summation in terms of a common unit of account. The measurement of output in physical terms is just not feasible for the entire economy, as one could hardly count the number of units not produced in each and every firm or organization with alcohol-troubled workers.

An alternative measure of lost production expressed in terms such as productive man-years lost would be feasible, but the *value* of the lost production would not be conveyed by such a measure. Any estimate of the value of lost production would require some estimate of the value of a man-year lost or the value of labor in production. The value of labor in production—the opportunity cost of labor—is the very information that is provided by a well-functioning market, wherein the earnings of labor reflect labor's economic value in production. Hence, in order to estimate the value of lost production, a reasonably well-functioning price system is a necessary condition.

To the extent possible, we will attempt to estimate the market value of lost production by estimating the amout of reduced earnings of workers with alcohol problems. The validity of this approach depends critically upon whether or not people are paid according to the value of their contribution to output. Technically, lost production could be valued by earnings if and only if workers were paid the value of their marginal product. Practically, however, the application of the economic calculus requires not the strict assumption that every worker receives as earnings the value of his marginal product, but rather the assumption that there is a tendency for earnings to reflect economic productivity. If average earnings tend to reflect productivity, then lost earnings will be a reasonable approximation to lost production.

Before we turn our attention to specific methods of measuring lost production, an example of the breadth of information transmitted by market prices can be noted. The wages and salaries of workers simultaneously represent costs to producers and income to families and individuals. Within the context of alcohol abuse, the reduced earnings of workers can be taken as a measure of what was not produced. At the same time, those reduced earnings represent a decline in family or household incomes. When prices are examined as income, we are afforded a more general view of the economic consequences of alcoholism. A decline in family income will reduce the family's welfare, since fewer goods and services can be purchased. In an attempt to minimize the loss in family welfare occasioned by a decline in income, the economic roles played by various family members may be restructured. Thus, for example, if a husband's drinking problem results in a reduced family income, the wife may enter the labor force in order to arrest the decline in the family's standard of living. It would be incorrect to subtract the wife's output in the market sector from the lost production related to alcoholism, for, in the broader economic view, the change in the economic structure of the family is not costless. The concept of economic cost involves foregone output. Within the family context, the movement of the wife into the labor force involves foregone production within the home or foregone leisure. Thus, what is produced in the market sector by the wife of an alcohol-troubled worker is, in effect, cancelled out by the production and leisure that must be foregone within the family.[1]

The Measurement of Lost Production in the Market Sector

A reasonable basis for estimating the cost of lost production in the market sector would be to compare the income of a representative sample of alcohol abusers with the income of a matched sample of nonabusers. If the persons in the two samples were similar in all respects except that one group included only alcohol abusers and the other group included only nonabusers, then any difference in earnings would represent a reliable estimate of the impact of alcohol abuse on income. Given the prevalence of alcohol abuse, and the reasonable assumption that earnings tend to reflect productivity, such an estimate of the impact of alcohol abuse would allow one to generate an estimate of the total cost of lost production due to alcohol abuse.

In a similar way, if one could obtain the per-capita income from employment for both alcohol-abusing workers and nonabusing workers, it would be possible to generate a reasonable estimate of the total cost of lost production due to alcohol abuse. The difference in earnings between abusing and nonabusing workers would be due in part to the effect of alcohol abuse and in part to other factors which influence earnings, such as age, experience, and education. If the gross difference in earnings between abusers and nonabusers was adjusted to account for other factors known to influence earnings, the result could be taken as an estimate of the net effect of alcohol abuse on income.

In this chapter, a method similar to the latter technique will be used to estimate the cost of lost production due to alcohol abuse and alcoholism for the major component of the labor force, namely, males between the ages of 21 and 59. We were able to apply this estimation procedure beause specific income and problem-drinking prevalence data were available for households that included a male between the ages of 21 and 59.

Unfortunately, very little is known about either the problem-drinking prevalence or the economic and social behavior of other groups within society whose economic productivity may have been reduced because of alcohol abuse. In particular, prevalence and behavioral research to date has been inadequate for such groups as women, persons in institutions, and skid row alcoholics. As a consequence, reliable estimates of the cost of lost production are most difficult to make for these groups.

It is important to restate the general principle that reliable cost estimation in the alcohol field depends not only on economic analysis but also on what is known about the social and economic behavior of people with alcohol problems. At present, the necessary process of integrating knowledge and data from such diverse fields as alcohol research, economics, other social sciences, and the health sciences is just beginning. In time, as a better understanding is gained of the role of alcohol in affecting social behavior, the magnitude of the economic consequences of alcohol abuse will be estimated more precisely.

Lost Production in the Nonmarket Sector

In the market sector, the availability of factor or resource prices enhances the possibility of estimating the cost of lost production. When production takes place in nonmarket settings, however, the lack of prices renders the problem of estimating the cost of lost production essentially insoluble. We have already noted the importance of the family or household in the production of nonmarket goods and services. A recent development in economic analysis has been to view the household as an economic unit having the social objective of maximizing its welfare or utility subject to certain constraints such as family income, the time of family members, and the skills, energy, health status, and other assets of the family. This objective is achieved in part by combining goods and services purchased in the market with other family assets to produce the outputs that the family deems necessary to increase its well-being. The family produces child care, housekeeping services, meals, recreation, and a host of other goods and services consonant with its preferences.

In deciding what and how much of these several goods and services to produce, the family is faced with the classic economic problem of allocating scarce resources to achieve an objective. The family presumably solves the problem by allocating its resources in such a way as to make the family unit as well off as possible given its resource constraints. Consideration of this solution reveals an analog to the market solution. The opportunity cost of using a scarce family resource for one purpose is the value in family satisfaction or welfare that is foregone by not using that resource for an alternative purpose. The family is able to allocate its resources efficiently because scarcity values or "prices" are perceived by the family in the form of foregone activities. However, since these prices are expressed in subjective terms of family utility, they can not be compared across families, and they do not lend themselves to aggregation beyond the family level.

We might consider a specific example in the context of alcohol abuse. If alcoholism begins to affect a family, a likely result is a decline in family production, which in turn leads to a reduction in family welfare. The decline in family welfare is tangible, in the form of such real losses as less or lower-quality child care, fewer housekeeping services, fewer well-prepared meals, less enjoyable recreation activities, and the like. As tangible as these events are, however, they can not be systematically measured and aggregated, because there is no convenient common unit of account. Family outputs and inputs, unlike goods and services that are usually found in the marketplace, have no simple market prices. Attempts are often made to price family outputs by determining the market prices of related market goods: thus, for example, the price of babysitting services may be taken to approximate the value of child care; the wages of maids or handymen may be taken to approximate the value of housekeeping services; or restaurant prices may be taken as surrogates for the value of meals prepared at home. Such estimates, however, particularly in the case of alcoholism, may tend to obscure the scope and magnitude of production loss within the family and, more importantly, the concomitant effect on family welfare.

Since very little is actually known about changes in the economic structure of the family under the impact of alcoholism, it is not really possible to estimate the cost of lost production in this most significant nonmarket sector. In particular, since very little is known about either the prevalence of alcohol abuse or the economic and social behavior among alcohol-abusing women, and since the major economic impact of women is likely to be in the nonmarket sector, no reasonable estimates can be made of the economic cost of lost production among women. On the other hand, there are sufficient, albeit somewhat limited, data to generate an estimate of the cost of lost production in one significant nonmarket context—the military.

On balance, however, any estimate of the economic cost of lost production in the nonmarket sector will be significantly understated.

A SELECTIVE REVIEW OF PAST RESEARCH

The issue of the economic cost of lost production has drawn some attention in past research. Most previous studies, however, have taken a less than total view of the problem. A review of past research also indicates that much of the empirical work was not based on the actual economic behavior of alcohol-troubled workers. On the basis of available research data, it is not possible to conclude that alcohol is definitely a causal factor in reducing production. On the other hand, there is certainly an abundance of evidence that reduced production is related to the alcohol problems of workers.

Past studies of the problem can be classified in general as adopting either a limited or aggregate perspective. Studies in the former category concentrate on determining the costs of alcoholism to a particular firm, organization, or industry or to some other productive sector of the economy. Studies in the latter category adopt the perspective of the total economy and attempt to determine what society as a whole foregoes in terms of output as a consequence of alcohol abuse. There is some advantage in analyzing both with the objective of discovering their respective strengths and weaknesses.

One study of less than the total economy that is of some interest is the 1970 study by the comptroller general of alcoholism among federal civilian employees.[2] Briefly, the study, based primarily on expert opinion, estimated the cost of alcoholism to the federal government in 1970 by a simple three-step technique. The first step was to develop alcoholism prevalence rates among federal civilian employees: the prevalence rate of alcoholism was set at between 4 and 8 percent of all federal employees. The second step was to develop rates of reduced efficiency among alcoholic federal workers:

the efficiency of alcoholic workers was estimated to be some 25 percent lower as a consequence of their affliction. The third step was to generalize these rates of prevalence and reduced efficiency to all federal civilian employees. Given a 25 percent reduction in efficiency, measured as 25 percent of the average annual salary per employee, and prevalence rates varying between 4 and 8 percent of total federal civilian employment, cost estimates were derived in the range of $275 to $550 million per annum.

Although this study can be criticized on the ground that the rates of prevalence and reduced efficiency were not developed from empirical analysis of actual behavior among federal civilian employees, the study does have certain merits. In particular, it asks some of the right questions: viz., what are the rates of prevalence and reduced efficiency associated with alcohol abuse? It should also be noted that the results implicitly rest on two assumptions. First, it had to be assumed that wages paid but not earned were an accurate measure of loss. Second, it had to be assumed that the distribution of alcohol-abusing workers among pay scales and presumably among job assignments was similar to the distribution of nonalcoholic workers. The first assumption, albeit not immune from criticism on theoretical and empirical grounds, is standard in applied economic research, and we will not quarrel with it. The second assumption, however, is a matter for more concern. It may be that workers in the same job classification receive the same wage or salary whether or not they are alcohol abusers. But do alcohol abusers have the same rate of advancement in job classification, for example, as their nonabusing counterparts? It is unlikely that the average wage paid to problem drinkers is more or less equal to the average wage paid to workers without alcohol problems.

Parenthetically, it should be noted that the intent of this review is not to belabor the comptroller general's study but rather to use its simple structure to get at the fundamental problems inherent in measuring lost production. Clearly, the rates of prevalence and efficiency loss are important. In addition, the implicit assumptions concerning labor-force characteristics of the civilian workers should be made explicit, for they will have much broader implications when an attempt is made to measure lost production in the aggregate.

A second, similar study is the report of the Program for Alcoholic Recovery (PAR), run by the Postal Service.[3] Since the PAR study is based on the methodology employed in the comptroller general's study of alcoholism among federal employees, it provides no new conceptual insights. On the other hand, consideration of the fact that both the PAR study and the comptroller general's study are aimed at measuring annual costs does serve to introduce an additional basic issue—the problem of time.

Ordinarily in an economic study, one should be concerned with future as well as present costs. The *present value* of future costs is determined by discounting those costs at some rate such as the market rate of interest. Thus, for example, the present value of $100 one year hence discounted at 10 percent would be $90.91; the present value of $100 two years hence, would be $82.65; the present value of $100 per year for five years discounted at 10 percent would be some $379.07. Obviously the present value is lower for years more distant at any given interest rate, and lower for any given year at higher interest rates.

The comptroller general's study was concerned with the cost of alcoholism among federal employees in 1970; the PAR study focused on the cost of alcoholism among postal service workers in 1971. Neither study attempted to assess the *future* costs. On the surface it might seem that the focus of each study on a particular year negated any need for concern with future costs; the latter could in principle be assigned to their respective future years. In many contexts this might well be so. In the context of alcohol abuse, however, it is not. Alcohol abuse can result in premature death. In assessing the economic cost of alcohol abuse in a given year, some account must be taken of premature deaths during that year that can be attributed to alcohol abuse. When an individual dies prematurely, all of that individual's future production is irretrievably lost to society. It seems reasonable to allocate those costs to the year of death.

Both the comptroller general's study and the PAR study are simple and straightforward. Although they may both have had program and policy impact, they leave the reader with low confidence with respect to solving the problem of actually measuring the relationship between lost output and alcohol abuse. Other studies of a more scientific nature have addressed themselves to the problem of measuring the lost production costs of alcoholism. One such study of interest was that completed by Winslow and his associates in the mid-1960s.[4]

Winslow et al. used three small samples ($N = 19$), identified as suspected-problem-drinking, miscellaneous-problem, and problem-free groups, and attempted to measure several economic costs, including impaired productivity. They found that the costs for the two problem groups were about the same, but considerably higher than the costs for the *problem-free* group. The implication of the costliness of problem drinkers is hardly significant for our purposes, since every study gives similar results. In fact, as noted by Trice and Roman in their comprehensive survey of the literature, ". . . regardless of the method used and the dollar amounts revealed, these studies all point out that the deviant drinker costs his employer *dollars* that might be used elsewhere."[5] Three aspects of the Winslow et al. study are of interest in light of our present purposes, however. First, they note that the cost of days absent without pay is borne by the worker; this is an example of a cost borne by society and not by the firm. A second and more intriguing feature is their choice of a miscellaneous-problem group as part of the research methodology. We are informed that problem workers, drinking and nondrinking, are equally costly. This finding is somewhat disturbing, in that it is consistent with certain prevalent beliefs about alcoholism to the effect that if people did not take to alcohol, they would take to something else; that is, if people are problem-prone, whether or not they abuse alcohol is not really significant. Of course, formulating or trying to formulate theories to fit known facts is not the scientific method. Rather, we must be aware of the fact that we do not really know if alcohol, at least in the aggregate, is dysfunctional. To know that alcoholic workers are more costly to a firm than nonalcoholic workers is not to know that the alcohol-abusing worker without alcohol would be more productive. Although the available evidence is certainly suggestive in support of the view that alcohol abuse unfavorably affects productivity, current knowledge is not sufficient to isolate the net impact of alcohol abuse, per se, on productivity.

The third and most significant aspect of the Winslow study is their finding that "apparently the company was already paying a higher base daily wage rate to the problem-free employees than to the suspected problem drinking employees. . . ."[6] What we have here is a finding consistent with economic theory, namely, that lower wages imply lower productivity. In effect, the market corrects for lower productivity in the form of lower wages.

For the most part, studies which have dealt with firms, organizations, or industries have not been designed to answer the question "How much more productive would alcohol-abusing workers be if they were not abusers?" Rather, these studies have been designed to approximate an answer to a more limited question: "Given the present productivity of the worker as measured by his present wage, what are the costs of alcohol abuse to the firm?'' Society in general needs an answer to the first question, and to date one has not been forthcoming.

One final set of more limited studies can be analyzed to some advantage for the purpose of designing a means to measure the economic cost of reduced output from the broader perspective of society as a whole. These studies come from the work of Pell and D'Alonzo. In their work Pell and D'Alonzo make no effort to quantify the economic costs of alcohol abuse, but they are nonetheless illuminating with respect to the nature of the problem. For example, in their mortality study they note that

> the cost of alcoholism to industry is made up of several components, including loss of efficiency, absenteeism, lost time on the job as well as off the job, faulty decision making, accidents, impaired morale of co-workers, and the cost of rehabilitation programs. A large and significant portion of the economic impact of alcoholism also includes premature disability and death, resulting in loss of many employees in their prime who have skills that are difficult to replace.[7]

An important finding in their work is that the present and past economic behavior of problem drinkers is significantly different from that of nonproblem drinkers.

In their earlier work on absenteeism, Pell and D'Alonzo reported that for each of three alcoholic-worker classifications—*known, suspected,* and *recovered*—the absences per annum were significantly higher than for each of three matched control groups.[8] While one might expect that problem drinkers in the *known* and *suspected* groups would have more absences than members of the respective control groups, the finding that those in the *recovered* group had more absences than those in the relevant control group is of special interest. It suggests perhaps that alcohol has a long-run deleterious effect on productivity even if one recovers from the disease, or possibly that the alcoholic person is a problem worker even when he does not drink.

An interesting aspect of Pell and D'Alonzo's work is that in the firm they studied they found an alcoholic prevalence rate considerably lower than the rate which is generally accepted. They found a prevalence rate of about 1 percent of the work force; the minimum rate generally accepted by experts in the field is some 4 percent of the work force. If the economic effects of alcoholism as measured by Pell and D'Alonzo and others are concentrated in a much smaller proportion of the labor force than is generally assumed, then estimates of economic cost based on higher prevalence rates will be considerably overstated.

On the other hand, it is quite possible that general prevalence rates may be much higher than the rate Pell and D'Alonzo report for their company. Although the company under study is not identified, it is clear that the company management was well aware of the problem and implications of alcohol abuse. The lower prevalence rate could be a result of a conscious effort by management to minimize alcoholism through a variety of programs. Alternatively, the lower rate noted by Pell and D'Alonzo may be due to the classification of the three types of alcoholics by a company medical staff with more restrictive standards for defining alcoholism than those used by other professionals in the alcohol field.

Two additional findings in the work of Pell and D'Alonzo are worthy of note. First, they report that 37.8 percent of the alcoholics had no absent sick days. This certainly suggests that some alcohol-abusing workers may be able to handle their problem with no adverse impact on their productivity. Second, they found a relatively greater proportion of alcoholics were paid an hourly wage than were paid a salary as compared with the entire work force of the company under study. Since those on wages generally have lower earnings than those on salary, this finding is certainly consistent with the view that the market tends to "correct" for the lower productivity of alcoholics in the form of lower pay.

On balance, past research which has concentrated on the cost of lost production to a single firm, organization, or industry does not provide a basis for estimating the economic cost of lost production to society in the aggregate. These studies do, however, provide some insight into the factors that need to be considered in making such an effort.

Two previous research efforts have attempted to treat the economic cost of alcoholism from the broader perspective of society as a whole. Holtmann attempted to quantify many of the economic costs attributable to alcoholism among males in the United States for the year 1959.[9] Pritchard, although apparently unaware of Holtmann's work, attempted to estimate the economic costs to Australia of alcoholism in the year 1965.[10] Both Holtmann and Pritchard attempted to estimate the economic cost of alcohol abuse as reflected in, for example, premature mortality, excess morbidity, absenteeism, and unemployment. Since each of these manifestations is related to lost production, and since the two researchers used somewhat different approaches, some insight can be gained by considering each study briefly.

One objective of Holtmann's study was to determine the present value of the costs of alcoholism for those who were alcoholics in 1959. In order to accomplish this, Holtmann attempted to estimate lost production costs due to premature mortality, unemployment, and absenteeism among alcoholics.

Holtmann relied on previously published mortality, occupation, and age data for alcoholics and occupational income data for the general population as a basis for estimating the present value of reduced earnings due to the premature death of alcoholics.[11] The first step in his calculation amounted to generating a single average-income figure for an occupationally composite alcoholic. Thus, for example, given the proportion of the 2,023 clinic patients in his source study in each occupation (see note 11), he multiplied these proportions by the actual median income for each occupation to obtain an estimated income for a "typical" alcoholic of some $5,334. Then, on the basis of the age distribution of the sample of alcoholics and the projected mortality of alcoholics based on Pearl's data (see note 11), he calculated the present value of lost earnings due to the premature death of alcoholics. In effect, he did not calculate the present value of alcoholics who died in 1959, but rather the present value of alcoholics who were alive in 1959 and might be expected to die prematurely in some future year.

Holtmann used the same general approach to estimate the present value of future losses due to alcohol-induced unemployment. Employing data from the same, previously published sources (see note 11), he estimated unemployment rates and average income for alcoholics. Holtmann used an unemployment rate due to alcohol abuse of 25 percent among labor-force alcoholics to calculate the present value of future losses from unemployment caused by alcoholism. Again, his estimate of the cost of unemployment due to alcoholism is an estimate not of lost production in 1959, but rather of projected lost production in future years. His estimate of the cost of unemployment amounted to assessing what the future earnings of alcoholics would be if they had the same unemployment rate as nonalcoholics.

Finally, Holtmann applied the same technique to estimate the present value of the cost of absenteeism among alcoholics. His estimate of the cost of absenteeism amounted to assessing what the future earnings of alcoholics would be if they had the same rate of absence as nonalcoholics.

On balance, although Holtmann's study took the broader social perspective, it really did not answer the question that we want to answer—viz., "What is the economic cost of lost production in a given year due to alcoholism?" Holtmann did not estimate the economic cost of lost production in 1959; rather, he estimated the present value of future lost production for those who were alcoholics in 1959.[12]

The objective of Pritchard's study was more in line with our present concern. Pritchard was attempting to answer the question "What were the economic costs to Australia of alcohol abuse in 1965?" Unfortunately, his efforts at quantification were quite limited. He attempted to measure the costs of alcoholism only as reflected in premature mortality and excess morbidity resulting in unemployment.

The approach that Pritchard used to calculate the costs of premature mortality is more relevant to our purpose than Holtmann's. Pritchard argued that earnings can be taken as a reasonable approximation of a worker's productivity. Moreover, he explicitly assumed that if alcoholism had not resulted in premature death in 1965, [13] the individual would have had an average life expectancy and would have experienced a stream of future earnings similar to that enjoyed by the average person of the same age and sex.

Pritchard employed a similar approach to estimate the economic cost of unemployment due to alcoholism. He used estimates of the unemployment rates among alcoholic workers, but he applied these rates to average earnings data rather than to the earnings of alcoholics. Thus, his estimates of the economic cost of unemployment due to alcoholism implicitly assumed that any difference in productivity and earnings between alcoholic workers and other workers is due to alcohol abuse.

On balance, although Pritchard's study took the broader social perspective and was cast in the context of the question that we want to answer, his answer was incomplete. What is the economic cost to society of lost production in a given year due to alcoholism? Alternatively, what would society gain in terms of economic output if alcohol abuse did not exist? Pritchard's study indicated what society would gain if alcoholics did not die prematurely but rather lived to produce at the same rate as nonalcoholics. His study also indicated what society would gain if unemployed alcoholics returned to the labor force to produce at the same rate as nonalcoholics. But his study did not indicate what society would gain if the surviving, employed alcoholics were to produce at the same rate as nonalcoholics. Although Pritchard did argue that earnings approximate productivity, and he did allow for the productivity of alcoholic workers to be lower than that of nonalcoholic workers in his calculations of the costs of premature mortality and unemployment, he did not attempt to measure the cost of lost production in the context of the lower productivity of alcoholics who were actually employed, Hence, his estimates did not include a very significant part of the total economic cost of lost production due to alcoholism.

Although a review of past research does not provide an answer to the question of what is the economic cost of lost production due to alcoholism, it does provide considerable insight into the factors that must be considered if the question is to be answered. It should be clear that we must have answers to three specific questions if we hope to answer the general question. First, we need some estimate or indication of the prevalence of alcohol abuse. Second, we need some estimate or indication of the extent to which alcohol abuse unfavorably affects productivity. Third, we need to know the incidence of premature mortality among alcohol abusers. Given answers to these questions, we could estimate the cost of lost production—albeit only in the market sector—due to alcohol abuse.

PRODUCTIVITY AND THE PREVALENCE OF ALCOHOL ABUSE

In order to estimate the value of lost production due to alcohol abuse, we need to know both the impact of alcohol abuse on productivity and the prevalence of alcohol abuse. Does the abuse of alcohol tend to lower a person's productivity? Do workers with lower productivity earn less? How many workers have alcohol problems?

Numerous studies of alcoholism within particular firms, organizations, and industries have found that workers with alcohol problems have higher average levels of absenteeism, tardiness, sickness, and the like than nonalcoholic workers. Certainly the studies outlined in the previous section indicate potential lower productivity among alcohol-abusing workers. Moreover, to the extent that virtually all such studies conclude that there are significant costs to the firm or organization, they indicate lower productivity among alcohol-abusing workers relative to the wages and salaries paid these workers.

There are some difficulties, however, with taking such indications as definite evidence of lower productivity relative to wages paid. It is quite possible that although alcohol-abusing workers are more frequently absent, tardy, and the like, their actual wage may reflect their lower productivity. In essence, the employer may recognize that alcohol-troubled workers have lower productivity and accordingly pay them less than other workers. From the perspective of the firm, the cost of alcohol abuse is minimized. Of course there is an economic cost to society in terms of lost production due to alcohol abuse, but it is borne by the worker, not by the firm.

But although there may be a tendency for the wages of alcohol-abusing workers to reflect their productivity, it is unlikely that the wage always measures the real value of the marginal product. A critical question is whether or not the firm is aware of a differential between what it pays, the wage, and what it gets, the dollar value of the marginal product of the worker. Even if the firm is cognizant of a productivity differential, it does not necessarily follow that all of that differential will be reflected in a wage differential. One consideration, of course, is that removing the differential may well involve costs: the firm would have to expend time and resources to identify alcohol-induced lower productivity. Moreover, in many instances the firm may want to consider future as well as present productivity. Certain workers may have potential or skills that can not readily be replaced. Firms may choose to "invest" in some workers by paying them more than the value of their present product. A comment in a study by Observer and Maxwell is illustrative of the relevance of this point of view in the context of alcohol abuse.

> It has been hypothesized that industry's greatest loss from problem drinking may well be the failure of certain promising young men, men with ten years and more in the company who were expected to show great talent and to assume high responsibility as they moved into their forties, but who fell (no longer "unaccountably") by the wayside.[14]

Finally, given a complex relationship between a firm and a worker organization such as a union, it just may not be "worth it" to try to root out the alcoholic workers, or to reduce their wages to reflect any productivity difference.

To the extent that the difference in productivity due to alcohol abuse is greater, for whatever reason, than the difference in wages, the firm will be absorbing part of the cost of lost production. The economic cost of lost production due to alcohol abuse remains the same, but it is not borne as directly by the alcohol abuser. In fact, of course, the firm may well be able to shift the burden to nonabusing workers in the form of lower average wages, or to consumers in general in the form of higher prices for its product.

On balance, we may expect that lower productivity will be reflected in lower wages. In order to estimate the value of lost production due to alcohol-induced lower productivity, it is necessary to use available market information. Lower earnings will be the best available approximation to lost production. In general and on the average, when the market is working reasonably well it will tend to correct for lower productivity. Still, the market does not often, if ever, work perfectly, and we would expect the correction to be less than perfect. To the extent that the adjustment in wages is less than a complete adjustment for lower productivity, any estimate of the value of lost production will be an understatement.

In effect, since we must rely on market information to estimate lost production, the estimate will be more or less accurate according as the market is working more or less well. At one extreme, if the market served to adjust each worker's wage so as to exactly reflect his relative productivity, an estimate of lost production generated by summing the lost earnings of alcohol abusers would result in a perfectly accurate measure. At the other extreme, if the market did not serve to adjust wages for relative productivity at all, an estimate of lost production generated by summing the lost earnings of alcohol abusers would result in a completely inaccurate estimate of zero. Hence, it might be more appropriate to note that the estimate derived is actually a measure of the lost production burden borne by the alcohol-abusing worker. As such, it will generally be an understatement of total lost production.

In general, the alcohol-troubled worker has usually been identified as one who has problems that are manifested in the form of absenteeism, tardiness, sickness, and the like. Very little is known about the alcohol-troubled worker who has lower productivity that is not recorded in terms of time off the job but his problems are manifested in more subtle forms. Part of the measurement problem is that nearly everyone drinks. Many people drink a great deal with apparently little effect on their productivity.

It might seem that one could measure income differences between abusing and nonabusing workers and consider such differences as a first approximation to the cost of alcohol abuse. But how would one determine which workers were abusers and which nonabusers? Surely one cannot conclude that a low-income drinker has a low income because of his drinking, anymore than one could conclude that a high-income drinker has a high income because of his drinking. If, however, one had an independently derived identification of alcohol-abusing workers, one could test the hypothesis that they have lower incomes, on the average, than their nonabusing counterparts.

The works of Cahalan and his colleagues on American drinking practices seemingly constitute a breakthrough in determining who might be classified as an abuser for purposes of measuring the economic cost of alcohol abuse. They have been engaged in a research program on the drinking practices of the general population over the past fifteen years.[15] During the course of this research they have conducted several surveys, including three national probability samples of households. These surveys have been concerned with drinking, on the one hand, and the consequences of drinking, on the other. Thus, respondents have been questioned both about their drinking practices and about problems they were having with other people, such as spouses, relatives, friends, neighbors, and co-workers, and problems they were having in managing themselves, such as financial and health problems. On the basis of individual drinking practices, Cahalan and his colleagues have identified five mutually exclusive groups: (1) nondrinkers; (2) those who drink but have no problems; (3) those who drink but have potential problems only; (4) heavy drinkers for whom drinking has no consequences; and (5) drinkers for whom drinking has high consequences.

The last group is seemingly the alcohol-abusing classification that is sought for present purposes. From an economic perspective, this group is most likely to be the major source of whatever may be the economic cost of lost production due to alcohol abuse, since they represent the drinkers apparently having difficulty functioning in society. If they are having difficulty functioning in their general social roles, problems in their work roles are to be expected. The extent of their work problems might be measured by comparing their incomes with the incomes of otherwise similar persons who are not in their category.

There is indeed some empirical evidence that can be used to test the hypothesis that alcohol abusers, defined as drinkers with high consequences, have lower incomes than nonabusers. The Social Research Group of the School of Public Health, University of California at Berkeley, provided us with household income data generated by their most recent national probability sample, conducted in 1969. The households surveyed were those that included a noninstitutionalized male aged 21 to 59 inclusive in 1968. The income distribution of households, classified according to whether or not a male alcohol abuser was present in the household, is outlined in table 2–1. The average income of households with male abusers is indeed lower than that of households with no male abusers.[16]

There are a disproportionate number of households with male abusers present in the lowest income groups; in fact, the percentage of households in the two lowest income groups is almost three times as great among abuser households as among nonabuser households. Similarly, there are proportionately fewer households with male abusers present in the highest income groups. Thus, for example, while less than one-third of nonabuser households had incomes below $8,000, just over one-half of the abuser households had incomes below $8,000.

The nonabusers include men in the first four groups of the Cahalan et. al. typology: nondrinkers; drinkers with no problems; drinkers with potential problems only; and heavy drinkers with no consequences. The abusers include only those men found to be drinkers with high consequences. Households that include male alcohol abusers have lower incomes than households that do not; this difference in average household income is consistent with the hypothesis that alcohol abusers have lower incomes than others.

The household income data in table 2–1 do not represent the earnings of workers alone, however, since they include transfer payments and nonlabor income such as interest income. The mean income data are particularly influenced by extreme observations, such as rather low income in the case of certain households which rely exclusively on transfer payments from welfare programs or rather high incomes that certain households may derive from nonlabor sources.[17] The median income data, on the other hand, will be less influenced by nonemployment income and may reflect more

TABLE 2–1. Distribution of Household Income in 1968 for Households That Included a Noninstitutionalized Male Aged 21–59

Household Income	No Alcohol-Abusing Male Present*		Alcohol-Abusing Male Present†		Both	
	Number of Households	Percentage	Number of Households	Percentage	Number of Households	Percentage
Under $2,000	21	1.6	4	1.4	25	1.6
2,000–3,999	50	3.9	41	14.4	91	5.8
4,000–5,999	128	10.0	42	14.7	170	10.9
6,000–7,999	192	15.1	58	20.4	250	16.0
8,000–9,999	266	20.9	49	17.2	315	20.2
10,000–14,999	373	29.2	61	21.4	434	27.8
15,000 and over	246	19.3	30	10.5	276	17.7
Total	1276	100.0	285	100.0	1561	100.0
Median Household Income	$ 9,861		$7,931		$ 9,556	
Mean Household Income‡	10,689		8,725		10,330	

*Nonabusers include: nondrinkers; drinkers with no problems; drinkers with potential problems only; and heavy drinkers with no consequences.
†Abusers include drinkers with high consequences.
‡Calculated by assuming $18,000 as the midpoint of the open-end income class.
Source: Social Research Group, School of Public Health, University of California at Berkeley. The data are from a national probability sample of households.

closely earnings from employment alone.[18] Strictly speaking, a difference between the earnings of abusing and nonabusing workers cannot be inferred directly from these data. These data are consistent, however, with the hypothesis that alcohol abusers, defined as drinkers with high consequences, have lower earnings than others.

Of course, determinants of income include many and varied factors. Experience, education, age, luck, intelligence, creativity, health status, and other factors all have something to do with one's level of income. One's ability to function within society might also be associated with productivity and, hence, be a determinant of one's level of income. If a person drinks with high consequences, he might be expected to have a lower income than others of the same experience, education, age, luck, intelligence, creativity, health status, and so forth. In effect, we would postulate that, all other things being equal, alcohol abuse will lower productivity and be reflected in lower earnings. The data in table 2–1 do indicate the extent to which alcohol abusers tend to have lower incomes. They do not indicate the extent to which other things that affect income are or are not equal, however. If the income data summarized in table 2–1 are to be used to estimate lost production due to alcohol abuse, some account must be taken of and an appropriate adjustment made for the likelihood that other things are indeed not equal.

It would appear that Cahalan and his colleagues have succeeded in delineating a group that is composed of persons that have difficulty functioning in society and that they are drinkers. It seems reasonable to infer that this dysfunction affects their productivity and that their lowered productivity is reflected in their earnings. This inference rests on two assumptions: first, that a dysfunctional group has been identified; and, second, that factor markets will tend to correct for the productivity implications of the dysfunction. Certainly the income data collected by Cahalan and his colleagues tend to support this conclusion. We are implicitly assuming, of course, that alcohol abuse is the cause of the dysfunction. Actually, Cahalan and his colleagues have argued only that drinking is involved and that high consequences attend such drinking.

ESTIMATED PRODUCTION LOSS IN 1971 AMONG NONINSTITUTIONALIZED MALES AGED 21–59

If alcohol abuse were a factor in lowering the earnings of workers, it would show up as a difference between the average annual earnings of alcohol abusers and nonabusers. If an adjustment were made for any differences in the composition of the abusing and nonabusing groups in terms of other factors that affect income (such as age, education, experience, cultural background, and the like), the net difference between the average annual earnings of the two groups would be a reasonable basis for estimating the cost of lost production due to alcohol abuse.

It would not be appropriate to take the gross difference in income between the abusing and nonabusing groups as a measure of the effect of alcohol abuse on earnings unless the two groups were the same with respect to all other factors that affect income. Unfortunately, the data provided by the Social Research Group at Berkeley are such that only age differences can be adjusted for directly. The respective average annual household incomes in 1968 by age of noninstitutionalized males included in the household are given in Table 2–2. Analysis of the data in table 2–2 indicates that some 9.3 percent of the gross difference in mean household income— approximately $183 of the $1,964 difference in mean income between households with and without alcohol-abusing males present— can be accounted for by age differences between the two groups.

Although age is undoubtedly correlated with other factors (such as experience) that affect income, an additional adjustment would be desirable to account for factors that affect income and are not correlated with age.[19] What is needed is an adjustment factor to apply to the gross difference in income between the abusing and nonabusing groups that will serve to net out that part of the difference that is due to factors other than alcohol abuse that are known to influence income.

In a recently published comprehensive study, Luft utilized such an approach to measure the impact of poor health on earnings.[20] His empirical results provide the basis we need for computing the adjustment factor. Utilizing data from the 1967 Survey of Economic Opportunity, a national sample of all adults aged 18 to 64, Luft calculated the mean annual earnings of sick and well workers for the year 1966. As one would expect, the earnings of those in good health were considerably higher than the earnings of those in poor health. By means of multiple regression, Luft was able to analyze the gross difference and determine the net effect of poor health on earnings, taking account of such other factors as age, education, family structure, and the like. Even after controlling for other factors, Luft found a net difference between the annual earnings of those in good

TABLE 2–2. Average Annual Household Income in 1968 by Age of Noninstitutionalized Males Included in the Household

Age Group	Number of Households			Mean Household Income			Median Household Income		
	No Male Abuser Present*	Male Abuser Present†	Total	No Male Abuser Present*	Male Abuser Present†	Difference	No Male Abuser Present*	Male Abuser Present†	Difference
21–29	284	108	392	$ 9,692	$7,875	$1,817	$ 8,857	$7,121	$1,736
30–39	330	66	396	11,252	9,303	1,949	10,808	8,857	1,951
40–49	331	59	390	11,118	8,983	2,135	10,026	7,934	2,092
50–59	331	52	383	10,556	9,462	1,094	10,023	8,756	1,267
All ages	1276	285	1561	10,689	8,725	1,964	9,861	7,931	1,930

*Nonabusers include: nondrinkers; drinkers with no problems; drinkers with potential problems only; and heavy drinkers with no consequences.
†Abusers include drinkers with high consequences.
Source: Social Research Group, School of Public Health, University of California at Berkeley. The data are from a national probability sample of households.

and poor health, but that difference, of course, was somewhat less than the gross difference.

Of particular interest, however, is the estimate Luft derived of the proportion of the gross difference in earnings that is accounted for by differences in such factors as age, education, family structure, and the like. In fact, some 23.9 percent of the gross difference in male earnings was accounted for by differences in these and other, related characteristics of the two groups. Thus, we might make an additional adjustment of some 14.6 percent (23.9—9.3) to account for other factors that affect income and that are not accounted for by age-specific differences in mean income between the abusing and nonabusing groups. Alternatively, we could make an adjustment of 23.9 percent of the gross difference.

Certainly some adjustment should be made for differences in the composition of the abusing and nonabusing groups with respect to other factors that affect income. It would not be appropriate to take the gross difference in income as a measure of the effect of alcohol abuse on earnings, since there is ample evidence that alcohol abusers do not have the same sociocultural/economic characteristics as non-abusers. It would obviously be better if we had sufficient data to ascertain the extent to which differences in these characteristics account for income differences, but the gross adjustment suggested by the Luft study seems a reasonable approximation for a number of reasons. First, the data available for alcohol abusers indicates that age-related factors account for some 9.3 percent of the gross differ-ence. Second, both the Social Research Group data and the Luft data came from national probability samples; hence, statistically the two samples would be expected to have similar sociocultural/economic characteristics in the aggregate. Of course, the Social Research Group sample was partitioned by alcohol abuse and the Luft sample was partitioned by health status, so the relevant subsamples would not necessarily have the same characteristics. Still, to the extent that alcohol abuse is a disease, one might expect the characteristics of the relevant subsamples to be somewhat similar as well. Finally, even if the adjustment is but an approximation, it serves to avoid overstating the net effect of alcohol abuse on earnings.

Given the data made available by the Social Research Group and the adjustment factor suggested by Luft's study, we now have sufficient data to generate an estimate of the economic cost of lost production due to alcohol abuse among noninstitutionalized males between the ages of 21 and 59. Of course the data are not ideal, and the flaws in them should not be forgotten when the results are considered, but they do make possible a better approximation than previously available data allowed.

Estimated annual average household income by age for 1971 is given in table 2–3. The mean 1968 income data have been adjusted for inflation to estimate the mean household income in 1971 and are summarized by age group in the first two columns. Nonabusers include the first four groups in the Cahalan et. al. typology: non-drinkers, drinkers with no problems; drinkers with potential problems only; and heavy drinkers with no consequences. Abusers include only those men found to be drinkers with high consequences. The gross age-specific differences in mean income between households with no male abuser present and households with a male abuser present are given in column 3. The estimated net differences—that is, the differences adjusted to account for other sociocultural/economic factors that affect earnings—are given in column 4. The estimated net differences in household income can be taken as reasonable approximations of the effect of alcohol abuse on earnings.

Since the original data were for 1968, we are assuming that there was no change in the net effect of alcohol abuse on household earnings over the period 1968 to 1971. Moreover, we are assuming that the alcoholism prevalence rates of the earlier period still prevailed in 1971. Finally, we are assuming that some 23.9 percent of the gross difference in earnings between abusers and nonabusers is accounted for by sociocultural/economic factors such as age, education, and family structure.[21] Given these qualifications, we can estimate the lower earnings due to alcohol abuse in 1971 as the product of the estimated net difference in average household income and the estimated number of households that included an alcohol-abusing male.

Our estimate of lower earnings due to alcohol abuse in 1971 by age is given in table 2–4. More than 6.5 million households included a male alcohol abuser between the ages of 21 and 59. In the aggregate, households with an alcohol-abusing male present had lower earnings due to alcohol abuse on the order of $11.4 billion. In fact, they actually had lower earnings of almost $15 billion, but sociocultural/economic factors accounted for some 23.9 percent of those lower earnings.

The lower earnings of these households due to alcohol abuse represents a reasonable approximation of the economic cost of lost production due to alcohol abuse among noninstitutionalized males between the ages of 21 and 59. In fact, since we have no reasonable empirical basis for refining this estimate, it will be taken as our best

TABLE 2–3. Estimated Average Annual Household Income in 1971 by Age of Noninstitutionalized Males Included in the Household

Age Group	Mean Household Income			Estimated Net Difference	Percentage of Households with Male Abuser Present
	No Male Abuser Present*	Male Abuser Present†	Gross Difference		
21–29	$11,242	$ 9,134	$2,108	$1,769	27.6
30–39	13,051	10,791	2,260	1,896	16.7
40–49	12,896	10,419	2,477	2,078	15.1
50–59	12,244	10,975	1,269	1,065	13.6
All ages	12,398	10,120	2,278	1,734	18.3

*Nonabusers include: nondrinkers; drinkers with no problems; drinkers with potential problems only; and heavy drinkers with no consequences.

†Abusers include drinkers with high consequences.

Source: Mean household income data in columns 1 and 2 were derived by inflating 1968 data in table 2–2. The prevalence data in column 4 were derived from number of households in each category, as outlined in table 2–2.

TABLE 2–4. Estimated Lower Earnings in 1971 of Households Having an Alcohol-Abusing Male Present, by Age

Age Group	Total Number of Households Including a Male (in thousands)	Percentage of Households with Male Abuser Present	Estimated Number of Households with Male Abuser Present (in thousands)	Estimated Net Difference in Mean Household Income	Estimated Lower Earnings Due to Alcohol Abuse (in millions)
21–29	7,012	27.6	1,935.3	$1,769	$ 3,423.5
30–39	10,156	16.7	1,696.1	1,896	3,215.8
40–49	10,851	15.1	1,638.5	2,078	3,404.8
50–59	9,553	13.6	1,299.2	1,065	1,383.6
All ages	37,572		6,569.1		$11,427.7

Source: The total number of households including a male is from U.S. Bureau of the Census, *Family Composition 1970: Subject Report* (Washington, D.C.: U.S. Government Printing Office, 1973). For the percentage of households with male abusers present, see table 2–2. For the estimated net difference in mean household income, see table 2–3.

estimate of lost production in the market sector in 1971 due to alcohol abuse. If careful consideration is given to the several obvious ways in which this surrogate may be a biased estimate, it would seem that $11.4 billion does indeed represent a reasonably conservative estimate of the economic cost of lost production due to alcohol abuse in 1971.

On the one hand, we have not taken the gross difference in income between abuser and nonabuser households as a measure of the difference in earnings due to alcohol abuse. Rather, we have attempted to adjust the difference to account for other factors, such as age, education, and family structure, that undoubtedly influence earnings. Clearly, the gross difference in median income between abuser and nonabuser households represents more than the net effect of alcohol abuse. By adjusting the difference to account for other factors, we have avoided an obvious overstatement of the net loss due to alcohol abuse.

On the other hand, there are several ways in which the estimate derived will tend to understate the economic cost of lost production. To the extent that lower earnings of abusers were offset in part by transfer payments such as unemployment compensation or welfare payments, the difference in average income between abuser and nonabuser households would understate the loss due to alcohol abuse. The same holds true with respect to the extent that other household members moved into the labor force in order to counteract the loss of earnings.[22] Moreover, the age distribution was truncated at both ends. No amount is included in the estimate for alcohol-abusing workers below the age of 21 or over the age of 59. Finally, no amount is included in the estimate for working women who were alcohol abusers.

On balance, $11.4 billion would seem to be a conservative estimate of the economic cost of lost production due to alcohol abuse among the civilian labor force in 1971. In any event, it is a reasonable approximation, and it is the best approximation available at present of the economic cost of lost production in the market sector.

ESTIMATED PRODUCTION LOSS IN 1971 AMONG THE MILITARY

What is the output of the military services? The answer at the most abstract and possibly most useful level is national defense.

National defense, like the output of the housewife, is not sold in the marketplace. Hence there are no convenient data such as market prices to measure either the value of national defense or the value of lost national-defense production due to alcohol abuse. Still, national defense consumes a significant part of the nation's scarce resources, and some estimate should be made, if possible, of the economic cost of lost production due to alcohol abuse among the military.

Since no market prices for military output are available, an alternative approach would be to examine the economic costs of the labor inputs used to produce national defense and then use the reduced labor inputs times their wage as a measure of reduced military output. This procedure is a satisfactory approximation so long as it is understood that the figure arrived at measures not the value of lost military output but rather the cost of producing some unknown value of military output. If, for example, alcoholism, in the aggregate, causes the army to lose enough man-years to staff a division for a year, the loss is not the division per se but rather the amount of national defense that the division's worth of manpower could have produced.

In 1971, according to Department of Defense data, the total military payroll for all services was some $18.6 billion.[23] What proportion of that payroll was paid out for services not performed because of alcohol abuse? That amount could be taken to represent the cost, albeit not the value, of lost military production due to alcohol abuse.

In a recent study by Cahalan et al.,[24] some reasonable estimates were derived of the cost to the army of lost production due to alcohol abuse. They estimated that the army lost up to 18,748 man-years of military work in 1971 because of absence from duty and reduced efficiency among army personnel due to alcohol abuse. Since the army employed some 966,000 personnel in 1971, it lost approximately 2 percent of its potential labor productivity because of alcohol abuse.

These data are applied in table 2–5 to estimate the cost to the entire military of lost production in 1971. The estimate of $361 million can be interpreted in two ways. On the one hand, from the perspective of the military, military personnel were paid some $361 million for work not performed. On the other hand, from the more important perspective of the society that is buying military output, society was getting at least $361 million less of national-defense output than Defense Department budget data indicated was purchased for 1971.

TABLE 2–5. Estimated Cost of Lost Production in the Military Due to Alcohol Abuse in 1971

Army Personnel	Man-Years Lost Due to Alcohol Abuse in the Army	Man-Years Lost as a Percentage of Total Personnel	Total Military Payroll (in billions)	Estimated Cost of Lost Production (in millions)
966,000	18,748	1.94	$18.6	$361

Sources: Army personnel and total military payroll are from U.S. Bureau of the Census, *Statistical Abstract of the United States: 1973* (Washington, D.C.: U.S. Government Printing Office, 1973).

Man-years lost due to alcohol abuse in the army are from D. Cahalan, I. H. Cisin, G. L. Gardner, and G. C. Smith, "Drinking Practices and Problems in the U.S. Army, 1972," final report of a study conducted for the Deputy Chief of Staff, Personnel, Headquarters, Department of the Army, under Contract Report No. 73-6 (December 1972).

LOST PRODUCTION AND PREMATURE MORTALITY

Throughout this chapter we have concentrated on estimating the value of the production that society had to forego in 1971 because of alcohol abuse. But what of the persons who died prematurely in 1971 as a direct or indirect consequence of alcohol abuse? When an individual dies prematurely, all of that individual's future production is irretrievably lost. It seems reasonable, as we have noted, to assign the present value of lost future production to the year of premature death.

How many people died in 1971 who would not have died if they had not been alcohol abusers? In the absence of alcohol abuse, how many more productive years would those persons have had? If we had answers to these questions, we could estimate the present value of the lost future production as the discounted stream of future earnings that these workers might have been expected to earn if they were not alcohol abusers and had not died prematurely.

If alcohol abuse did not contribute to premature death, alcohol abusers would have the same mortality rate as nonabusers—that is, their *relative mortality rate* would be 1.0.[25] To the extent that alcohol abuse does contribute to premature death, alcohol abusers will have a higher mortality rate than nonabusers. Their relative mortality rate will then be greater than 1.0; and excess deaths will be attributable to alcohol abuse.

There is a considerable literature on the relationship between alcohol and mortality. Indeed, there are almost too many estimates of the relative mortality rates of alcohol abusers. Several estimates of the age-specific relative mortality rates of alcohol abusers are summarized in table 2-6. Although the studies cited consistently indicate excess mortality among alcohol abusers, some care should be exercised in interpreting the results.

The literature concerned with excess mortality and alcohol abuse has been summarized and analyzed in two recent comprehensive reviews.[26] These reviews serve to indicate the extent to which previous empirical evidence was derived from samples with special characteristics and, hence, should not be generalized without specific adjustment or qualifications.

For example, the first three studies summarized in table 2-6 were carried out to compare relative mortality rates among persons covered by life insurance. In effect, these studies compared a group of policy holders judged to be "substandard" on the basis of evidence in their records indicating adverse drinking behavior with the group of policy holders judged to be "standard." Although these studies probably reflect excess mortality among heavy drinkers, it is unlikely that the specific rates can be generalized to the population at large. On the one hand, "standard" policy holders of insurance companies presumably have lower than average mortality rates; good insurance risks are good precisely because they are better in this respect than the general population. On the other hand, those who are judged substandard with respect to drinking habits may also be substandard on other mortality-related factors. Moreover, males are generally overrepresentated in insurance data, as are persons with higher incomes and those with families. On balance, estimated relative mortality rates from insurance studies are probably biased upwards, even for the insurance populations in question.

The second three studies summarized in table 2-6 were undertaken to compare the mortality rate of males who had been in treatment for alcoholism with that of the male population in general.[27] The estimates of relative mortality derived from such follow-up studies of alcoholic patients are rather consistent and the overall rates range from 2.02 to 2.36.[28] It is unlikely that the results of such clinical studies are representative for alcohol abusers in general. It seems reasonable to assume that persons who end up in alcoholism treatment centers have an extended history of relatively heavy drinking. It is unlikely that such patients are typical even of all heavy

TABLE 2–6. Age-Specific Relative Mortality Rates of Alcohol Abusers, as Estimated in Several Studies

Age Group	Insurance Studies			Clinical Studies			Population Studies		
	Menge 1950	Davies 1965	Gundy 1965	Schmidt & deLint 1972	Sundby 1967	California 1961	Dahlgren 1951	Pearl 1926	Room & Day 1974
10–19	3.89	3.41	3.10	2.50	*	*	*	*	*
20–29	4.85			2.50	2.95	3.26	.98	*	*
30–39	3.92	2.38	1.87	2.92	2.25	3.87	1.05	1.29	3.30
40–49	2.95			3.52	2.96	2.63	1.46	1.58	
50–59	2.08	2.93	1.44	1.94	2.58	1.44	1.32	1.51	2.08
60–69	2.01			1.37	2.21	*	.95	1.13	*
Overall	3.10	2.78	2.14	2.02	2.13	2.36	1.19	*	*

*Not estimated.

Sources: W. O. Menge, "Mortality Experience among Cases Involving Alcoholic Habits," *Proceedings, Home Office Life Underwriters' Association,* vol. 31 (1950), pp. 70–93. K. M. Davies, "The Influence of Alcohol on Mortality," *Proceedings, Home Office Life Underwriters' Association,* vol. 46 (1965), pp. 159–66. H. Gundy, "Discussion on Davies Paper," *Proceedings, Home Office Life Underwriters' Association,* vol. 46 (1965), pp. 167–77. W. Schmidt and J. deLint, "The Mortality of Alcoholic People," *Alcohol Health and Research World,* DHEW Publication No. (NIH) 74–652 (Washington, D.C.: U.S. Government Printing Office, 1973), pp. 16–20. P. Sundby, *Alcoholism and Mortality,* National Institute for Alcohol Research, Publication No. 6 (Oslo: Universitetsforlaget, 1967). California State Department of Public Health, Alcoholic Rehabilitation Division, "Follow-up Studies of Treated Alcoholics' Mortality," Publication No. 6, *Alcoholism and California* (Berkeley, May 1961). K. G. Dahlgren, "On Death-Rates and Causes of Death in Alcohol Addicts," *Acta Psychiatrica Scandinavica,* vol. 26 (1951), pp. 296–311. R. Pearl, *Alcohol and Longevity* (New York: Alfred A. Knopf, 1926). R. Room and N. Day, "Alcohol and Mortality," Special Report to the National Institute on Alcohol Abuse and Alcoholism (March 1974).

drinkers. Moreover, it is reasonable to assume that they have other health problems in addition to their drinking problems that may account for their being in hospitals and clinics in the first place. Excess mortality associated with drinking problems in clinical samples is likely to be greater, then, because the patients are more sick not only than the general population, but also than those with similar drinking habits who do not appear for alcoholism treatment.

The last three studies summarized in table 2–6 come closer to reflecting excess mortality among alcohol abusers in general, although the definition of alcohol abuse implied in each is quite different. Dahlgren's alcoholic sample included all men in Sweden with reported drinking habits, whether or not they had been institutionalized. The relative mortality rates from Dahlgren's study reflect the ratio of the mortality rate of all men with drinking habits to the mortality rate of the general population. It is not surprising that his relative mortality rates are consistently lowest.

Pearl's study was based on broad samples of drinkers; he classified drinkers in terms of both quantity consumed and frequency of consumption. The relative mortality rates from Pearl's study are for heavy drinkers, both frequent and occasional. The fact that his results fall between those of the clinical studies and Dahlgren's is consistent with the fact that his definition of alcohol abuse is less restrictive than that used in the former but more restrictive than the latter's.

The study by Room and Day was based on information pooled from four general population samples; the samples were followed for varying periods of between four and eleven years. Their analysis of mortality experience was quite extensive, and in general their findings are consistent with those from other studies. They found higher mortality rates among frequent heavy drinkers, with the highest relative mortality rate among those under fifty years of age. But their analysis revealed that the relationship between alcohol and mortality was specific to those who were frequent heavy drinkers; there was no apparent excess mortality among frequent light drinkers or occasional heavy drinkers. The relative mortality rates found by Room and Day, as summarized in table 2–6, are specific to the some 5 percent of the population who are frequent heavy drinkers.

Thus, the literature does provide evidence that alcohol abuse is associated with excess mortality. The excess mortality is found to be more pronounced for younger abusers than for older abusers, and it is concentrated among those who are frequent heavy drinkers. Not all alcohol abusers are subject to the risk of excess mortality, and alcohol consumption per se is not related to mortality.[29] Any estimate of the economic cost of lost production due to premature death must reflect these findings.

It would be inappropriate to apply the relative mortality rates found in either the insurance studies or the clinical studies to general alcohol-abuse prevalence data and general-population mortality data. Such an estimate of excess deaths due to alcohol abuse would clearly be an exaggeration that would result in an overstatement of the cost of lost production due to premature mortality. There are two practical alternatives. On the one hand, the relative mortality rates of the Room and Day study, which more closely approximated a general population study, could be applied to their estimates of the prevalence of frequent heavy drinking and general-population mortality data. On the other hand, the relative mortality rates from the clinical studies could be applied to prevalence data for frequent heavy drinkers and general mortality data.

Two such alternative estimates of excess deaths due to frequent heavy drinking are summarized by age in table 2–7. The first estimate is based on the relative mortality rates found in the clinical

TABLE 2–7. Estimated Excess Male Deaths in 1971 Due to Frequent Heavy Drinking, by Age

Age Group	Total Deaths	Estimated Prevalence of Frequent Heavy Drinking (percentage)	Excess Deaths Due to Frequent Heavy Drinking	
			(1)	(2)
20–29	32,889	5.2	2,707	4,150
30–39	29,810	5.2	3,138	3,760
40–49	69,960	5.2	9,351	8,826
50–59	149,367	6.1	9,115	10,483
60–64	111,902	2.2	927	*
Total	393,928		25,238	27,219

*Not estimated because relative mortality rate not estimated (see table 2–6).

Sources: Total deaths by age group are from U.S. Department of Health, Education, and Welfare, National Center for Health Statistics, Vital Statistics of the United States: 1971, vol. II–Mortality, part A (Washington, D.C.: U.S. Government Printing Office, 1975). Estimated prevalence of frequent heavy drinking is from R. Room and N. Day, "Alcohol and Mortality," Special Report to the National Institute on Alcohol Abuse and Alcoholism (March 1974). Excess deaths (1) are based on relative mortality data from Schmidt and deLint (see table 2–6). Excess deaths (2) are based on relative mortality data from Room and Day (see table 2–6).

study by Schmidt and deLint; the second on those obtained by Room and Day.[30] Although there are minor differences, the two estimates tend to be quite similar, and we can take an average of the two as a reasonable single estimate. Hence, the empirical evidence in the literature suggests that excess mortality due to alcohol abuse accounted for something on the order of 6.5 to 7 percent of all deaths in 1971 among males in the productive years between 20 and 64.

Given the number of men who died prematurely in 1971 because of alcohol abuse, we can estimate first the number of lost productive man-years, and then the present value of the lost future production as the discounted stream of future earnings that these men would have earned if they had not died prematurely. These estimates are summarized in table 2-8. An estimated 26,693 men died prematurely in 1971 because they were alcohol abusers. If these men had not died prematurely, but, in the absence of alcohol abuse, had experienced the same survival probabilities as other men in their age cohort, they would have enjoyed more than 480,000 additional productive man-years among them. During their expected working lives, they would have been expected to produce future goods and services with a present value in 1971 of some $3.1 billion. It seems reasonable to assign the present value of their lost future production to 1971—the year of their premature death.

Of course, this estimate of lost future production in no way captures the real social cost of premature death; it only identifies and approximates the value of one aspect of the economic cost.

Finally, we might ask how these 26,693 premature deaths were distributed in terms of the reported major cause of death. The excess mortality was due to alcohol abuse, but it was manifested in deaths from a number of causes. In their study of excess mortality among alcohol abusers, Schmidt and deLint have analyzed cause-specific mortality.[31] They found that alcohol abusers in their sample had a significantly higher rate of death from the causes usually associated with alcoholism. Specifically, excess mortality was found to be particularly "high from cancers of the upper digestive and respiratory organs, alcoholism, pneumonia, cirrhosis of the liver, and violent causes which include accidents, suicides, and homicides."[32] We have used the data reported by Schmidt and deLint to estimate the distribution of the excess mortality due to alcohol abuse by major cause of death. These cause-specific excess mortality estimates are presented in table 2-9. They follow, obviously, the pattern found by Schmidt and deLint. The largest absolute excess mortality is as-

TABLE 2–8. Estimated Lost Productive Man-Years and the Present Value in 1971 of Lost Future Production Due to Excess Mortality among Male Alcohol Abusers in 1971, by Age

Age Group	Excess Mortality	Productive Man-Years Lost	Present Value of Lost Production (in millions)
20–29	3,429	127,182	$ 543.8
30–39	3,449	94,932	554.1
40–49	9,089	169,612	1,170.6
50–59	9,799	91,227	777.6
60–64	927	2,008	34.6
Total	26,693	484,961	$3,080.7

Sources: Excess mortality is derived from table 2–7 as the average of the two estimates of excess deaths due to frequent heavy drinking.

Productive man-years lost were derived by assigning survival probabilities of age cohort in the general male population to excess mortality.

Present value of lost production is derived from earnings data discounted at 6 percent in B. S. Cooper and W. Brody, "1972 Lifetime Earnings by Age, Sex, Race, and Education Level," Research and Statistics Note No. 14 (Washington, D.C.: Office of Research and Statistics, Social Security Administration, September 30, 1975).

sociated with heart disease, because it is the major cause of death and heavy drinkers have a relative mortality rate from heart disease of 1.90. Proportionately, excess mortality is especially high for alcoholism, cirrhosis of the liver, accidental deaths, and suicide. The excess mortality from cancers reveals the same interesting pattern noted by Schmidt and deLint, namely, significant excess mortality arising from cancers of the upper digestive tracts and respiratory organs and a considerably lower number of deaths than might be expected from other cancers. As they concluded, "it would appear that at least in some cases, alcoholism affects only the site of the cancer and not the likelihood of its development."[33]

The distribution of excess mortality by cause is interesting in its own right, but it also provides us with information that will be most useful in aggregating the economic cost of alcohol abuse. We have estimated the present value of lost future production of the 26,693 men who died prematurely in 1971 at some $3.1 billion. In later chapters we will be estimating the economic cost of motor vehicle accidents and fires. Some part of the total economic cost of these will include the present value of lost production due to premature death in motor vehicle accidents and fires. Thus, there is the danger

TABLE 2–9. Estimated Excess Male Deaths in 1971 Due to Frequent Heavy Drinking, by Major Cause

Cause of Death:	Relative Mortality Rate of Heavy Drinkers	Percentage of Excess Deaths	Number of Excess Deaths
All causes	2.13	100.00	26,693
Cancer of the upper digestive and respiratory organs	5.15	4.12	1,100
Cancer of the lung	2.11	4.03	1,076
Cancer of other digestive organs	1.00	0.00	0
Cancer of reproductive organs	2.64	1.74	464
Other cancers	0.36	− 5.08	(1,356)
Alcoholism	24.63	8.08	2,157
Vascular lesions of central nervous system	1.32	2.21	590
Arteriosclerotic and degenerative heart disease	1.90	31.22	8,334
Pneumonia	3.44	4.89	1,305
Cirrhosis of the liver	12.71	15.99	4,268
Stomach and duodenal ulcer	3.67	2.60	694
Accidental falls	5.77	3.80	1,014
Accidental poisoning	14.71	4.76	1,271
Accidents caused by fire	9.70	2.98	795
Motor vehicle accidents	1.45	1.34	358
Other accidents	1.65	1.71	456
Suicide	6.17	10.91	2,912
Other causes	1.30	4.70	1,255

Sources: Relative mortality rates and percentage of excess deaths are derived from data in W. Schmidt and J. deLint, "The Mortality of Alcoholic People," *Alcohol Health and Research World*, DHEW Publication No. (NIH) 74–652 (Washington, D.C.: U.S. Government Printing Office, 1973), pp. 16–20. The total number of excess deaths is from table 2–8.

of double-counting certain deaths and hence the economic cost of those deaths. The data in table 2–9 indicate the extent to which motor vehicle deaths and fire deaths have been counted; an adjustment will be made in the relevant chapters to avoid double-counting these deaths.

LOST PRODUCTION MEASURED AND NOT MEASURED

Lost production is synonymous with the concept of foregone output, and lost production due to alcohol abuse reflects the op-

portunity cost of the adverse impact of alcohol abuse on productivity. We have been able to estimate the value of lost production in
several contexts, but not in all contexts. We have estimated lost
production due to alcohol abuse among the male civilian labor force
in 1971 at some $11.4 billion. We have estimated lost production
due to alcohol abuse in the military in 1971 at some $361 million.
Finally, we have estimated the present value in 1971 of lost future
production due to premature mortality of alcohol abusers at some
$3.1 billion. In sum, we have estimated a total economic cost of lost
production due to alcohol abuse of some $14.9 billion.

Our estimates of lost production due to alcohol abuse are summarized in table 2–10. The format of the table is intended to serve as
a reminder that the estimates are conservative and incomplete. They
clearly represent a lower limit to the economic cost of lost production.

This estimation of the economic cost to society of lost production was made possible by the significant simplification provided by
the market system. The market provides prices that tend to measure
a person's productivity. The procedure we used was possible because
we were able to obtain empirical data and qualitative information on
the number of male alcohol abusers, their average income, and
certain of their demographic and social characteristics. But our
estimates of the cost of lost production are incomplete. Unfortunately, very little is known about either the prevalence or the

TABLE 2–10. A Summary of Estimated Lost Production Due to Alcohol Abuse
in 1971

Economic Cost	Estimate (in millions)
Lost market production among males aged 21–59	$11,427.7
Lost production among military personnel	360.8
Present value in 1971 of lost future market production among males aged 20–64 who died prematurely in 1971	3,080.7
Total measured	$14,869.2

Not measured

Lost market production among males under 21 and over 59
Lost market production among women
Lost nonmarket production
Present value in 1971 of lost future production among those who
   died prematurely in 1971 who were not males aged 20–64

economic and social behavior of certain groups within society whose economic productivity may have been lowered by alcohol abuse. In particular, prevalence and behavioral research to date has been inadequate for women, persons in institutions, and skid row alcoholics.

The understatement of lost production in the market sector is real but relatively less significant; the most significant understatement is in the context of family or household production. When a family member has a problem with alcohol, the family suffers the consequences in many ways, including in the form of lost family production. Goods and services produced by and within the household may not have market prices, but they are nonetheless valuable. A lower level of household production represents foregone output and is a real economic cost.

NOTES

1. If this point is not intuitively obvious, the reader should reflect on the fact that the family *always* had the choice of having the wife in the labor force. If, in the absence of alcohol abuse, the family chose to have the wife stay out of the labor force, it must have been because the family valued her household production and other nonmarket activities higher than the income she might have earned.

2. U.S. General Accounting Office, *Comptroller General's Report to Special Subcommittee on Alcoholism and Narcotics, Committee on Labor and Public Welfare, U.S. Senate: Substantial Cost Savings from Establishment of Alcoholism Program for Federal Civilian Employees* (Washington, D.C.: U.S. Government Printing Office, 1970).

3. National Council on Alcoholism, "Postal Service Keeps up with PAR," *Labor–Management Alcoholism Newsletter,* vol. 2, no. 2 (September–October 1972), pp. 1–16.

4. W. W. Winslow, K. Hayes, L. Prentice, W. E. Powles, W. Seeman, and W. D. Ross, "Some Economic Estimates of Job Disruption," *Archives of Environmental Health*, vol. 13 (August 1966), pp. 213–19.

5. H. M. Trice and P. M. Roman, *Spirits and Demons at Work: Alcohol and Other Drugs on the Job* (Ithaca, N.Y.: New York State School of Industrial and Labor Relations, Cornell University, 1972), p. 7.

6. Winslow et al., p. 217.

7. S. Pell and C. A. D'Alonzo, "A Five-Year Mortality Study of Alcoholics," *Journal of Occupational Medicine*, vol. 15 (February 1973), p. 120.

8. S. Pell and C. A. D'Alonzo, "Sickness Absenteeism of Alcoholics," *Journal of Occupational Medicine*, vol. 12 (June 1970), pp. 198–210.

9. A. G. Holtmann, Jr., "The Value of Human Resources and Alcoholism" (unpublished Ph.D. dissertation, Washington University, St. Louis, 1963).

10. H. M. Pritchard, "Economic Costs of Abuse of and Dependency on Alcohol in Australia," *Twenty-Ninth International Congress on Alcoholism and Drug Dependence, Sydney, Australia, February, 1970,* ed. L. G. Kiloh and D. S. Bell (Butterworths, 1971).

11. The alcoholic mortality data he used were from Raymond Pearl, *Alcohol and Longevity* (New York: Alfred A. Knopf, 1926). The alcoholic occupation and age data he used were reported in two studies: R. Straus and S. D. Bacon, "Alcoholism and Social Stability: A Study of Occupational Integration of 2,023 Male Alcoholism Clinic Patients," *Quarterly Journal of Studies on Alcohol*, vol. 12 (1951), pp. 231–60; and U.S. Public Health Service, *Patients in Mental Institutions, 1959*, parts 2 and 3 (Washington, D.C.: U.S. Government Printing Office, 1961). The general occupational income data he used were from U.S. Bureau of the Census, *Statistical Abstract of the United States: 1959* (Washington, D.C.: U.S. Government Printing Office, 1959).

12. In fairness to Holtmann, it should be noted that he was trying to answer a somewhat different question. His objective was to determine the present value of costs attributable to the *present number* of alcoholics, given their *present economic status.*

13. Pritchard's data on premature deaths attributable to alcoholism are from a study by E. H. Derrick, "A Survey of Mortality Caused by Alcohol," *Medical Journal of Australia*, vol. 2 (1967), p. 915.

14. Observer [Anon.] and M. A. Maxwell, "A Study of Absenteeism, Accidents and Sickness Payments in Problem Drinkers in One Industry," *Quarterly Journal of Studies on Alcohol*, vol. 20 (1959), p. 310.

15. The final stages of the research program are now being carried out by the Social Research Group, School of Public Health, University of California at Berkeley. For a more complete description of this research and a comprehensive analysis, see the most recent publication, D. Cahalan and R. Room, *Problem Drinking Among American Men*, Monograph No. 7 (New Brunswick, N.J.: Rutgers Center of Alcohol Studies, 1974).

16. The difference is statistically significant. In fact, the t-statistic for the $1,964 difference in mean household income is 6.6, which is extremely significant.

17. In fact, to the extent that alcohol abuse results in lower earnings due to unemployment, absenteeism, or lower wages consonant with lower productivity, the lower earnings will tend to be reflected in the difference between the mean income of the two groups. To the extent that some part of the loss in earnings is replaced by transfer payments such as unemploy-

ment compensation or welfare payments, the actual difference in mean household income will understate the difference in earnings.

18. Of course, if other family members enter the labor force to arrest the decline in household income occasioned by the lower earnings of an abusing worker, their earnings will serve to lower the difference between the median household income of the two groups. To the extent that such is the case, the actual difference between the median income of the two groups will understate the difference in earnings between abusing and nonabusing workers.

19. Of course, since age is "picking up" the influence of factors correlated with age, an adjustment of 9.3 percent for age would account for more than just the net age effect.

20. H. S. Luft, "The Impact of Poor Health on Earnings," *The Review of Economics and Statistics*, vol. 57 (February 1975), pp. 43–57.

21. We know that 9.3 percent of the difference is accounted for by age difference; we are assuming the balance.

22. Thus, for example, suppose alcohol abuse caused a husband's earnings to fall by $5,000, but his wife took a part-time job and earned $3,000 to help maintain the household's standard of living. The gross difference in household income would be only $2,000, but that understates the loss due to alcohol abuse by $3,000. Lost production in the market sector has been reduced at the expense of lost production in the nonmarket sector.

23. U.S. Bureau of the Census, *Statistical Abstract of the United States: 1973* (Washington, D.C.: U.S. Government Printing Office, 1973), table 423, p. 265.

24. D. Cahalan, I. H. Cisin, G. L. Gardner, and G. C. Smith, "Drinking Practices and Problems in the U.S. Army, 1972," final report of a study conducted for the Deputy Chief of Staff, Personnel, Headquarters, Department of the Army, under Contract Report No. 73–6 (December 1972).

25. The *relative mortality rate* of a group is simply the ratio of their mortality rate to the mortality rate in general.

26. U.S. Department of Health, Education, and Welfare, *Second Special Report to the U.S. Congress on Alcohol and Health from the Secretary of Health, Education, and Welfare, June 1974*, DHEW Publication No. (ADM) 75–212 (Washington, D.C.: U.S. Government Printing Office, 1975); and R. Room and N. Day, "Alcohol and Mortality," Special Report to the National Institute on Alcohol Abuse and Alcoholism (March 1974). The former review is apparently based in large part on the latter, as is the material that follows.

27. The Schmidt and deLint study actually included separate samples of males and females, but the relative mortality rates included in table 2–6 were those for males.

28. In fact, of course, the mortality data for the population in general includes
   that for alcoholics. If alcoholic mortality rates were compared relative to
   nonalcoholic mortality rates, the relative mortality rate would be somewhat
   higher.

29. Moderate drinkers, in fact, not only have lower mortality rates than heavy
   drinkers, but have lower mortality rates than abstainers. Virtually all studies
   have obtained this thought-provoking result: see, for example, U.S. Department of Health, Education, and Welfare, *Second Special Report to the U.S.
   Congress on Alcohol and Health*, chapter 5.

30. Excess deaths, or excess mortality, is the difference between the actual
   mortality experience and that which would have obtained if the mortality
   rate of nonabusers had prevailed for abusers and nonabusers alike. In effect,

$$EM = \dot{P}P - \dot{N}P, \text{ with } \dot{N}P = \dot{P}P[1-K(A/P)]/N/P,$$

   where: EM = excess mortality
       $\dot{P}$ = mortality rate of population
       $\dot{N}$ = mortality rate of nonabusers
       $\dot{A}$ = mortality rate of abusers
       K = relative mortality rate $(K = \dot{A}/\dot{P})$
       A = abusers
       N = nonabusers
       P = population $(P = A + N)$

31. W. Schmidt and J. deLint, "The Mortality of Alcoholic People," *Alcohol
   Health and Research World*, DHEW Publication No. (NIH) 74–652 (Washington, D.C.: U.S. Government Printing Office, 1973), pp. 16–20.

32. Ibid., p. 17.

33. Ibid.

CHAPTER THREE

THE HEALTH CARE COSTS
OF ALCOHOL ABUSE AND ALCOHOLISM

The economic cost of lost production due to alcohol abuse is indeed significant. By conservative estimate, society had to forego at least $11.4 billion in output in 1971 because workers were less productive than they would have been if it were not for the adverse impact of alcohol on their productivity. Moreover, society lost future production with a present value in 1971 of some $3.1 billion because of the premature death of almost 27,000 alcohol abusers. But economic cost is manifested in ways other than lost production as well. It is necessary to produce certain goods and services to cope with the consequences of alcohol abuse; as a result, society must forego the alternative goods and services that could have been produced if alcohol abuse had not generated such consequences. The most obvious, and perhaps most significant example of this kind of cost involves the extra health care that must be produced to treat the disease of alcoholism and the diseases exacerbated by alcohol abuse.

In 1971, total national health expenditures were just over $80 billion. The purpose of the analysis outlined in this chapter is to estimate the proportion of this total which represented excess expenditures due specifically to alcohol abuse and alcoholism.

ALCOHOL AND HEALTH

The question of the effect of alcohol abuse on health care costs is different from that of the effect of alcohol abuse on health, since it involves the additional element of a decision (and the ability) to obtain medical treatment given the fact of poor health. However, it is useful to begin by considering some of the possible sources of ill health among alcoholics, so as to provide an outline of the causes of excess use of the health care system by alcoholics. Certainly the cause-specific excess mortality data outlined in the previous chapter suggest that alcohol abuse affects health care costs across a rather broad spectrum of diseases. Excess mortality is particularly high for alcoholism and cirrhosis of the liver, the diseases usually associated with alcohol abuse; and significant relative mortality rates obtain for several other causes, including heart disease, certain cancers, pneumonia, and stomach and duodenal ulcer.[1]

Clearly, given the pattern of excess mortality, one would expect considerable excess morbidity as well. If excess mortality of male heavy drinkers accounted for almost 7 percent of all male deaths in 1971, what proportion of the total national health care expenditures of just over $80 billion were accounted for by excess morbidity among alcohol abusers?

There are a number of different processes by which alcohol abuse could cause higher mortality and morbidity rates.

1. Alcohol abuse can promote a disease process either by diminishing the normal capacity to defend against a disease or by providing support for the development of a pathological condition. Depending on the level of severity, this may promote a subclinical disease to a clinically recognizable one, may change a mild disease state to a more severe disease state, or may increase the likelihood of fatality in the case of a severe disease state. This type of mechanism could account for increased morbidity and mortality rates for a number of diseases, even those for which there is no direct evidence that alcohol abuse, per se, has a role in the disease or for which the evidence suggests only a relatively minor role.

2. Alcohol abuse can initiate a disease process, which is subsequently characterized by continual repair and recovery until some critical point is reached at which the process is no longer reversible. The total impact would be somewhat affected by accumulated exposure but would also be affected by the level of drinking at any given point. Cessation of drinking would result in a rapid reduction of risk, provided the critical level initiating an irreversible process had not been reached.

3. Alcohol abuse can initiate a disease process by producing progressive irreversible damage. In this case, the total effect would be

approximately proportional to the accumulated amount of abuse experienced over the years. Cessation of drinking leaves impaired functioning which will not improve appreciably and may deteriorate through aging or through exposure to other harmful agents.

4. Alcohol abuse may be related to excess morbidity through behavioral factors on the part of abusers or others, such as failure to follow medical advice, failure on the part of the abuser to recognize that his health has been impaired until a very late state in the disease process, or rejection of the alcohol abuser or his disease by the health care system.

5. Alcohol abuse may be artifically related to excess disability or death through close association with some other condition or exposure (such as smoking) which is found more frequently among drinkers than among nondrinkers, and which is itself responsible for the disease.

Alcohol abuse seems to be a factor primary or causally related to a number of conditions, some of which are listed in table 3–1.

There are three conceptual alternatives that might provide a basis for estimating the excess health care costs due to alcohol abuse and alcoholism. First, for each disease entity for which there is excess morbidity for alcoholics—whether or not a causal relationship is known to obtain—an estimate of the health care costs due to excess morbidity among alcoholics could be based on a comparison of the relative costs of treating alcoholic and nonalcoholic patients suffering from the disease entity. This approach, though conceptually straightforward, would require more detailed data than are currently available.

Second, the total amount of health care that alcohol abusers consume could be compared directly with the total amount of health care that nonabusers consume to estimate the excess health care costs due to alcohol abuse. In order to accomplish such a comparison it would be necessary to obtain health care consumption data from an analysis of health care histories. Again, such an approach, though conceptually straightforward, would require data that are not currently available.

Third, the total amount of health care consumed by alcoholics could be estimated from their proportionate use of such medical services as hospital care, physicians' services, drugs, and so forth. Then, given the prevalence of alcoholics and the per-capita health care expenditures of the rest of the population, the excess health care costs due to alcoholism could be estimated by comparing the

TABLE 3–1. Alcohol-Related Disorders

Gastrointestinal	*Neurologic and Psychiatric*
Esophagitis	Peripheral neuropathy
Esophageal carcinoma	Convulsive disorders
Gastritis	Alcoholic hallucinosis
Malabsorption	Delirium tremens
Chronic diarrhea	Wernicke's syndrome
Pancreatitis	Korsakoff's psychosis
Fatty liver	Marchiafava's syndrome
Alcoholic hepatitis	
Cirrhosis (may lead to cancer of liver)	
Cardiac	*Muscle*
Alcoholic cardiomyopathy	Alcoholic myopathy
Beriberi	
Skin	*Hematologic*
Rosacea	Megaloblastic anemia
Telangiectasia	
Rhinophyma	
Cutaneous ulcers	
Metabolic	*Vitamin Deficiency Disease*
Alcoholic hypoglycemia	Beriberi
Alcoholic hyperlipemia	Pellagra
	Scurvy

Source: U.S. Department of Health, Education, and Welfare, *First Special Report to the U.S. Congress on Alcohol and Health from the Secretary of Health, Education, and Welfare, December 1971,* DHEW Publication No. (HSM) 73-9031 (Washington, D.C.: U.S. Government Printing Office, 1971), p. 45.

per-capita health care expenditures of alcoholics with those of the rest of the population. Available data do allow for at least two variants of this third conceptual alternative.

THE SCOPE OF THE PROBLEM AND AN ANALYTICAL SOLUTION

What is sought is an estimate of the health care costs due to alcohol abuse and alcoholism in 1971. A review of relevant literature and assessment of available data suggest that it is possible to estimate these excess health care costs by employing variants of the third conceptual alternative outlined above. A number of specific preliminary estimates are needed:

1. an estimate of the total expenditures on health care in 1971 by category of expenditure, including such medical services as hospital care, physicians' services, drugs, and so forth;
2. an estimate of the proportionate use of such medical services by alcohol abusers and alcoholics;
3. an estimate of the prevalence of alcohol abusers and alcoholics in the general population; and
4. an estimate of the per-capita health care expenditures of the general, nonalcohol-abusing population.

Given these estimates, it is possible to estimate the excess health care costs due to alcoholism by comparing the per-capita expenditures of alcoholics on such care with those of the rest of the population.

A detailed estimate of the total expenditures on health care in 1971, by category of expenditure is presented in table 3–2. The estimates are rather straightforward: total expenditures for health services and supplies by type of expenditure in 1971 have been published by the Social Security Administration. It seems appropriate, however, to make two specific adjustments in the context of estimating the excess cost of health care due to alcohol abuse and alcoholism. First, it seems appropriate to add to the health care expenditures the costs of training and educating health professionals, since such costs represent the use of resources in the educational sector and presumably reflect the opportunity cost of such resources. Second, and more specifically pertinent to our purposes, it seems appropriate to subtract the health care expenditures of the nonadult (under 19) population from the total. Health care expenditures for children should have little relationship to alcoholism.

Given the estimated total expenditures of the adult population by type of expenditure, it is next necessary to estimate the proportionate use of such services by alcohol abusers and alcoholics. Certain estimates are available in direct or indirect form in the existing literature. Much of the literature suggests rather significant excess utilization by alcohol abusers and alcoholics. Unfortunately, the literature does not provide much evidence with respect to utilization of many types of health services.

An additional source of information that can be employed to some advantage in estimating the proportionate use of health care services by alcohol abusers and alcoholics is the Alcohol Treatment Center (ATC) Program, sponsored by the National Institute on Alcohol Abuse and Alcoholism. The staff of the NIAAA provided us with data on hospital utilization for some 17,000 ATC clients.

TABLE 3–2. National Health Expenditures, by Type of Expenditure: Adult and Nonadult Population in 1971

Type of Expenditure	Total (in billions)	Nonadult Population (in billions)	Adult Population (in billions)
Health services and supplies:			
Hospital care	$31.1	$ 3.3	$27.8
Physicians' services	15.7	3.8	11.9
Dentists' services	4.9	1.1	3.8
Other professional services	1.6	0.4	1.2
Drug and drug sundries	7.7	1.5	6.2
Eyeglasses and appliances	2.0	0.3	1.7
Nursing home care	3.5	0.1	3.4
Expenses for prepayment and administration	2.6	0.4	2.2
Government public-health activities	1.9	0.3	1.6
Other health services	3.0	0.8	2.2
Research and medical facilities construction	5.8	1.0	4.8
Training and education	1.8	0.3	1.5
Total	$81.6	$13.3	$68.3

Sources: Total Expenditures for health services and supplies and research and medical facilities construction are from Barbara S. Cooper and Nancy L. Worthington, "National Health Expenditures, Calendar Years 1929–71," Research and Statistics Note No. 3 (Washington, D.C.: Office of Research and Statistics, Social Security Administration, 1973), p. 4.

Nonadult-population expenditures for health services and supplies and research and medical facilities construction have been estimated from data in Barbara S. Cooper and Nancy L. Worthington, "Age Differences in Medical Care Spending, Fiscal Year 1972," Social Security Bulletin, vol. 36 (May 1973), pp. 3–15.

Training and education expenditures were estimated from data in National Academy of Sciences, Institute of Medicine, Cost of Education of the Health Professions (Washington, D.C.: National Academy of Sciences, 1973).

Finally, during the course of our research, a survey was conducted to provide more information on the proportionate use of health care services by alcohol abusers and alcoholics. The survey was limited by time and budget constraints and was not intended to be exhaustive or definitive. It did, however, serve two useful purposes. First, it provided a check of sorts on the relative orders of magnitude of the estimates previously available; and it covered a broader spectrum of health care services and consequently allows estimating utilization of more specific types of health services.

In the next few sections, an attempt is made to marshall information from these several sources in order to estimate the proportionate use of the several types of health services by alcohol abusers and alcoholics.

The Literature on Hospital Utilization by Alcohol Abusers

Hospital care for the adult population is the largest single health care expenditure, some $27.8 billion in 1971. Several studies reported in the literature provide some insight into hospital utilization by alcoholics. The results of the major studies in this context are summarized briefly in table 3–3. For each of the ten studies, the table gives the size of the sample employed in the study, the study's estimate of the proportion of alcohol abusers among the admissions or patients of general hospitals, some indication of the criterion employed by each author in defining alcohol abuse, and a brief comment concerning the sample composition or study interest.

The proportion of alcohol abusers among the population in hospitals is found in these studies to vary widely from a low of 5 percent to a high of 60 percent. But on balance, the proportion of alcohol abusers appears to be significant—especially so, in light of the fact that it might be expected that the reported observed rates are lower limits, owing to the difficulties inherent in identifying and diagnosing alcohol abuse and alcoholism.

The methodology employed in most of these studies involved some form of patient interview. Occasionally other techniques were employed, such as interviews with relatives, consideration of past history of treatment for alcoholism, and noting the presence of a diagnosis of an alcoholism-related disorder such as cirrhosis or pancreatitis.

It is well known and adequately documented that alcoholism is difficult to identify. For example, in a well-conducted household survey, about one-half of a group of known alcoholics that had been included in the survey sample were not identified or picked up.[2] Generally, alcohol abusers from the higher socioeconomic classes are less likely to be identified in surveys. Alcohol abusers who are at an earlier stage of abuse or who are less sick with a specific disease entity are also less likely to be identified. In this context, perhaps less weight should be given to the Kearney study outlined in table 3–3, since his study employed a rather limited set of criteria for identifying alcohol abuse and the sample composition involved an upper-middle-class population.

TABLE 3–3. Some Evidence from Relevant Literature Concerning the Proportion of Alcoholics in General Hospitals

Author	Sample Size	Alcohol Abusers as a Percentage of All Admissions or All Patients			Author's Criteria for Defining Alcohol Abuse	Sample Composition or Study Interest
		Male	Female	Total		
Pearson	100	29 (plus 9% possible)	—	29 (plus 9% possible)	By interview, four or more of the following criteria: 1. Alcoholic blackouts 2. Sneaking drinks 3. Loss of control 4. Morning "eye-openers" 5. Loss of friends, family, job due to drinking 6. Hospitalization due to drinking	Prevalence of white male adults, North Carolina medical and surgical patients, 1962
Nolan	826	15	10	14	Questionnaire on functional interference of alcohol with health, job, family	Admissions of adults, Connecticut, 1965
Kearney et al.	416	—	—	8.7 (plus 17% possible)	Known to MDs as alcoholic or history of treatment for alcoholism, or treated for a diagnosed complication of alcoholism such as DTs, cirrhosis, etc. Information basically obtained from chart	Admissions of in-patients aged 14–75, upper-middle-class excluding obstetric patients, Connecticut, 1967, and hospitalized under a diagnosis of alcoholism or with a disease in which alcoholism can be a factor (i.e., GI or respiratory problems)

				Criteria	
Kearney et al.	235	—	—	13.4 (plus 27% possible)	Same criteria as above	Admissions of lower-class out-patients, otherwise same criteria as above
Moore	200	18	5.5	10 (plus 3.5% possible)	Michigan alcoholism screening test	Prevalence of patients 21 years or older, California, 1971, excluding obstetric patients, 65% female
Barchha et al.	392	28 (plus 7% possible)	6 (plus 2% possible)	16 (plus 5% possible)	Drinking history interview	Admissions of general medical patients over 20 years of age, 1968
Ewing & Rouse	130	40	9	28	Barchha criteria	Prevalence of medical and surgical adult patients, North Carolina, 1969, data evaluated by three sets of criteria
Neustadt	67	8	0	5	Pearson criteria	Prevalence in Baltimore City Hospital medical wards, 1960
		14	9	12	Hospital record	
		59	18	39	Physician rating on basis of drinking enough to be a problem	
Neustadt	65	72	36	60	Same criteria as above	Prevalence in Baltimore City Hospital medical wards, 1964
Neustadt	109	44	18	34	Same criteria as above	Prevalence in Johns Hopkins Hospital medical wards, 1964

Sources: W. S. Pearson, "The 'Hidden' Alcoholic in the General Hospital," *North Carolina Medical Journal,* vol. 23 (1962), pp. 6–10. J. P. Nolan, "Alcohol as a Factor in the Illness of University Service Patients," *American Journal of Medical Science,* vol. 249 (1965), pp. 135–42. T. R. Kearney, H. Bonime and G. Cassimatis, "The Impact of Alcoholism on a Community General Hospital," *Community Mental Health Journal,* vol. 3 (1967), pp. 373–76. R. A. Moore, "The Prevalence of Alcoholism in a Community General Hospital," *American Journal of Psychiatry,* vol. 128 (1971), pp. 638–39. R. Barchha, M. A. Steward, and S. B. Guze, "The Prevalence of Alcoholism among General Hospital Ward Patients," *American Journal of Psychiatry,* vol. 125 (1968), pp. 681–84. J. A. Ewing and B. A. Rouse, "Identifying the 'Hidden Alcoholic,'" paper presented at Twenty-Ninth International Congress on Alcohol and Drug Dependence, Sydney, N.S.W., Australia, February 3, 1970. J. Neustadt, "The Vise of Alcohol," *Maryland State Medical Journal* (May 1966), pp. 29–30.

The studies can be divided into two groups, depending upon whether the sample was a random selection of patients in the hospital or a random sample of admissions. Generally, it is to be expected that an alcoholic admitted to a hospital with a given diagnosis in addition to alcoholism will be sicker than a nonalcoholic admitted with the same diagnosis. Thus, it seems likely that the alcohol abuser will probably spend, on the average, a longer time in the hospital once admitted. The studies by Nolan, Kearney, and Barchha appear to involve samples of admissions, while the remaining six studies appear to involve samples of patients in the hospital. This distinction is critical, since excess utilization can be expected to be associated with either excess admissions, excess length of stay, or both.

The studies based only on admissions tend to have prevalence rates of approximately 15 percent, if the suspected or possible alcohol abusers are counted. The study design in these cases is not sufficient to capture excess length of stay. The studies based on patients in the hospital tend to have prevalence rates of approximately 25 percent. These results are consonant with the expectation that alcohol abusers once admitted tend to have longer lengths of stay than nonabusers.

In still another study, for example, Middleton, as reported by Straus, found that alcoholic patients in Kentucky, when compared with nonproblem drinkers, were generally sicker and had more complex problems. The average length of stay was 11.2 days for problem drinkers versus 7.7 days for nonproblem drinkers, or 45 percent longer.[3] If the prevalence rates obtained in those studies based only on admissions were adjusted to reflect longer lengths of stay, they would be in the same range as those found in studies based on patients. Thus, adjusting them by the 45-percent higher lengths of stay found in the Middleton study, for example, results in an adjusted prevalence rate of approximately 20 percent.

It seems reasonable to summarize these studies as implying that about 20 to 25 percent of all general-hospital bed-days are used by alcoholics, with the proportion higher in big cities and higher among males.

Additional insight can be gained from studies based on official records of hospitals as to how many people are treated in hospitals with a diagnosis of alcoholism per se. In 1970, for example, less than one-tenth of one percent of all patient days were for patients with a primary diagnosis of alcoholic psychosis.[4] In 1968, according to the

National Health Survey, about two-tenths of one percent of all patient days were used by people diagnosed under the general heading of acute brain disorders, which includes the smaller diagnostic categories in which alcoholics may be classified.[5] Each of these figures represents a lower limit on the number of people who are recognized as alcoholics, diagnosed as alcoholics, and receive treatment in general hospitals for alcoholism; these figures come nowhere near representing the number of alcohol abusers receiving hospital care. They lead to the conclusion that the vast majority of hospital care received by abusers is not for alcoholism per se.

The Literature on the Use of Physicians' Services by Alcohol Abusers

On balance, the literature provides much less useful information with respect to estimating the cost of physicians' services due to alcohol abuse and alcoholism than it does for hospital utilization.

There appear to be no large-scale surveys which give information on the proportion of a physician's practice that is devoted to treating alcoholics for any medical condition, including alcoholism. There are two national surveys, however, which bear on the question of the amount of treatment provided by physicians to alcoholics.

Jones and Helrich surveyed 13,000 general practitioners, osteopaths, internists, and psychiatrists in 1970 and discovered that they had seen problem drinkers in the previous two months at a level that projected to 108,000 nationally.[6] Clearly, this represents a very small fraction of the total number of patients seen by physicians, and Jones and Helrich add that "an astonishing number of alcoholics are being seen by physicians and treated for other diseases or symptoms, but are not being recognized as alcoholics." Another interesting result is that the proportion of alcoholics reported gets smaller as the practice size gets larger: ". . . physicians (excepting psychiatrists) report seeing approximately the same number of problem-drinking patients irrespective of the size of their practice. . . ." A possible explanation is that the physician with a large practice may not have the time to recognize problem drinkers who disguise or do not report the symptoms of alcoholism; or he may not have time to work with problem drinkers.

The *National Disease and Therapeutic Index* has reported on the basis of their ongoing surveys that patient visits to private practitioners for treatment of alcoholism in 1972 numbered slightly more than three million, and that there were 200,000 visits for the treatment of alcoholic psychosis.[7]

The Literature on the Use of Other Health Care Services by Alcohol Abusers

In general, the literature is even less valuable as a source of information on the use of other types of health services by alcohol abusers. There is very limited information concerning dental services and nursing home utilization.

The existing literature does suggest that the dental needs of the alcoholic are higher than those of the rest of the population. A study by Dunkley and Carson provides some insight into their dental needs.[8] They found that permanent tooth loss among alcohol abusers was three times higher than the national average for corresponding ages. The cost of a dental rehabilitation program is significantly higher for alcohol abusers, primarily because of a greater need for dental laboratory services for the construction of fixed and removable dentures. In a study of patients at a Veterans Administration hospital, both alcoholic and psychiatric patients exhibited severe oral neglect, but the alcoholics had more missing teeth and more nonrestorable teeth than the psychiatric patients.[9] However, it is not at all clear that the poorer dental health of alcoholics is reflected in greater utilization of dental services.

There is one study in the literature that provides limited information concerning the use of nursing home services by alcoholics. In a study of 700 male patients transferred from a Veterans Administration hospital into nursing homes, Greenwald and Linn found that 23 percent of those under 50 were alcoholics and 4 percent of those over 50 were alcoholics.[10] While this group is not typical of the nursing home population, their finding does provide some evidence that a substantial number of alcoholics do receive services in nursing homes. The most striking statistic, of course, is the apparent disproportionate number of alcohol abusers under 50 years of age.

Additional Information and Some Cost Estimates

This, then, represents the information available in the relevant literature regarding health services provided to alcoholics. The evidence tends to imply that alcoholics do use a substantial amount of health care services. It would seem, for example, that about 20 to 25 percent of adult hospital services are utilized by alcoholics. Given that adult hospital care expenditures in 1971 amounted to some $27.8 billion, the implication is that the cost of hospital care for alcohol abusers amounted (in 1971) to over $5 billion. This figure seems surprisingly large when compared with the $2 billion cited in *Alcohol and Health* as the cost of all health and welfare services provided to alcoholic persons and their families.[11] It was in large part to check the relative order of magnitude of this estimate, based only on the information available in the relevant literature, that a special survey was conducted. In effect, the survey was designed to obtain from experts throughout the country data that would serve as a check on the validity of prior estimates. Information was also sought with regard to a broader spectrum of health care services. By means of personal interviews, a small number of experts were asked a series of questions about the proportion of local health services which were furnished to alcoholics, whether or not the person was recognized as an alcoholic by those providing treatment and independent of what condition the person was being treated for. In all, twenty-nine experts were interviewed at seven alcoholism-treatment centers and two other treatment facilities. The interview subjects were divided into two groups, those representing large cities and those in smaller cities and rural areas. Generally, the responses tended to indicate that alcoholics in large cities used more health services. The results of the interviews are summarized in table 3–4. The data were subjected to analysis and median responses were calculated in order to reduce the effect of extreme answers.

These survey data and the data on hospital utilization by the clients of the Alcohol Treatment Centers that were provided by the staff of NIAAA were analyzed to gain further insights into the health care cost of alcohol abuse. The ATC data are outlined in table 3–5.

Four different sets of information that can be employed as a basis for estimating the amount of hospital services that alcoholics use have been identified:

1. Analysis of the literature implies that about 20 to 25 percent of all hospital beds are occupied by alcoholics.
2. The interviews conducted in the special survey imply that a minimum of 20 to 25 percent of all hospital beds are occupied by alcoholics and that if more weight were given to results from large cities, the figure might be as high as 30 percent.

TABLE 3–4. Summary of Interview Data from Special Survey of Alcohol-
Treatment Experts Concerning Utilization of Health Services by Alcohol
Abusers

Type of Health Service	Median Best Estimates of Experts		
	Group I Large Cities	Group II Smaller Cities & Rural Areas	Overall
Days of in-patient care per year in medical hospitals	9.5	8.3	8.6
Number of ambulatory medical visits per year	8.0	9.5	8.5
Expenditures on drugs per year	$67.0	$77.0	$75.0
Dental visits per year	0.25	0.8	0.7
Percentage of hospital beds occupied by alcoholics	30	15	22.5
Percentage of nursing home beds occupied by alcoholics	15	6	8.5
Percentage of physicians' practice represented by alcoholics	20	15	17

Source: Derived from responses of twenty-nine experts to specific questions concerning the utilization of health services by alcohol abusers.

3. The interviews conducted in the special survey imply that an
   alcohol abuser uses about 8.6 days of hospital care per year.
   (This question was intentionally included as a check against
   the answer to the question concerning the proportion of beds
   occupied by alcohol abusers.)
4. Analysis of the ATC data provided by NIAAA results in an
   estimated utilization by alcohol abusers of about 11.1 days of
   hospital care per year.

If estimates based on these four sets of information are approximately equal, somewhat more credibility should attach to that estimate.

It is clear that the interviews conducted in the special survey
undertaken as part of this study tend to reinforce the estimates
derived from the literature review. Actually, to estimate the cost of
hospital services due to alcohol abuse from the information outlined
above, it is necessary to have an estimate of the prevalence rate of
alcoholism. The generally accepted estimate of the number of alcohol abusers and alcoholics in the United States is some 9 million. [12]
Hence, as a first approximation, a prevalence rate of 7.5 percent for

TABLE 3—5. Hospital Utilization by Clients of Alcohol-Treatment Centers in 1971, by Sex

Number of Clients	Sex	Hospitalized in Last Year	Total Hospital Days	Hospital Days per Client per year
6,045	Male	Yes	123,300	
8,255	Male	No	–	
14,300			123,300	8.6
1,424	Female	Yes	66,200	
1,384	Female	No	–	
2,808			66,200	23.6
17,108	Both		189,500	11.1

Source: Derived from data provided by the staff of the National Institute on Alcohol Abuse and Alcoholism.

alcoholism among adults—corresponding to 9 million alcoholics among 120 million adults—will be assumed. It should be obvious that estimates based on information concerning the proportion of total hospital utilization that is accounted for by alcoholics will be inversely related to the prevalence rate, while estimates based on information concerning the number of days of hospital care used per alcoholic will be directly related to the prevalence rate. Thus, for example, a higher prevalence rate means that the fixed proportion of hospital costs implied by the proportion of all beds occupied by alcohol abusers is spread over a larger number of alcohol abusers and hence implies a lower cost per abuser. In fact, if the prevalence rate of alcoholism were in the range of 20 to 25 percent, then the fact that 20 to 25 percent of all hospital beds were occupied by alcoholics would imply that there was no excess hospital utilization due to alcohol abuse. The lower the prevalence rate, the greater the gap between the proportion of the population that are alcohol abusers and the proportion of hospital utilization accounted for by those abusers; hence the greater is the excess utilization due to alcohol abuse. On the other hand, if a lower prevalence rate is applied to the number of days of hospital care utilized per alcoholic per year, the resulting estimate of the total cost of hospital care due to alcohol abuse will decrease.

In fact, since the available information includes independent estimates from the literature and from the special survey of the proportion of hospital utilization accounted for by alcohol abusers, on the one hand, and estimates from the special survey and from the ATC data of the number of days of hospital care used by alcoholics, on the other, the extent to which the estimates based on the two types of information are consistent should provide some indication of the approximate prevalence rate of alcoholism.[13]

The actual estimates of hospital care costs due to alcohol abuse are straightforward in each case and are outlined in table 3–6. For the hospital utilization by alcoholics implied by the relevant literature, for example, using the lower estimate of 20 percent, .20 × $27.8 billion = $5.6 billion was spent on hospital care for alcohol abusers, or $622 for each of the estimated 9 million alcoholics. The remaining $22.2 billion ($27.8 − $5.6), or $200 for each of the remaining 111 million nonalcoholics, was spent on hospital care for the rest of the adult population. The difference, $422 per alcoholic, is the amount spent on each alcoholic for hospital care in excess of what would have been spent if his pattern of utilization were the same as that of nonabusers. This amounts to a total of $3.8 billion for 9 million alcoholics ($422 × 9,000,000).

Using the upper estimate of 25 percent utilization by alcoholics, we have .25 × $27.8 billion = $7.0 billion, or $778 per alcoholic; the associated nonabuser expenditure is $187. The difference, $591 per

TABLE 3–6. Estimated Hospital Care Expenditures Due to Alcohol Abuse

	Range of Estimate (in billions)		
Basis for Estimate	Lower Bound	Upper Bound	Midpoint
(1) Alcoholic proportion of total hospital utilization, as derived from relevant literature (20 to 25%)	$3.8	$5.3	$4.6
(2) Alcoholic proportion of total hospital utilization, as derived from special survey (20 to 30%)	3.8	6.7	5.3
(3) Number of hospital days used per alcoholic, as derived from special survey (8.6)	–	–	5.4
(4) Number of hospital days used per alcoholic, as derived from ATC data (11.1)	–	–	7.6

Sources: Derived by applying the relevant utilization rates from tables 3–3, 3–4, and 3–5 to the total adult population expenditures on hospital care services from table 3–2.

alcoholic, implies an estimated $5.3 billion of hospital care costs due to alcohol abuse. Thus, the information derived from the relevant literature implies a range of excess hospital care costs due to alcohol abuse and alcoholism of between $3.8 and $5.3 billion.

These calculations can be repeated for the hospital utilization implied by the information gathered in the special survey conducted as part of this project. In that case, the range of excess hospital care costs due to alcohol abuse and alcoholism is between $3.8 billion (for the lower limit of 20 percent) and $6.7 billion (for the upper limit of 30 percent).

Estimates of the cost of hospital care due to alcohol abuse based upon the number of days of use per alcoholic are equally straight-forward. In 1971, a typical day of adult hospital care cost $91. [14] Given this cost and the information from the special survey that alcohol abusers use some 8.6 days of hospital care per person per year, it is possible to generate an estimate as follows: 8.6 days × $91/day × 9 million alcohol abusers = $7.04 billion spent on hospital care for abusers, or $782 for each of 9 million abusers. The remaining $20.76 billion ($27.8 −7.04), or $187 for each of the 111 million nonabusers, was spent on hospital care for the rest of the adult population. The difference, $595 per abuser, is the amount spent per abuser for hospital care in excess of what would have been spent if the pattern of utilization were the same for abusers as it is for nonabusers. This amounts to a total of $5.4 billion for 9 million abusers ($595 × 9,000,000).

The calculations can be repeated using the information from the ATC data that an alcohol abuser uses some 11.1 days of hospital care per year. The resulting estimate of excess hospitalization cost due to alcohol abuse and alcoholism is some $7.6 billion. Thus, the range of excess hospital care costs due to alcohol abuse implied by the information from the special survey and the ATC data on the number of days of hospital care used by alcoholics is between $5.4 billion and $7.6 billion. The range implied by the four different sets of information is between $3.8 and $7.6 billion.

Given the quality of the data on which these four estimates are based, the results appear to be quite consistent. It would seem that the lower bound of the range, $3.8 billion, would be a conservative estimate and perhaps constitute the lower limit of the cost of hospital care due to alcohol abuse and alcoholism. The midpoint of the range, something on the order of $5.7 billion, is consistent with the information derived from the relevant literature and the special

survey conducted as part of this project. In order to provide a
somewhat conservative estimate of the health care costs of alcohol
abuse, we will take as our estimate of hospital care expenditures due
to alcohol abuse and alcoholism some $5.3 billion. Such an estimate
represents the midpoint of the range derived from the special survey,
and is to be preferred to the $5.7 billion estimate because it is not
beyond the range derived from the relevant literature.

Two separate estimates of the amount of physicians' services
used by alcoholics can be generated from data gathered in the special
survey, and they are presented in table 3—7. According to the
responses of experts surveyed:

1. Seventeen percent of an average physician's practice involves
   alcoholics.
2. The alcoholic has an average of 8.5 ambulatory medical visits
   a year.

Seventeen percent of the $11.9 billion spent for physicians' services
for adults in 1971 is $2.0 billion, which implies a per-capita expendi-
ture of $224 per year for physicians' services for alcoholics. The
remainder, $9.9 billion, is spent on the nonalcoholic adult popula-
tion, yielding a per-capita figure of $89. The difference, $135 × 9
million alcoholics, represents an estimate of the cost of physicians'
services due to alcohol abuse and alcoholism and amounted to some
$1.2 billion in 1971.

The adult population in the United States makes, on the average,
5.3 ambulatory visits to a physician in the course of a year.[15] If the
8.5 visits per year made by the alcoholic population (9 million) are
netted out, then the rest of the population averages some 5.0 visits
per year. The number of excess visits made by an alcoholic is 3.5

TABLE 3—7. Estimated Physicians' Services Expenditures Due to Alcohol
Abuse in 1971

Basis for Estimate	Estimated Expenditure (in billions)
(1) Proportion of average physician's practice involving alcoholics, as derived from special survey (17%)	$1.2
(2) Number of ambulatory medical visits per alcoholic per year, as derived from special survey (8.5)	0.6

visits per year, which comes to 3.5 × 9 million = 31.5 million visits for the total alcoholic population. This represents some 5 percent of all visits (5.3 × 120 million = 636 million). Hence, 5 percent of the total expenditures on physicians' services or some $595 million represents an estimate of the cost of physicians' services due to alcohol abuse and alcoholism.

The data available for estimating the cost of physicians' services is limited to the special survey information; the range implied by this information is between $595 million and $1.2 billion. Although the special survey was exceedingly limited in scope and technique, the fact that the estimates generated by the survey information were consistent with estimates based on other information in the case of hospital care costs does provide us with some basis for limited confidence in the survey-based estimates for physician services costs and other health services costs. (Unfortunately, there are no alternative sources of information in other than the hospital care case.)

No estimate of excess dental services costs due to alcoholism is offered. Although there is evidence that alcoholics have poorer dental health than the average adult, there is no evidence to suggest that they use more dental care. In fact, lower utilization of dental services may be a contributing factor in the poorer dental health of alcoholics. The fact that no estimate of dental services costs is attempted should not be interpreted as implying that alcoholism does not result in some real costs in a dental health context, however; rather, no basis exists for estimating those costs.[16] To the extent that no such estimate is possible, the total health care cost of alcohol abuse and alcoholism will be somewhat understated. It is not likely to introduce a serious bias into the overall estimate, however.

The special survey information did provide information that can form the basis for estimating nursing home care costs and drug costs due to alcohol abuse and alcoholism. These estimates are presented in table 3–8. In the case of nursing home costs, the survey results imply that 8.5 percent of nursing home beds were used by alcoholics in 1971. This implies that about 8.5 percent of the $3.4 billion spent on nursing home care by the adult population in 1971, some $289 million, was spent for the care of alcohol abusers—which amounts to $32 per alcohol abuser. The per-capita expenditure for nursing home care for the nonalcoholic adult population was $28; thus, the estimated cost of nursing home care due to alcohol abuse and alcoholism in 1971 was $4 × 9 million alcoholics, or some $36 million.

TABLE 3–8. Estimated Nursing Home Care Expenditures and Drug Expenditures Due to Alcohol Abuse in 1971

Basis for Estimate	Estimated Expenditure (in millions)
(1) Alcoholic proportion of total nursing home utilization, as derived from special survey (8.5%)	$ 36
(2) Amount spent on drugs per alcoholic per year, as derived from special survey ($75)	297

The average American adult spent some $45 for drugs in 1971. [17] According to the information provided by the special survey, the typical alcohol abuser used some $75 worth of drugs. If alcoholics' expenditures for drugs are netted out of total expenditures for drugs, the average nonalcoholic adult spent some $42 for drugs. The difference, $33 per alcoholic, is the estimated per-capita cost of drugs due to alcohol abuse, and implies an aggregate drug cost due to alcohol abuse of some $297 million.

There is no information on use of the remaining health services by alcohol abusers. The estimates that have been made for hospital care, physicians' services, drugs, and nursing home care exhibit quite a variation in the proportion of total adult-population expenditures that expenditures due to alcohol abuse represent in these four cases. Some 19.1 percent of all hospital care costs have been estimated to be due to alcohol abuse, but only 1.1 percent of all nursing home care costs have been estimated to be so. Over all four types of expenditures, the expenditures due to alcohol abuse have been estimated to be some 13.2 percent of total adult-population expenditures, but given the wide variation in the various proportions and the dominance of hospital care costs in the aggregate proportion, some care should be exercised in choosing a basis for estimating the expenditures due to alcohol abuse in the several other categories. Any choice, of course, will be arbitrary, but some figures seem more reasonable than others. Table 3–9 lists our best estimates of expenditures due to alcohol abuse and alcoholism for the several types of health care expenditures in 1971. The estimates for hospital care, physicians' services, drugs, and nursing home care have been explained in detail above. The estimates for each of the other types of service are based on reasonable assumptions. Thus, for example, other professional services expenditures have been estimated as occurring at the same rate as physicians' services expenditures; expenses

TABLE 3–9. Estimated National Health Expenditures Due to Alcohol Abuse in 1971, by Type of Expenditure

Type of Expenditure	Total Adult Population Expenditures (in billions)	Expenditures Due to Alcohol Abuse (in millions)	Expenditures Due to Alcohol Abuse as a Percentage of Total Expenditures
Health services and supplies:			
Hospital care	$27.8	$5,300	19.1
Physicians' services	11.9	900	7.6
Dentists' services	3.8	–	–
Other professional services	1.2	91	7.6
Drugs and drug sundries	6.2	297	4.8
Eyeglasses and appliances	1.7	–	–
Nursing home care	3.4	36	1.1
Expenses for prepayment and administration	2.2	420	19.1
Government public-health activities	1.6	211	13.2
Other health services	2.2	290	13.2
Research and medical facilities construction	4.8	634	13.2
Training and education	1.5	114	7.6
Total	$68.3	$8,293	12.2

for prepayment and administration have been estimated as occurring at the same rate as hospital care expenditures; training and education expenditures have been estimated as occurring at the same rate as physicians' services expenditures; and expenditures for dentists' services and eyeglasses and appliances have been estimated as occurring at a rate of zero percent.[18] The remaining types of expenditures have been estimated as occurring at a rate of 13.2 percent.[19]

Overall, national health expenditures due to alcohol abuse and alcoholism have been estimated to be some $8.3 billion—12.2 percent of total adult-population expenditures in 1971, or some 10.2 percent of total health expenditures. At the beginning of this chapter we noted that excess mortality among male heavy drinkers amounted to almost 7 percent of all male deaths in 1971, and we asked what proportion of total national health care expenditures were accounted for by the excess morbidity of alcohol abusers. Our estimated answer—10.2 percent—does not seem unreasonable when juxtaposed with an excess mortality rate among heavy drinkers of 7 percent.

Summary: Estimated Health Care Costs

The data in table 3—9 have been discussed in some detail. Any reader who has followed the discussion and analysis throughout this chapter is well aware of the limited nature of the information upon which the estimates there have been based; has been alerted to the potential shortcomings of the specific techniques employed in the estimation procedures; and has been reminded that in some cases the estimates of expenditures do not reflect real economic cost. Still, it is in the nature of such exercises that somehow once all the qualifications have been put forward, all the disclaimers made, and all the caveats issued, when numbers are presented in tabular form they tend to take on a new meaning and to be accepted less and less critically. It is unlikely that anything will alter this particular phenomenon, but in order to modify its implication somewhat, the ranges of the estimates we derived for national health expenditures due to alcohol abuse and alcoholism are presented in table 3—10. The estimated range of total national health expenditures due to alcohol abuse and alcoholism in 1971 is between $6 billion and $11.7 billion; the single estimate given in table 3—9 above, $8.3 billion, lies just below the midpoint of this range.

TABLE 3–10. Ranges of Estimated National Health Expenditures Due to Alcohol Abuse in 1971, by Type of Expenditure

Type of Expenditure	Range of Estimate (in millions)	
	Lower Bound	Upper Bound
Health services and supplies:		
Hospital care	$3,800	$ 7,600
Physicians' services	600	1,200
Dentists' services	–	–
Other professional services	60	121
Drugs and drug sundries	297	297
Eyeglasses and appliances	–	–
Nursing home care	36	36
Expenses for prepayment and administration	301	601
Government public-health activities	152	306
Other health services	209	420
Research and medical facilities construction	456	917
Training and education	75	152
Total	$5,986	$11,650

CONCLUDING COMMENTS AND FUTURE RESEARCH NEEDS

Health care costs due to alcohol abuse and alcoholism, then, do indeed represent a significant economic cost. The orders of magnitude of the estimates of health care costs derived and presented in this chapter suggest that this is an appropriate area of both policy concern and further research.

Hospital care costs tend to dominate health care costs due to alcohol abuse, as they tend to dominate health care costs in general. In fact, their dominance in the alcohol-abuse context is even more pronounced. The general consistency of the several estimates of hospital care costs due to alcohol abuse based on information from different and hopefully somewhat independent sources has been noted. This consistency is encouraging and does provide some basis for limited confidence in the general range of the estimates. Still, the limited nature of the information on which these estimates are based should not be ignored. Further research would most certainly be appropriate.

The studies cited in the literature are indeed somewhat difficult to compare, because different definitions of alcohol abuse are employed in them. In fact, the study of Ewing and Rouse specifically addresses this question and, by applying different operational definitions to the same population of hospital patients, derives estimates of the number of alcoholics that differ by more than a factor of five. [20] Moreover, of course, the information derived from the studies available in the general literature as well as the information available from the ATC data and the special survey conducted as part of this project is not of such a nature that it can be reliably extrapolated as representative of all hospitals in the United States. A most significant extension of the research drawn upon in this project would involve a systematic study of the proportion of hospital utilization due to alcohol abuse and alcoholism.

If alcoholics are, in fact, receiving as large a proportion of the care offered by our health care delivery system as the estimates derived imply, there is a good possibility that this system could serve the health needs of the alcoholic population better, and with the use of fewer resources, by explicitly recognizing this phenomenon. Of course, if appropriate changes were made and as a consequence real resources were saved, the health care delivery system would be serving the general population better as well.

In order to ascertain the potential for increased efficiency and potential resource saving, a national or at least regional study of hospitals selected so as to be representative of all general hospitals should be undertaken.

NOTES

1. See Table 2–9 and W. Schmidt and J. deLint, "The Mortality of Alcoholic People," *Alcohol Health and Research World,* DHEW Publication No. (NIH) 74–652 (Washington, D.C.: U.S. Government Printing Office, 1973), table 2, p. 17.

2. U.S. Department of Health, Education, and Welfare, National Center for Health Statistics, *Identifying Problem Drinkers in a Household Health Survey,* Vital and Health Statistics Series 2, No. 16 (Washington, D.C.: U.S. Government Printing Office, May 1966).

3. Robert Straus, "Alcohol and Society," *Psychiatric Annals,* vol. 3 (1973), p. 72.

4. Commission on Professional and Hospital Activities, *Length of Stay in PAS Hospitals, United States, 1970* (Ann Arbor, Mich., October 1971).

5. U.S. Department of Health, Education, and Welfare, National Center for Health Statistics, *Inpatient Utilization of Short-Stay Hospitals by Diagnosis*, Vital and Health Statistics Series 13, No. 12 (Washington, D.C.: U.S. Government Printing Office, March 1973).

6. R. Jones and A. Helrich, "Treatment of Alcoholism by Physicians in Private Practice," *Quarterly Journal of Studies on Alcohol*, vol. 33 (1972), pp. 117–31.

7. "Alcoholism," *NDTI Review*, vol. 4 (1973), pp. 7–8.

8. R. Dunkley and R. Carson, "Dental Requirements of the Hospitalized Alcoholic Patient," *Journal of the American Dental Association*, vol. 76 (1968), pp. 800–803.

9. W. King and K. Tucker, "Dental Problems of Alcoholic and Nonalcoholic Psychiatric Patients," *Quarterly Journal of Studies on Alcohol*, vol. 34 (1973), pp. 1208–11.

10. S. Greenwald and M. Linn, "The Younger Nursing Home Patient," *Journal of Gerontology*, vol. 27 (1972), pp. 393–98.

11. U.S. Department of Health, Education, and Welfare, *First Special Report to the U.S. Congress on Alcohol and Health* (see table 3–1), p. viii.

12. Ibid.

13. Thus, if the resulting estimates are approximately equal, the assumed 7.5 percent prevalence rate tends to be supported. Of course, approximately equal estimates could also obtain if the prevalence rate were different from 7.5 percent and either the proportion of hospital utilization accounted for by alcohol abusers or the number of days of hospital care used by alcoholics or both were in error. That is why the somewhat independent estimates can reinforce the credibility of each other and of the assumed prevalence rate. In fact, the experts estimated that approximately 25 percent of general-hospital days were accounted for by abusers. We know that there were 242 million patient days in 1971. Hence, abusers used 60.5 million days. Given the experts' estimate that the typical abuser used 8.6 days per year, the implied number of abusers is just over 7 million, which implies a prevalence rate of 5.9 percent.

14. B. S. Cooper and N. L. Worthington, "Medical Care Spending for Three Age Groups," *Social Security Bulletin*, vol. 35 (May 1972), pp. 3–16.

15. U.S. Department of Health, Education, and Welfare, National Center for Health Statistics, *Current Estimates from the Health Interview Survey: United States, 1971*, Vital and Health Statistics Series 10, No. 79 (Washington, D.C.: U.S. Government Printing Office, February 1973).

16. Of course, the fact that no expenditures for dental care are made does not

mean that no real cost has been incurred. Quite the contrary, if alcoholism and alcohol abuse contribute to a deterioration in dental health, then such a deterioration is a real economic cost. If the alcoholic chose to repair the deterioration by incurring dental expenses, these expenses would provide a basis for estimating the value of eliminating the deterioration.

17. Cooper and Worthington, "Medical Care Spending for Three Age Groups."

18. The reader is reminded that the estimates herein are of *expenditures*, and these items tend to be neglected by alcohol abusers. The implication is that expenditures do not occur, not that there is no real cost associated with such neglect.

19. That is, the proportion that the sum of the estimates for hospital care costs, physicians' services costs, drug costs, and nursing home care costs due to alcoholism is of the total adult-population expenditure for these four types of services.

20. J. A. Ewing and B. A. Rouse, "Identifying the 'Hidden Alcoholic,'" paper presented at Twenty-Ninth International Congress on Alcohol and Drug Dependence, Sydney, N.S.W., Australia, February 3, 1970.

CHAPTER FOUR

THE ECONOMIC COST OF MOTOR VEHICLE ACCIDENTS DUE TO ALCOHOL ABUSE

INTRODUCTION

The automobile is more than representative of the technology of our society; in many ways, it is an integral part of our culture. But the automobile, like most of our technological advances, is somewhat of a mixed blessing. Long before attention was focused on the automobile in the contexts of energy consumption and environmental pollution, we had come to realize that motor vehicle accidents represented a tremendous social cost. Holiday weekend death tolls are dramatic and provide the most readily available statistics. The morbid fact is that although the automobile has been around for a relatively short time, it has managed to kill more of us than all of our wars. In addition, of course, motor vehicle accidents result in countless injuries, many resulting in permanent disability, and extensive property damage. Some part of this significant social cost is due to alcohol abuse.

The National Highway Traffic Safety Administration (NHTSA) of the United States Department of Transportation completed a comprehensive study of the economic costs of motor vehicle accidents in 1971.[1] The NHTSA cost estimate ranged as high as $46 billion. What part of this cost can be reasonably attributed to alcohol abuse?

In order to answer this question we need to assign to alcohol abuse a proportion of the total economic cost of motor vehicle accidents in 1971. Given the total cost data, the problem that remains is to determine the proportion of accidents that might reasonably be attributed to alcohol abuse. A reasonable solution to the problem would proceed in two steps. First, it is necessary to estimate the specific proportion of accidents that involve alcohol abusers. Second, an adjustment should be made to account for the fact that alcohol abusers would in all probability have had accidents at the same rate as nonabusers if they had not been abusers. Such a procedure would allow us, in effect, to estimate the extra costs to society of motor vehicle accidents that might have been due to alcohol abuse.

ESTIMATING THE ECONOMIC COSTS OF MOTOR VEHICLE ACCIDENTS

The NHTSA study was, as noted, quite comprehensive. They undertook to assess the economic cost of the almost 17 million motor vehicle accidents that occurred in the United States in 1971. Data on these accidents are presented in table 4–1; they serve to highlight the magnitude of the death, personal injury, and property damage occasioned by highway disaster. In 1971, some 55,000 lives were lost in motor vehicle accidents. Almost 4 million persons were injured, more than 250,000 of them suffering some permanent disability. In addition to the staggering human losses, motor vehicle accidents caused inordinate property damage as well.

The perspective and basic economic approach adopted in the NHTSA study were essentially the same as those employed in our

TABLE 4–1. Motor Vehicle Accidents in the United States in 1971, by Type of Accident

Type of Accident	Number of		
	Accidents	Persons	Vehicles
Fatality	47,000	55,000	69,000
Personal injury	2,469,600	3,800,000	4,510,000
Property damage	14,000,000	–	24,000,000
Total	16,516,600	3,855,000	28,579,000

Source: U.S. Department of Transportation, NHTSA, *Societal Costs of Motor Vehicle Accidents*, Preliminary Report (April 1972).

analysis of the economic cost of alcohol abuse and alcoholism. The major tangible economic costs of motor vehicle accidents were seen as including the economic value of the lost production of those who died or were disabled and the value of the foregone output of resources diverted to provide the goods and services made necessary because of motor vehicle accidents. The NHTSA study actually went somewhat further in attempting to assign some dollar cost estimates to less tangible items, such as lost production in nonmarket sectors, and even to nontangible things, such as pain and suffering.

In some instances the NHTSA study staff was able to obtain rather reliable quantitative data; in other instances the available data were considerably less reliable. In certain instances, the data available were minimal or nonexistent. A summary of the societal costs of motor vehicle accidents in the United States in 1971 as estimated in the NHTSA study is presented in table 4–2; brief descriptions of the several cost categories as defined by the NHTSA are given in table

TABLE 4–2. A Summary of the Societal Costs of Motor Vehicle Accidents in the United States in 1971, by Type of Accident and Type of Cost (in billions)

	Type of Accident			
Cost Category*	Fatality	Personal Injury	Property Damage	Total
Property damage	$ .082	$ 2.715	$4.320	$ 7.117
Medical care	.061	1.879	–	1.940
Funeral	.051	–	–	.051
Legal and court	.164	.806†	.072	1.042
Wage loss	7.220	10.821‡	–	18.041
Miscellaneous	.011	.204	.600	.815
Insurance administration	.257	3.945	2.400	6.602
Loss to others	.071‡	.735‡	–	.806‡
Loss to employers	.055‡	.008‡	–	.063‡
Community service	.383‡	.506‡	–	.889‡
Pain and suffering	.547‡	3.255‡	–	3.802‡
Nonwork duties	1.805‡	2.707‡	–	4.512‡
Loss of assets	.274‡	.016‡	–	.290‡
Total Cost	$10.981	$27.597	$7.392	$45.970

*See table 4–3 for an elaboration of the several cost categories.
†Estimates are based on relatively unreliable data.
‡Estimates are based on minimal quantitative data.
Source: U.S. Department of Transportation, NHTSA, *Societal Costs of Motor Vehicle Accidents,* Preliminary Report (April 1972).

TABLE 4-3. An Elaboration of the NHTSA Cost Categories

Cost Category	Description
Property damage	Property damage estimates are based on several accident cost studies sponsored by state highway departments, the Federal Highway Administration, and the National Safety Council.
Medical care	Medical care costs include hospital costs and other medical costs.
Funeral	Represents the difference between funeral costs incurred because of fatal accidents in 1971 and the present value of funeral costs if they had occurred at end of normal life expectancy.
Legal and court	Includes civil court costs, legal fees, criminal court costs, and police costs due to motor vehicle accidents.
Wage loss	Includes the present value in 1971 of lost future earnings of all persons killed and injured in motor vehicle accidents.
Miscellaneous	Includes the costs of loss of vehicle use, accommodations away from home, telephone calls, replacing damaged clothing, and vehicle repair arrangements.
Insurance administration	Represents the difference between premiums paid to insurance companies and claims paid—in effect, the overhead cost of accident insurance.
Loss to others	Includes the time and money costs to others involved in attending funerals, visiting patients in hospitals, and attending to home care of persons injured in accidents.
Loss to employers	Includes the cost to employers of restaffing and of retraining a replacement worker. Estimated at $1,000 per employee lost.
Community service	Includes the loss of voluntary community service activities related to churches, youth organizations, neighborhood organizations, charity fund drives, etc. Estimated at 5 percent of wage loss.
Pain and suffering	Includes the loss associated with pain and suffering caused by motor vehicle accidents. Based on an analysis of court awards for pain and suffering.
Nonwork duties	Includes lost home or family production during evenings or weekends. Estimate based on 10 hours per week of lost household production per person killed or injured. (The lost household production of housewives was included in the estimate of wage loss.)

Continued

TABLE 4–3 (Continued)

Cost Category	Description
Loss of assets	Includes the difference between the market value of accumulated assets and the satisfaction derived from them by persons killed or totally disabled by an accident. The actual estimate assumes a value difference of $5,000 for fatalities and $2,500 for total disabilities.

Source: U.S. Department of Transportation, NHTSA, *Societal Costs of Motor Vehicle Accidents,* Preliminary Report (April 1972).

4–3. The total societal cost incurred was estimated to be on the order of $46 billion.

The NHTSA study included estimates for some thirteen categories of cost for each of the several types of accidents. The most significant economic cost of motor vehicle accidents was estimated to be that of lost production, as approximated by wages lost due to death and personal injury. The study estimated the cost of lost production due to motor vehicle accidents at just over $18 billion. Viewed another way, society had to forego more than 1 percent of its potential production of goods and services in 1971 because of motor vehicle accidents.[2]

In terms of magnitude, property damage was the second most significant economic cost generated by motor vehicle accidents; the study estimated property damage at over $7 billion. Clearly, the resources that society must use to repair or replace such damaged property implies considerable foregone alternative production. Indeed, such a loss was equivalent to almost 20 percent of the value of the output of the automobile industry in 1971.

The consequences of motor vehicle accidents also required that considerable resources be diverted to the production of goods and services in other sectors. Significant medical care services, funeral services, legal and court services, and insurance services were necessitated by motor vehicle accidents.

Finally, of course, the account taken in the NHTSA study of such real costs as loss of nonmarket production and pain and suffering serves to increase the estimate of the social costs of motor vehicle accidents. Although the estimates of such less tangible and nontangible items were based on rather scanty data, they do serve to remind us that estimates of economic cost in the market sector are often very conservative estimates of the real economic and social costs.

Although the NHTSA study was comprehensive, it is certainly not immune to criticism. While the analytical method employed by the NHTSA staff was sound, in several instances they had to rely on rather scanty data, and often their estimates were based on rather heroic assumptions. On balance, it may be appropriate for our purposes to revise the NHTSA estimates downwards somewhat.

There is an alternative source of data on the costs of motor vehicle accidents. The National Safety Council (NSC) estimates the costs of motor vehicle accidents each year. Their estimates, unfortunately, are not as comprehensive as those of the NHTSA. They do not include such costs as legal and court costs, indirect costs to employers, lost nonmarket production, the cost of pain and suffering, and the like. The NSC estimated the cost of motor vehicle accidents in 1971 at some $15.8 billion; their estimates are outlined in table 4–4.

Actually, the significant difference in the estimates of the NHTSA and the NSC is rather easy to explain. Two factors account for almost 90 percent of the difference. First, approximately $12.5 billion of the difference represents items counted by the NHTSA but not counted by the NSC. Second, some $14.3 billion of the difference falls in the single category of lost production, as estimated by wages or earnings lost. A consideration of these two factors should serve our purpose.

Clearly, to the extent that the NSC estimate does not count certain real costs, it represents an understatement. It would seem reasonable to conclude that legal and court costs, funeral expenses, and miscellaneous accident-related costs such as those attending loss of vehicle use and replacing damaged clothing are tangible, quantita-

TABLE 4–4. A Summary of the Costs of Motor Vehicle Accidents in the United States in 1971, as Estimated by the National Safety Council

Cost Category	Estimated Cost (in billions)
Losses in earnings	$ 3.7
Medical expenses	1.1
Property damage	5.0
Insurance administration	6.0
Total	$15.8

Source: National Safety Council, Accident Facts, 1971 (Chicago: National Safety Council, 1972).

tive items and should be included in an estimate of the costs of motor vehicle accidents. On the other hand, several of the cost categories included in the NHTSA estimates represent a variety of less tangible or nontangible things. The estimates of nontangibles are valid conceptually; they do represent real social losses. But the lack of data and the somewhat tenuous assumptions upon which the estimates in money terms are based render the reliability of these estimates uncertain. It may be more reasonable to recognize the relevance of these items in social terms but not include them in dollar estimates of the cost of motor vehicle accidents. In effect, to reduce an estimate by these amounts is to make a more conservative estimate of motor vehicle accident costs.

The significant difference in the two estimates of lost production would appear to derive from three sources. First, the NHTSA estimated lost production for all persons killed or injured. They included not only lost production in the market sector, but also lost production in the nonmarket sector, in the form of the services of housewives. In effect, the NHTSA estimate values housewife services at their opportunity cost, as represented by the market wage of working women.

Second, the two studies use different definitions of injuries. The NSC defines a disabling injury as one that prevents a person from performing any of his usual activities for a full day beyond the day of an accident. The NHTSA uses the National Health Survey definition of a bed-disabling injury, viz., one that confines a person to bed for more than half of the daylight hours on the day of the accident or on some subsequent day. The NSC definition appears to include a smaller group of injuries than the NHTSA definition and would consequently result in a lower cost estimate.

Finally, the NHTSA used a rather low discount rate to estimate the present value in 1971 of lost production in future years. In fact, they generated three different estimates, using discount rates of 5, 7, and 10 percent. In each case, however, the earnings data were adjusted for a 3-percent productivity growth; thus, the net discount rates were 2, 4, and 7 percent. The final NHTSA estimate of lost wages of some $18 billion was based on a net discount rate of 4 percent. Although any discount rate choice is somewhat arbitrary and there is no universal agreement on an appropriate discount rate, 4 percent would certainly seem rather low. Of course, a lower discount rate will result in a higher estimate of the present value of lost future production, while a higher discount rate will result in a lower estimate. If the NHTSA had chosen a net discount rate of 7 percent, for example, their estimate of lost wages would have been some $12.9 billion.

The NHTSA study, then, was comprehensive, but some of their estimates of less tangible items are of uncertain reliability and their estimate of lost production is based on a rather low net discount rate. The NHTSA estimate of some $46 billion might be viewed as an upper limit to the economic costs of motor vehicle accidents; it would seem appropriate to take a more conservative estimate. The NSC estimate of some $15.8 billion, on the other hand, might be viewed as a lower limit to the economic costs of motor vehicle accidents; it probably represents an understatement of the actual costs. Some intermediate figure would be preferred as a reasonable and conservative estimate of the costs of motor vehicle accidents.

Several alternative estimates are summarized in table 4–5, including the original estimates by NHTSA and NSC as upper and lower bounds and three intermediate estimates. The NHTSA estimate minus the less tangible items is summarized in column 3. In column 4 we have given the NHTSA estimate at a net discount rate of 7 percent. Finally, the NHTSA estimate at a net discount rate of 7 percent and minus the less tangible items is given in column 5.

In fact, a reasonable argument could be made for each of these alternatives. The original NHTSA estimate has the advantage of being comprehensive. Each of the several categories represents a real economic cost, either in terms of lost production or in terms of the need to forego production of certain goods and services in order to cope with the consequences of motor vehicle accidents.

The original NSC estimate has the advantage of being particularly conservative. The four categories included represent the most obvious economic costs of motor vehicle accidents and those for which reasonably reliable market prices are available to quantify the losses involved. Since no attempt was made to estimate the less tangible items, there is no danger of overstating the costs. The NSC estimates were apparently based upon conservative estimates even for the four types of loss included.

The advantage of the NHTSA estimate minus the less tangible items is that it is more comprehensive than the NSC estimate, yet like the NSC estimate it excludes the less tangible items and therefore cannot overstate less tangible losses. Of course, these two estimates do understate the less tangible losses. There is a trade-off between comprehensiveness and conservativeness.

The NHTSA estimate at a net discount rate of 7 percent has the

TABLE 4–5. Alternative Estimates of the Economic Costs of Motor Vehicle Accidents in the United States in 1971, by Type of Cost

| | Estimates (in billions) | | | | |
Cost Category	Original NHTSA (1)	Original NSC (2)	NHTSA Minus Less Tangible Items (3)	NHTSA at 7% Net Discount (4)	NHTSA at 7% Net Discount and Minus Less Tangible Items (5)
Property damage	$ 7.1	$ 5.0	$ 7.1	$ 7.1	$ 7.1
Medical care	1.9	1.1	1.9	1.9	1.9
Funeral	0.1	—	0.1	0.1	0.1
Legal and court	1.0	—	1.0	1.0	1.0
Wage loss	18.0	3.7	18.0	12.9	12.9
Miscellaneous	0.8	—	0.8	0.8	0.8
Insurance administration	6.6	6.0	6.6	6.6	6.6
Loss to others	0.8	—	—	0.8	—
Loss to employers	0.1	—	—	0.1	—
Community service	0.9	—	—	0.9	—
Pain and suffering	3.8	—	—	3.8	—
Nonwork duties	4.5	—	—	4.5	—
Loss of assets	0.3	—	—	0.3	—
Total cost	$45.9	$15.8	$35.5	$40.8	$30.4

advantage of being based on a more conservative discount rate. It is as comprehensive as the original NHTSA estimate but more conservative than the latter because of the discount rate employed.

Finally, the NHTSA estimate at a net discount rate of 7 percent and minus the less tangible items also has certain advantages. It is more comprehensive than the NSC estimate but cannot overstate less tangible losses. It is less comprehensive than the original NHTSA estimate, but it does include a more conservative estimate of lost production because it is based on a more conservative discount rate.

The choice would seem to be between the NHTSA estimate at a net discount rate of 7 percent and the NHTSA estimate at a net discount rate of 7 percent and minus the less tangible items. The former estimate is more comprehensive—it includes all real costs—but there is the possibility that less tangible costs are overstated. The latter is more conservative, but the less tangible costs are clearly understated, since they are excluded. On balance, it seems appropriate for present purposes to choose the NHTSA estimate at a net discount rate of 7 percent and minus the less tangible items. For one, we have consistently chosen to err on the conservative side throughout our analysis of the economic cost of alcoholism. Furthermore, eliminating the less tangible items is consistent with our procedure in estimating other costs of alcohol abuse. As we noted earlier, it is difficult to measure less tangible types of loss without detailed behavioral studies. Thus, in the previous chapters, such less tangible items as lost production in the nonmarket sector and the home care of patients necessitated by alcohol abuse were not included in our estimates. Thus the choice of the NHTSA estimate at a net discount rate of 7 percent and minus the less tangible items is consistent with our conservative bias and provides an estimate comparable to the others in our analysis.

Of course, our concern with the cost of motor vehicle accidents was prompted by the need to assign a proportion of the total economic cost of such accidents to alcohol abuse. Our task is eased somewhat by the available estimates of the cost of motor vehicle accidents. In fact, we now have the basis for a reasonable estimate of the total cost of such accidents. This estimate appears in table 4–6. The remaining task is to estimate the proportion of accidents that involve alcohol abusers and to determine the extra costs of motor vehicle accidents that might have been due to alcohol abuse. What part of the revised estimate of the cost of motor vehicle accidents of $30.5 billion can reasonably be attributed to alcohol abuse? In order to answer that question, we first need an estimate of the proportion of accidents that involved alcohol abusers.

DETERMINING THE PRESENCE OF ALCOHOL ABUSE IN A MOTOR VEHICLE ACCIDENT

There is no single measure of what constitutes driving under the influence of alcohol. The most reliable measure involves determining the amount of alcohol present in the bloodstream of the individual. The *blood alcohol content* (BAC) provides a specific numerical magnitude that indicates the presence of alcohol. Since the purpose of our analysis is to estimate the economic costs of the behavior of alcohol abusers in actual motor vehicle accidents, a numerical magnitude that indicates the presence of alcohol in an amount that would generally impair performance would serve our analytical needs.

It has been well documented that alcohol can have an adverse effect on drivers. Loomis and West, for example, have demonstrated that simulated driving tasks are performed with less skill at all levels of blood alcohol content.[3] Studies of the component skills that make up "driving skill" indicate that vision, coordination, judgment, and concentration begin to deteriorate at rather low levels of blood alcohol content.[4] The deleterious effect of alcohol on task perfor-

TABLE 4–6. A Summary of the Economic Cost of Motor Vehicle Accidents in the United States in 1971, by Type of Accident and Type of Cost (in billions)

Cost Category	Type of Accident			
	Fatality	Personal Injury	Property Damage	Total
Property damage	$0.082	$ 2.715	$4.320	$ 7.117
Medical care	0.061	1.879	–	1.940
Funeral	0.051	–	–	0.051
Legal and court	0.164	0.806	0.072	1.042
Lost production	5.157	7.743	–	12.900
Insurance administration	0.257	3.945	2.400	6.602
Miscellaneous	0.011	0.204	0.600	0.815
Total cost	$5.783	$17.292	$7.392	$30.467

Source: Derived from data in tables 4–2 and 4–5 above.

mance is less for heavy drinkers, for whom there may be little impairment with a blood alcohol content of less than .05 percent. For occasional drinkers, however, there is a significant deterioration in performance of a wide range of tasks at levels of blood alcohol content lower than .05 percent. Although some persons may drive as safely at .05 percent blood alcohol content as they do at zero percent BAC, most people do not.

Indeed, the selection of a .05 percent BAC as indicative of alcohol abuse in the context of motor vehicle accidents has considerable empirical justification. In his major review of factors associated with traffic accidents, Goldstein identified youth, old age, unfavorable records with local agencies and institutions, and *a blood alcohol content of .05 percent or higher* as the factors most strongly related to high accident vulnerability.[5] In assessing several studies of motor vehicle accidents that included a population-at-risk control group, Zylman concluded that "these and other studies indicate that the risk of traffic accident is increased by alcohol, particularly if the BAC is over 0.05%.."[6]

Perhaps the most convincing empirical evidence that a BAC of .05 percent or higher in the context of traffic accidents indicates alcohol abuse comes from the major study of traffic accidents by Borkenstein and his colleagues.[7] Their analysis of data on almost 6,000 drivers involved in traffic accidents in Grand Rapids, Michigan, indicated that alcohol was the most important factor in predicting accidents and that the first significant increase in accident vulnerability occurred for drivers with a blood alcohol content of .05 percent. Drivers with a BAC just under .04 percent were about as likely to cause accidents as drivers with a zero BAC. But the estimated probability of causing an accident with a BAC of .06 percent was twice as high. In fact, as the blood alcohol content increased beyond .05 percent, the relative probability of causing an accident increased dramatically.

On balance, an extensive review of the literature suggests that an immediate blood alcohol content at the time of a motor vehicle accident of .05 percent or higher can be taken as an indication of alcohol abuse.

Although the *presence* of alcohol in an accident case can be easily determined, the *causal* role of alcohol abuse is a more complex question. A large number of factors, including but not limited to alcohol abuse, may have contributed to the occurrence of an accident. In the Grand Rapids study, for example, eight factors in addition to alcohol were found to be associated with motor vehicle accidents. The age of the driver and his or her driving experience had an especially strong relationship to motor vehicle accidents. Accidents were found to vary considerably with the time of day. Such driver characteristics as marital status, occupation, race, sex, and even drinking experience were also related to accident vulnerability. Moreover, in most cases, these other factors were associated with alcohol to some degree. Experts in the field disagree strongly as to the relative importance of these and other factors such as speed, highway design, traffic density, and the condition of the vehicle that may be related to traffic accidents of various types. When an accident occurs that involves a young, relatively inexperienced driver who was exceeding the speed limit on a wet road at 2:00 A.M. and was found to have a BAC in excess of .05 percent, it is one thing to determine that alcohol abuse was present; it is still another to determine the net causal role of alcohol abuse.

To the extent possible, we will avoid the notion of causation and, rather, will rely on observed associations between various factors and the occurrence of traffic accidents of varying degrees of severity. In order to assign responsibility to alcohol abuse in motor vehicle accidents of various types, a practical estimation technique based on actual data will be employed.

ASSIGNING RESPONSIBILITY TO ALCOHOL ABUSE IN MOTOR VEHICLE ACCIDENTS

Research concerned with the behavioral aspects of motor vehicle accidents has demonstrated that the probability of alcohol abuse being involved tends to vary with the severity of the accident. Alcohol is much more likely to be involved in more severe traffic accidents. Any attempt to assign responsibility for motor vehicle accidents to alcohol abuse should take this fact into account and disaggregate total accidents by levels of severity. Moreover, any estimate of the proportion of accidents to be assigned to alcohol abuse should reflect the obvious fact that alcohol abusers would have motor vehicle accidents even if they were not abusers, although presumably at a lower rate. We have developed a simple method for assigning responsibility to alcohol abuse for three types of motor vehicle accidents: fatal accidents, accidents resulting in personal injury, and accidents resulting in property damage. The procedure employed in assigning responsibility to alcohol abuse involves two steps. First, on the basis of the considerable empirical literature on the subject, we have estimated the proportion of accidents of each type in which alcohol abuse was present. Second, we have adjusted that proportion to account for the probability that the individuals involved would have had accidents even if they had not been alcohol abusers. The result is an estimate of the net proportion of accidents that can be attributed to alcohol abuse.

Ideally, we want to know what proportion of drivers who have accidents are alcohol abusers and what proportion of all drivers are alcohol abusers. Perhaps a simple example will serve to illustrate the proposed technique. Suppose that 100,000 motor vehicles pass by a given place in a given space of time and 100 of those vehicles are involved in an accident. The overall accident rate is thus one in a thousand, or .001.

Now suppose it were possible to determine how many of the 100,000 drivers had a blood alcohol content of .05 percent or higher. In fact, let us assume that we were able to measure the blood alcohol content of all 100,000 drivers and found 10,000 to be alcohol abusers. Thus, alcohol abusers, in our example, constitute 10 percent of all drivers.

Suppose further that among the 100 drivers involved in accidents, 40 were abusers and 60 were nonabusers. Then, alcohol abusers, who account for only 10 percent of all drivers, were involved in 40 percent of the accidents.

We can summarize the data assumed in our example in tabular form and use it to determine the extra accidents that can be attributed to alcohol abuse.

	All Drivers	Accident-Free Drivers	Drivers Involved in Accidents	Accident Rate
Abusers	10,000	9,960	40	.004
Nonabusers	90,000	89,940	60	.00067
Total	100,000	99,900	100	.001

Thus, the overall accident rate is one in a thousand (.001); the accident rate among abusers is four in a thousand (.004); and the accident rate among nonabusers is only two-thirds (i.e., less than one) in a thousand (.00067).

It seems reasonable to assume that in the absence of alcohol abuse, those who were abusers would face the same risk of accident as nonabusers. If abusers had had accidents at the same rate as nonabusers, there would have been fewer accidents. In fact, if we applied the .00067 accident rate among nonabusers to abusers, we would estimate only 6.7 accidents for abusers. It would appear, then, that 33.3 (40 − 6.7) accidents can be attributed to alcohol abuse. Alternatively, we could estimate the extra risk of accident attributable to alcohol abuse. Alcohol abusers have an accident rate of .004, while nonabusers have an accident rate of .00067. The difference, .00333, is the net accident rate that can reasonably be attributed to alcohol abuse. Thus, the proportion of accidents in which alcohol abuse was present was 40 percent; the extra proportion of accidents attributable to alcohol abuse is 33.3 percent.

Of course we do not have the necessary data for applying this technique to the general population. We do not know, for example, what proportion of the almost 17 million motor vehicle accidents in 1971 involved alcohol abusers. Nor do we know what proportion of all drivers in 1971 were alcohol abusers. There is, however, considerable empirical literature on the subject that does allow us to estimate the proportion of accidents in which alcohol abuse was present. Furthermore, several studies have employed the technique of sampling a control group of drivers who were at the same place at the same time of day as those involved in an accident, but who were not themselves involved in an accident. Thus, it is possible to generate an estimate of the proportion of accidents in which alcohol abuse was present, an estimate of the proportion of alcohol abusers on the road, and, consequently an estimate of the net or excess proportion of accidents that can be attributed to alcohol abuse.

Thus, suppose, in the example outlined above, we did not have the blood alcohol content for each of the entire 100,000 drivers, but rather had the blood alcohol content only for the drivers in the accident group and a sample of the population at risk in a control group selected at random from the 99,900 accident-free drivers. Let us assume, for convenience, that a sample of 1,000 drivers had been selected at random as a control group and that the proportions of alcohol abusers and nonabusers had been determined to be 10 percent and 90 percent, respectively. From this information it would be a simple matter to estimate the excess proportion of accidents that could be attributed to alcohol abuse.

Since we know the proportions of abusers and nonabusers involved in accidents and have an estimate of the proportions of abusers and nonabusers in the population at risk, we can estimate the relative accident rates of abusers and nonabusers: the relative accident rate of each is simply their proportion in the accident group divided by their proportion in the control group. Or, in tabular form:

	Proportion in Accident Group	Proportion in Accident-Free Control Group	Relative Accident Rate
Abusers	.40	.10	4.00
Nonabusers	.60	.90	0.67

In effect, if we know the relative proportion of drivers who are alcohol abusers and the relative proportion of accidents in which alcohol abuse is present, we can estimate the extra proportion of motor vehicle accidents that might be attributable to alcohol abuse:

$$\begin{array}{l} \text{Extra proportion of} \\ \text{accidents attributed} \\ \text{to alcohol abuse} \end{array} = \begin{array}{l} \text{Proportion of} \\ \text{accidents with} \\ \text{alcohol abuse} \end{array} - \left(\begin{array}{l} \text{Proportion of} \\ \text{alcohol abusers} \\ \text{on the road} \end{array} \right) \times \left(\begin{array}{l} \text{Relative} \\ \text{accident rate} \\ \text{of nonabusers} \end{array} \right)$$

In our example:

Extra proportion of accidents attributed to alcohol abuse $= .40 - [(.10) \times (.67)]$

$$= .333.$$

In general:

If a = proportion of accidents with alcohol abuse present
   b = proportion of alcohol abusers in the population at risk
   c = proportion of nonabusers in the accident group
   d = proportion of nonabusers in the population at risk

Then,

Extra proportion of accidents attributed to alcohol abuse $= a - b(c)/(d)$

EMPIRICAL EVIDENCE IN THE LITERATURE

There is a good deal of evidence that a significant relationship exists between motor vehicle accidents and alcohol abuse. Virtually all studies of motor vehicle accidents indicate that the proportion of alcohol abusers involved in accidents is higher than the prevalence of alcoholism in the general population. But the general population is not the population at risk with respect to motor vehicle accidents. Rather, the population at risk includes only those who are on the road. Thus, the studies that are of signal concern for our present purposes are those which have employed the technique of selecting a matched control group of accident-free drivers who were at risk, for comparison with a specific study group of drivers who were involved in accidents.

The earliest motor vehicle accident research that used a population-at-risk control group was done by Holcomb in 1938.[8] He obtained the blood alcohol content of 270 drivers involved in motor vehicle accidents that resulted in personal injury in Evanston, Illinois, over a three-year period. He also obtained the blood alcohol content of 1,750 drivers selected at random from among drivers on the road over a one-week period in an area and at a time of day similar to that experienced by the accident group. He found that 33.2 percent of the accident group but only 6.3 percent of the accident-free group had blood alcohol contents of .05 percent or higher.

A group of researchers employed a similar methodology to study motor vehicle accidents occurring during evening hours in Toronto, Canada, in 1952.[9] While some 22.4 percent of drivers involved in evening motor vehicle accidents had a BAC of .05 percent or higher, the proportion of 2,015 accident-free drivers in their control group that had a BAC of .05 percent or higher was only 8.7 percent. Again the accident rate of alcohol abusers was disproportionately high relative to their proportion in the population at risk.

A similar study, limited to fatal accidents, was conducted by McCarroll and Haddon in New York City.[10] Among some 34 drivers fatally injured and surviving less than six hours, 55.9 percent had BACs of .05 percent or higher. On the other hand, in a control group of some 252 accident-free drivers selected at random from among drivers who were at the place of fatal accidents at the same time of day, only 13.9 percent had BACs of .05 percent or higher. The same research group did a related study of pedestrians fatally injured by motor vehicles in New York City.[11] Among 19 adult pedestrian fatalities in their study group, some 47.4 percent had a blood alcohol content of .05 percent or higher. Among 177 pedestrians in their matched control group, only 18.1 percent had a BAC of .05 percent or higher.

On balance, these several studies indicate that the accident rate of alcohol abusers is greater than that of nonabusers—there is an apparent extra accident rate that can be attributed to alcohol abuse.

Furthermore, it would appear that the extra accident rate increases with the severity of the accidents under consideration.

The most comprehensive study of motor vehicle accidents that used a population-at-risk control group was that conducted by Borkenstein and his colleagues in the Department of Police Administration at Indiana University.[12] Their study group included some 9,353 drivers involved in all types of motor vehicle accidents in Grand Rapids, Michigan. Their control group included 8,000 drivers selected at random over the year from July 1962 to June 1963 at a location, hour, day, and month at which an accident had occurred during the previous three years. They were able to conduct interviews with and analyze breath samples for some 5,985 drivers in the accident study group and 7,590 drivers in the control group. Among the 5,985 drivers in the accident study group, some 9.8 percent had a BAC of .05 percent or higher, while among the 7,590 drivers in the control group, only 3.2 percent had a BAC of .05 percent or higher. The Grand Rapids study also provides additional evidence that the proportion of accidents in which alcohol abuse is present increases with the severity of the accident. Thus, for example, among 300 drivers seriously injured in motor vehicle accidents in the Grand Rapids study group, some 17 percent had a BAC of .05 percent or higher.

We have summarized in table 4–7 selected study data on the relationship between blood alcohol content and motor vehicle accidents from these five studies that included a population-at-risk control group. Although these data must be considered with some care, they certainly do serve to summarize the nature of the relationship between alcohol abuse and motor vehicle accidents. In all cases, the proportion of alcohol abusers involved in accidents is considerably higher than the proportion of alcohol abusers in the control group that represents the population of risk. It seems reasonable to conclude, therefore, that a net accident rate can be attributed to alcohol abuse. Furthermore, the apparent net accident rate associated with alcohol abuse is higher for more serious types of accidents. The proportion of alcohol abusers seriously injured in accidents is higher than the proportion of alcohol abusers in all accidents, and the proportion of alcohol abusers killed is highest of all. Finally, the proportion of alcohol abusers in the population at risk is higher for more serious accidents than for less serious accidents. This phenomenon serves to indicate the importance of the interrelationships between alcohol abuse and several other factors related to motor

TABLE 4-7. A Summary of Selected Study Data on the Relationship between Blood Alcohol Concentration and Motor Vehicle Accidents in Five Studies That Included a Population-at-Risk Control Group

Study	Group	Group Size	Proportion of Alcohol Abusers*	Comments
Evanston, Illinois, 1938	Accident	270	33.2%	Drivers seriously injured
	Control	1,750	6.3	Drivers at a place and time similar to that experienced by the accident group
Toronto, Canada, 1952	Accident	Not reported	22.4	Drivers involved in evening accidents
	Control	2,015	8.7	Drivers at evening-accident sites
New York City, 1959–60	Accident	34	55.9	Drivers fatally injured and surviving less than six hours
	Control	252	13.9	Drivers at time and place of fatal accidents
New York City, 1959	Accident	19	47.4	Adult pedestrian fatalities
	Control	177	18.1	Adult pedestrians matched to fatalities
Grand Rapids, Michigan, 1962–63	Accident	5,985	9.8	Drivers in all accidents
	Accident	300	17.0	Drivers seriously injured
	Control	7,590	3.2	Drivers at time and place of all accidents

*Blood alcohol content of .05 percent or higher.

Sources: Derived from data reported in the following publications:

Evanston: R. L. Holcomb, "Alcohol in Relation to Traffic Accidents," *Journal of the American Medical Association*, vol. 3 (1938), pp. 1076–85.

Toronto: G. W. H. Lucas, W. Kalow, J. D. McColl, B. A. Griffith, and H. W. Smith, "Quantitative Studies of the Relationship between Alcohol Levels and Motor Vehicle Accidents," *Proceedings, Second International Conference on Alcohol and Road Traffic* (Toronto: Garden City Press Cooperative, 1955), pp. 139–42.

New York: J. R. McCarroll and W. Haddon, Jr., "A Controlled Study of Fatal Automobile Accidents in New York City," *Journal of Chronic Diseases*, vol. 15 (1962), pp. 811–26.

New York: W. Haddon, Jr., P. Valien, J. R. McCarroll, and C. J. Umberger, "A Controlled Investigation of the Characteristics of Adult Pedestrians Fatally Injured by Motor Vehicles in Manhattan," *Journal of Chronic Diseases*, vol. 14 (1961), pp. 655–78.

Grand Rapids: R. F. Borkenstein, R. F. Crowther, R. P. Shumate, W. B. Ziel, and R. Zylman, *The Role of the Drinking Driver in Traffic Accidents* (Bloomington, Ind.: Indiana University, Department of Police Administration, 1964).

vehicle accidents such as speed, highway conditions, time of day, and driver experience.

The data available from the several studies that included a popu-lation-at-risk control group provide the basis for estimating the extra proportion of accidents that might be attributed to alcohol abuse. It will be recalled that in order to estimate this extra proportion we need: (1) the proportion of accidents in which alcohol abuse was present; (2) the proportion of alcohol abusers in the population at risk; and (3) the relative accident rate of nonabusers. Each of these either is available directly or can be derived from the data in table 4–7. The necessary data implied by each of the several studies and the extra proportion of accidents that might be attributed to alcohol abuse in each case are outlined in table 4–8.

Thus, for example, the Grand Rapids study implies that the extra proportion of all accidents that might be attributed to alcohol abuse is on the order of 6.8 percent. Estimates of the extra proportion of more serious accidents that might be attributed to alcohol abuse are considerably higher. The extra proportion of accidents resulting in serious injury, for example, were on the order of 14.3 percent in the Grand Rapids study and 28.7 percent in the Evanston study. The extra proportion of accidents involving fatalities implied by the two New York City studies were some 48.8 percent for driver fatalities and 35.8 percent for pedestrian fatalities.

The data derived from these five studies are on the whole, consistent. Still, there are differences among the several estimates. When there is a choice to be made, it would seem appropriate for several reasons to rely more often than not on the Grand Rapids study. First, that study is the most recent of the five. Second, it was more comprehensive and included more observations than the other four studies combined. Third, the study design, sampling techniques, and measurement procedures were perhaps most reliable in the Grand Rapids study. Finally, it would seem that the driving popula-tion under study in the Grand Rapids case could be more reliably projected to represent that of the entire United States than could that of any of the other four.

Unfortunately, the Grand Rapids study does not provide any basis for estimating the extra proportion of fatal accidents that might be attributed to alcohol abuse. The New York City studies do, but the number of observations is exceedingly small, and New York City is perhaps not representative of the United States as a whole. There

TABLE 4–8. The Extra Proportion of Accidents Attributable to Alcohol Abuse in Studies That Included a Population-at-Risk Control Group

Study	Proportion of Accidents with Alcohol Abuse Present	Proportion of Alcohol Abusers in the Population at Risk	Relative Accident Rate of Nonabusers	Extra Proportion of Accidents Attributable to Alcohol Abuse
	(1)	(2)	(3)	(4)
Evanston (serious injuries)	33.2%	6.3%	.71	28.7%
Toronto (evening accidents)	22.4	8.7	.85	15.0
New York City (driver fatalities)	55.9	13.9	.51	48.8
New York City (pedestrian fatalities)	47.4	18.1	.64	35.8
Grand Rapids (all accidents)	9.8	3.2	.93	6.8
Grand Rapids (serious injuries)	17.0	3.2	.86	14.3

Sources: Column 1 is the proportion of alcohol abusers involved in accidents, taken directly from table 4–7. Column 2 is the proportion of alcohol abusers in the control group representing the population at risk, taken directly from table 4–7. Column 3 is simply the ratio of the proportion of nonabusers in the accident group to the proportion of nonabusers in the population at risk (100 − column 1)/(100 − column 2). Column 4 is derived by subtracting the product of column 2 and column 3 from column 1.

are, however, several studies of fatal accidents in the literature that
provide data on the proportion of accidents in which alcohol abuse
was present. These studies are summarized in table 4–9. Of course,
since none of them included a population-at-risk control group, they
provide no indication of the relative accident rate of alcohol abusers.

TABLE 4–9. A Summary of Selected Study Data on the Relationship
between Blood Alcohol Concentration and Fatal Motor Vehicle Accidents

Study	Number of Cases Studied	Proportion of Alcohol Abusers*
Single-Vehicle Accidents Resulting in Fatalities		
Westchester County, N.Y., 1950–57	83	68%
Dade County, Fla., 1956–65	221	64
California, 1965–66	1,403	61
New Jersey, 1961–63	469	63
Combined	2,176	62
All Accidents Resulting in Nonpedestrian Fatalities		
California, 1965–66	2,794	51
New Jersey, 1961–63	820	52
Baltimore, Md., 1951–56	145	63
Dade County Fla., 1956–65	485	45
Combined	4,244	51
All Accidents Resulting in Pedestrian Fatalities		
Baltimore, Md., 1951–56	137	44
New Jersey, 1961–63	414	37
California, 1950–67	246	43
Combined	797	40

*Blood alcohol content of .05 percent or higher.
Sources: Derived from data reported in the following publications:
   Westchester: W. Haddon, Jr. and V. A. Bradess, "Alcohol in the Single Vehicle
    Fatal Accident Experience of Westchester County, New York," *Journal of
    the American Medical Association,* vol. 169 (1959), pp. 1587–93.
   Dade County: J. H. Davis and A. J. Fisk, "The Dade County, Florida, Study
    on Carbon Monoxide, Alcohol, and Drugs in Fatal Single Vehicle Auto-
    mobile Accidents," *Proceedings, National Association of Coroners,* 1964–
    66, pp. 197–204.
   California, 1965–1966: R. A. Nielson, *Alcohol Involvement in Fatal Motor
    Vehicle Accidents,* California Traffic Safety Foundation, San Francisco,
    1965; and R. A. Nielson, *A Survey of Post-Mortem Blood Alcohols From
    Forty-One California Counties in 1966,* California Traffic Safety Founda-
    tion, San Francisco, 1967.
   California, 1950–67: J. A. Waller, E. M. King, G. Nielson, and A. W. Tarkel,
    "Alcohol and Other Factors in California Highway Fatalaities," *Journal of
    Forensic Sciences,* vol. 14 (1969), pp. 429–44.
   New Jersey: *New Jersey Alcohol Determination Program in Fatal Traffic
    Accident Cases: Report of Three-Year Study, 1961–1963,* New Jersey
    Department of Law and Public Safety, Division of Motor Vehicles, Traffic
    Safety Service, Trenton, 1964.
   Baltimore: H. C. Freimuth, S. R. Watts, and R. S. Fisher, "Alcohol and High-
    way Fatalities," *Journal of Forensic Sciences,* vol. 3 (1958), pp. 65–71.

On the other hand, however, they do provide considerable insight into the proportion of alcohol abusers involved in fatal accidents in a variety of locations. By and large, they are consistent with the implications of the New York City studies.

The first four studies outlined in table 4–9 dealt with single-vehicle accidents resulting in fatalities. Alcohol abuse was present in over 60 percent of the accidents in each of the four studies. (Overall, among the 2,176 accidents represented by these four studies, alcohol abuse was present in 62 percent.) Since these accidents did not involve other vehicles and drivers, there is perhaps less uncertainty about the role of alcohol abuse in causing them.

The second four studies summarized in table 4–9 dealt with all accidents resulting in nonpedestrian fatalities. Alcohol abuse was present in a somewhat lower proportion of the accidents analyzed in these four studies, but it was still present in 51 percent of the 4,244 accidents represented by these four studies.

Finally, the last three studies referred to in table 4–9 dealt with all accidents resulting in pedestrian fatalities. Taken together, the three studies represented some 797 pedestrian fatalities; 40 percent of these had a blood alcohol content of .05 percent or higher. This is a lower proportion than was obtained in the other groups of studies, but it should be noted that the pedestrian fatality studies do not make allowance for alcohol abuse on the part of drivers involved in the accidents.

There is sufficient empirical evidence in the literature to allow us to estimate the extra proportion of the several types of motor vehicle accidents that might be attributed to alcohol abuse. All of the studies provide data on the proportion of accidents in which alcohol abuse is present. The studies that included a population-at-risk control group provide data on the proportion of alcohol abusers in the population at risk. What remains is to select specific estimates for the several types of accidents. In order to apply the empirical evidence to the task at hand, then, we need to make a few choices. In making our choices we have followed two reasonable criteria. First, for the reasons noted above, we prefer to rely more often than not on the Grand Rapids study. Second, as has been the case throughout our analysis of the economic cost of alcohol abuse, we prefer to choose relatively conservative estimates.[13] Our estimates for the several types of motor vehicle accidents of the proportion of accidents in which alcohol abuse is present, the proportion of alcohol abusers in the population at risk, the relative accident rate of nonabusers, and the extra proportion of accidents attributable to alcohol abuse are given in table 4–10.

An estimate of the proportion of fatal accidents with alcohol abuse present on the order of 50 percent would seem to be reasonable and conservative. This estimate is somewhat lower than the empirical evidence in the literature would suggest, but it does allow for the somewhat lower incidence of alcohol abuse among pedestrian fatalities, which represented approximately 20 percent of all motor vehicle accident fatalities in 1971.

The estimates of the proportions of personal injury accidents and property damage accidents with alcohol abuse present are derived from the Grand Rapids study. The 17 percent figure for personal injury accidents is taken directly from the Grand Rapids study— among the 300 drivers seriously injured in motor vehicle accidents in the Grand Rapids study group, some 17 percent had a BAC of .05 percent or higher. The 8.4 percent estimate for property damage accidents with alcohol abuse present represents an adjustment of the Grand Rapids figure for the proportion of all accidents with alcohol abuse present. An adjustment seems reasonable in light of the evidence that the proportion of accidents with alcohol abuse present is lower for less serious accidents and higher for more serious accidents, and is consistent with our preference for conservative estimates.[14]

The several estimates of the proportions of alcohol abusers in the populations at risk are derived from the data in the several studies that included control groups representing the populations at risk. The 15.6 percent estimate for fatal accidents represents a weighted average of the pedestrian and nonpedestrian control groups in the two New York City studies. It may represent somewhat of an overstatement, but, if so, it will serve to lower the estimated extra proportion of accidents attributed to alcohol abuse and thereby result in a more conservative estimate of the economic cost of motor vehicle accidents due to alcohol abuse.

The Evanston study provides the most direct evidence of the proportion of alcohol abusers in the population at risk in the case of personal injury accidents. Some 6.3 percent of the drivers in the control group selected to represent the population at risk for serious injury accidents were alcohol abusers. To the extent that the proportion might be lower for less serious personal injury accidents, 6.3 might be somewhat of an overstatement. Given our preference for more conservative estimates, however, we have chosen to take the 6.3 percent figure as our estimate.

TABLE 4–10. Estimated Extra Proportion of Accidents Attributable to Alcohol Abuse, by Type of Accident

Type of Accident	Proportion of Accidents with Alcohol Abuse Present	Proportion of Alcohol Abusers in the Population at Risk	Relative Accident Rate of Nonabusers	Extra Proportion of Accidents Attributable to Alcohol Abuse
Fatality	50.0%	15.6%	.59	40.8%
Personal injury	17.0	6.3	.89	11.4
Property damage	8.4	3.2	.95	5.4
All	9.8	3.2	.93	6.8

Finally, our estimate of the proportion of alcohol abusers in the population at risk with respect to property damage accidents is taken to be some 3.2 percent—the proportion of alcohol abusers among all 7,590 drivers in the control group in the Grand Rapids study.

Given these several estimates of the proportions of accidents with alcohol abuse present and the proportions of alcohol abusers in the populations at risk, the respective relative accident rates of non-abusers and extra proportions of accidents attributable to alcohol abuse are derived in a straightforward manner.[15]

The several estimates derived reflect the necessary adjustments that should be made to take into account what is known about the relationship between motor vehicle accidents of different types and alcohol abuse. Furthermore, the extra proportion of motor vehicle accidents attributed to alcohol abuse is an adjusted proportion which accounts for the fact that alcohol abusers would have had accidents even if they had not been abusers. These extra proportions of motor vehicle accidents can be used to assign part of the total economic costs of motor vehicle accidents to alcohol abuse.

THE ECONOMIC COST OF MOTOR VEHICLE ACCIDENTS DUE TO ALCOHOL ABUSE

At the outset of this chapter we noted that in order to estimate the economic cost of motor vehicle accidents due to alcohol abuse we would need an estimate of the total cost of such accidents by accident type, some measure of the proportion of accidents that involved alcohol abuse, and an adjustment factor to account for the fact that alcohol abusers would have accidents even if they were not abusers. We now have all the necessary components to estimate the economic cost of motor vehicle accidents due to alcohol abuse. Our estimates are given in table 4–11 by type of accident.

The estimated economic cost of the several types of accident was derived in the second section of this chapter and was outlined in detail in table 4–6 above. It will be recalled that the revised estimate of some $30.5 billion for all accidents represented the conservative choice of the NHTSA estimate at a net discount rate of 7 percent and minus the less tangible items.

The estimated extra proportions of accidents attributable to alcohol abuse were derived in the last section and were outlined in

TABLE 4–11. Estimated Economic Cost of Motor Vehicle Accidents Attributable to Alcohol Abuse in 1971, by Type of Accident

Type of Accident	Estimated Economic Cost (in billions)	Estimated Extra Proportion of Accidents Attributed to Alcohol Abuse	Estimated Economic Cost Attributed to Alcohol Abuse (in billions)
Fatality	$ 5.783	40.8%	$2.359
Personal injury	17.292	11.4	1.971
Property damage	7.392	5.4	.399
All	$30.467	6.8	$4.729

detail in table 4–10 above. These were also based on relatively conservative estimates from among the empirical evidence in the literature.

On balance, our estimate of the economic cost of motor vehicle accidents attributed to alcohol abuse is a rather conservative one. Of the $30.5 billion estimated as the cost of all motor vehicle accidents, 15.5 percent, some $4.7 billion, is attributed by us to alcohol abuse.

Although these estimates were derived with some care, certain problems remain that should not go unnoted. There is the problem of alcohol-abusing drivers inflicting costs on nonabusers and non-abusers inflicting costs on abusers, for example. In both these instances, our method of assigning costs will result in the cost being counted against the wrong group. Since alcohol-abusing drivers are consistently associated with more than their share of accidents, however, it seems reasonable to conclude that the net effect of this error has been to understate the total costs due to alcohol abuse.

Included in our estimate of the economic costs of motor vehicle accidents attributed to alcohol abuse are some $239 million in medical care costs and $3.0 billion in lost production, including $2.1 billion as the present value in 1971 of future production lost owing to premature death. Since separate estimates of the cost of lost production and medical care due to alcohol abuse were also made for the economy as a whole, there is the distinct possibility that we have engaged in some double counting. However, our definition of alcohol abuse in the context of motor vehicle accidents was based on the immediate blood alcohol content at the time of a motor vehicle accident rather than on the drinking history or drinking problems of the individuals involved. Clearly not all accidents that occur after drinking involve alcoholics or alcohol abusers in the more traditional sense of these terms. The costs associated with occasional drinking are included in the motor vehicle context, but not in the lost production or medical care contexts. Thus, although some double counting has occurred, it is less than complete.

Actually, we do have a basis for assessing the extent of double counting in the case of lost production due to premature death. It will be recalled that 358 premature deaths in motor vehicle accidents were included in our estimate of lost production due to excess mortality of heavy drinkers in chapter 2. In effect, some $41.3 million of the economic cost of motor vehicle accidents has already been counted in chapter 2. Indeed, as suspected, the relative magnitude of double counting was rather insignificant: it amounted to less than 2 percent in the case of lost future production and there is no reason to expect it to be greater with respect to other lost production or medical care costs. Still, when the economic cost of alcohol abuse is aggregated, we shall subtract the amount that has been counted twice. On the whole, it seems reasonable to expect that to the extent that double counting overstates the economic cost due to alcohol abuse, it is more than balanced by the understatement that results from conservative estimation and noncounting of less tangible items.

In this latter context, it is revealing to reflect on the dollar estimate of the cost of fatal accidents attributed to alcohol abuse as a measure of the "cost" of the human lives that were lost in motor vehicle accidents in 1971. We have alluded several times to the fact that it is just not possible to measure the total social impact of the adverse consequences of alcohol abuse. More than 22,000 persons were killed in motor vehicle accidents attributed to alcohol abuse in 1971. Some part of the real social loss associated with these deaths is expressed in the $2.4 billion estimate of the economic cost of fatal motor vehicle accidents, but a dollar figure cannot convey the very real nontangible losses sustained, such as pain and suffering, family anguish, and other adverse consequences that affect the family and friends of the deceased and society in general.

Our analysis has relied on published estimates of the cost of motor vehicle accidents and the presence of alcohol abuse in such accidents. The data available suffered from certain weaknesses that have been pointed out throughout the chapter. We have had to rely on studies made at various times and various places. Unfortunately, there is no guarantee that these studies can be readily generalized to the country as a whole. The study locations may have been atypical relative to driving behavior, drinking behavior, driving-after-drinking behavior, or all three. Perhaps, in the future, analysis can be carried out on matched accident and control groups selected so as to be representative of the entire nation. In the meantime, however, we have made do with the empirical evidence that is available. Given the state of our knowledge concerning alcohol abuse and driving behavior and the state of available data, it would seem that our estimate of the economic cost of motor vehicle accidents due to alcohol abuse is a reasonable one and will serve our present purposes.

NOTES

1. U.S. Department of Transportation, National Highway Traffic Safety Administration, *Societal Costs of Motor Vehicle Accidents*, Preliminary Report (April 1972).

2. Actually, the estimate of $18 billion includes production lost in future years because of death and permanent disability occurring in 1971. But the figure is probably not far from the actual 1971 loss, since the actual output in any given year is lower as a consequence of death and permanent disability occurring in previous years.

3. T. A. Loomis and T. C. West, "The Influence of Alcohol on Automobile Driving Ability," *Quarterly Journal of Studies on Alcohol*, vol. 19 (1958), pp. 30–46.

4. See, for example, studies by J. A. Carpenter, "Effects of Alcohol on Psychological Processes," in B. H. Fox and J. H. Fox, ed., *Alcohol and Traffic Safety*, Public Health Service Publication No. 1043 (Washington, D.C.: U.S. Government Printing Office, May 1963), pp. 45–90; and L. Goldberg, "Tolerance to Alcohol in Moderate and Heavy Drinkers and Its Significance to Alcohol and Traffic," *Proceedings of the First International Conference on Alcohol and Road Traffic*, Stockholm, 1950 (Stockholm: Kugelbergs Boktrycheri, 1951), pp. 85–106.

5. L. G. Goldstein, "Human Variables in Traffic Accidents: *A Digest of Research, Traffic Safety Research Review*," vol. 8 (1964), pp. 26–31.

6. R. Zylman, "Accidents, Alcohol, and Single Cause Explanations: Lessons From the Grand Rapids Study," *Quarterly Journal of Studies on Alcohol,* supplement no. 4 (1968), p. 214.

7. R. F. Borkenstein, R. F. Crowther, R. P. Shumate, W. B. Ziel, and R. Zylman, *The Role of the Drinking Driver in Traffic Accidents*, (Bloomington, Ind.: Indiana University, Department of Police Administration, 1964).

8. R. L. Holcomb, "Alcohol in Relation to Traffic Accidents," *Journal of the American Medical Association*, vol. 3 (1938), pp. 1076–85.

9. G. W. H. Lucas, W. Kalow, J. D. McColl, B. A. Griffith, and H. W. Smith, "Quantitative Studies of the Relationship between Alcohol Levels and Motor Vehicle Accidents," *Proceedings, Second International Conference on Alcohol and Road Traffic* (Toronto: Garden City Press Cooperative, 1955), pp. 139–42.

10. J. R. McCarroll and W. Haddon, Jr., "A Controlled Study of Fatal Automobile Accidents in New York City," *Journal of Chronic Diseases*, vol. 15 (1962), pp. 811–26.

11. W. Haddon, Jr., P. Valien, J. R. McCarroll, and C. J. Umberger, "A Controlled Investigation of the Characteristics of Adult Pedestrians Fatally Injured by Motor Vehicles in Manhattan," *Journal of Chronic Diseases*, vol. 14 (1961), pp. 655–78.

12. Borkenstein, et al., *Role of the Drinking Driver.*

13. An estimate of the extra proportion of accidents attributable to alcohol abuse will be lower (i.e., more conservative) when: the proportion of accidents with alcohol abuse present is lower; the proportion of alcohol abusers in the population at risk is higher; and the relative accident rate of nonabusers is higher.

14. The adjustment was made by simply calculating what proportion of property damage accidents with alcohol abuse present would be consistent with a 9.8 percent proportion of all accidents with alcohol abuse present, assuming a distribution of accidents by type similar to that which prevailed in the United States as a whole in 1971.

15. It will be recalled that the relative accident rate of nonabusers is simply the ratio of the proportion of nonabusers in the accident group to the proportion of nonabusers in the population at risk; and the extra proportion of accidents attributed to alcohol abuse is the proportion of accidents with alcohol abuse present *minus* (the proportion of alcohol abusers in the population at risk *times* the relative accident rate of nonabusers).

CHAPTER FIVE

ALCOHOL AND THE ECONOMIC COST OF FIRES

INTRODUCTION

Fires are similar to motor vehicle accidents in many respects. Certainly the economic costs of fire are similar in kind to those of other types of accidents. The adverse consequences of fire are manifested as loss of life, personal injuries, and property damage. In each case, the economic consequences of fire involve some opportunity cost. The opportunity cost may take the form of production that does not occur, or it may take the form of alternatives foregone in order to produce goods and services necessary to cope with the consequences of fire. The economic costs of fire would certainly include the cost of lost production, medical costs, and costs associated with property damage.

Our current concern, of course, is not with the economic cost of fire per se, but rather with that part of this cost that might reasonably be attributed to alcohol abuse. Can alcohol abuse be linked as a causal factor to some proportion of the loss of life, personal injuries, and property damage resulting from fire? In effect, we are seeking an answer to the same question in the context of fire that we asked in the last chapter in the context of motor vehicle accidents. Conceptually, the problem is the same. Unfortunately, very little is known about the causes of fire that is directly useful for our present concerns. In fact, the whole area is surprisingly underresearched. Evidence and knowledge concerning fires is much more limited and much less revealing than would be necessary to allow particularly reliable answers. The state of knowledge concerning the relationship between fire and alcohol abuse is such that we can at best speculate about the economic cost of fire that might be attributable to alcohol abuse. Any estimate would be exceedingly limited and must be taken as a "soft" estimate.

Still, some evidence is available on the cost of fire, and some limited research has been done which is indicative of the relationships between alcohol and fire and between alcohol and the consequences of fire. It seems more appropriate to attempt to generate a tentative estimate, identified as such, than to ignore the economic cost of fire that might be due to alcohol abuse.

THE COST OF FIRE

The appropriate perspective toward and the basic approach to estimating the economic cost of fire are the same as those that have been employed in previous chapters. The major tangible economic costs of fire should include the economic value of the lost production of those who died or were injured in fires and the value of foregone output of resources diverted to provide goods and services made necessary because of fire.

We have no comprehensive study of the economic cost of fire to make our task somewhat easier, as we did in the case of motor vehicle accidents; rather, we must take information concerning the consequences of fire from a variety of sources and generate our own estimate of the economic cost of fire in 1971. The major consequences of fire in the United States in 1971 are outlined in table 5–1. Some 6,776 persons perished in fires, 107,000 people suffered personal injuries requiring medical attention, and property was damaged in 2,728,200 fires. These were the real consequences of fire in 1971. We seek an estimate of the economic costs implied by these adverse consequences of fire.

What does society forego in economic terms as a result of fire? The most obvious loss, perhaps, is the extensive property damage occasioned. Thus, the National Fire Protection Association estimated property damage from the 2,728,200 fires in 1971 at some $2.7 billion.[1] Society was clearly made worse off by this loss. To the extent that society chose to repair or replace the property damaged by fire, the resources used for that purpose were not available to produce other goods and services.

TABLE 5–1. The Major Consequences of Fire in the United States in 1971

Consequence	Number
Fatalities	6,776
Personal injuries requiring medical attention	107,000
Property damage fires	2,728,200

Sources: Fatalities are from U.S. Department of Health, Education, and Welfare, National Center for Health Statistics, *Vital Statistics of the United States: 1971,* vol. II–*Mortality,* part A (Washington, D.C.: U.S. Government Printing Office, 1975). Personal injuries requiring medical attention are as reported by fire departments to the National Fire Protection Association. Property damage is from National Fire Protection Association, "Fires and Fire Losses Classified, 1971," *Fire Journal,* vol. 66 (September, 1972).

Fires also claim a significant number of human lives. In 1971 there were 6,776 deaths due to fire in the United States.[2] These lives, of course, have both social and economic value. Lost production due to premature deaths is but a part of the total value, but even this part is a significant economic cost when we are dealing with almost 7,000 fire deaths. We have estimated the present value in 1971 of lost production due to premature death caused by fire to be some $386.8 million. This estimate, derived from expected lifetime earnings discounted at 6 percent, is broken down by age in table 5–2.

The age-specific death rates given there reflect the fact that the very young and the very old are particularly prone to die in fires. This fact should serve as a reminder that the value of lost future production is an incomplete and imperfect measure of the real value of a life lost. The value of human life has many dimensions, most of which virtually defy quantification. Lost future production due to premature death is but a part of the total value, and it clearly understates the real loss.[3]

Finally, fires result in personal injuries that imply lost production and the diversion of resources to treat the injured persons. The National Fire Protection Association collects data as reported by fire departments on the number of injuries requiring medical attention; in 1971, some 107,000 persons injured in fires required medical treatment. Unfortunately, no breakdown of this figure by age or extent of injury is available. In order to estimate lost production and medical treatment costs occasioned by personal injuries caused by fire, we must rely on other data.

In fact, there are reliable sample data available for injuries from

TABLE 5–2. Estimated Present Value in 1971 of Lost Future Production
Due to Premature Death Caused by Fire in 1971, by Age

Age Group	Deaths Per 100,000	Number of Deaths	Present Value in 1971 of Lost Future Production (in millions)
0–4	5.4	925	$ 41.0
5–14	1.5	590	39.1
15–24	1.1	427	52.5
25–44	2.1	1,010	129.8
45–64	4.2	1,778	109.9
65 and over	10.0	2,034	13.7
Not stated		12	0.8
		6,776	$386.8

Sources: Death rates are from *Insurance Facts, 1975* (New York: Insurance Information Institute, 1975).

Deaths by age group are from U.S. Department of Health, Education, and Welfare, National Center for Health Statistics, *Vital Statistics of the United States: 1971*, vol. II–*Mortality*, part A (Washington, D.C.: U.S. Government Printing Office, 1975).

Present value in 1971 of lost future production is derived from earnings data discounted at 6 percent in B. S. Cooper and W. Brody, "1972 Lifetime Earnings by Age, Sex, Race, and Education Level," Research and Statistics Note No. 14 (Washington, D.C.: Office of Research and Statistics, Social Security Administration, September 30, 1975).

burns associated with flammable fabrics. These data are compiled by the Injury Data and Control Center of the Bureau of Product Safety of the Food and Drug Administration, and are published in an annual report issued by the Secretary of Health, Education, and Welfare. Thus, for example, the 1971 report included a breakdown by length of hospital stay for a sample of 688 fire injuries.[4] This breakdown is given in table 5–3. In the absence of any other empirical evidence, it seems reasonable to assume that length of hospital stay is distributed similarly over all injuries. Hence, we have assumed that the distribution which obtained for this sample applies for all 107,000 fire-related personal injuries.

The medical costs incurred in treating the 65 percent of those injured in fires who required hospitalization have been estimated as the average cost of hospital care. In 1971, a typical day of hospital care cost $91.00. Since fire injuries often involve intensive care, an estimate based on the average cost of hospital care is undoubtedly a conservative one.

The medical costs incurred in treating those who were injured in fires and required medical attention but did not require hospitaliza-

TABLE 5–3. Estimated Economic Cost of Personal Injuries Requiring Medical Attention Caused by Fire in 1971

Length of Hospital Stay (in days)	Percentage of Sample*	Number of Persons Injured	Estimated Medical Treatment Costs (in thousands)	Estimated Lost Production (in thousands)
None	34.2	36,594	$ 684.7	$ 238.5
1–5	17.9	19,153	5,228.8	748.9
6–10	9.9	10,593	7,711.7	1,104.6
11–20	9.7	10,379	14,639.6	2,096.8
21–30	7.3	7,811	18,125.4	2,596.0
31–50	10.0	10,700	39,434.9	5,648.8
50 or more	11.0	11,770	80,330.3	11,506.3
Total	100.0	107,000	$166,155.4	$23,939.9

Sources: Length of stay of sample distribution is from U.S. Department of Health, Education, and Welfare, *Flammable Fabrics: Third Annual Report to the President and the Congress*, Fiscal Year 1971, DHEW Publication (FDA) 72-7013 (Washington, D.C.: U.S. Government Printing Office, 1972), p. 71.

Total injuries are from National Fire Protection Association, Boston, Mass.

Medical treatment costs are based on cost of an average ambulatory visit to a physician ($18.71) and average cost of a typical day of hospital care ($91) in 1971.

Lost production costs are based on the average daily earnings of production workers ($27.44) in 1971.
*The sample size was 688.

tion have been estimated as the average cost of an ambulatory visit to a physician. In 1971, a typical ambulatory visit to a physician cost $18.71. In all, we have estimated the medical treatment costs of personal injuries caused by fire in 1971 to total some $166.2 million.

We have used a similar approach to estimate the cost of lost production associated with personal injuries caused by fire. In the absence of any other empirical evidence, we have assumed that the age distribution of persons injured in fires is similar to that of persons killed in fires. In effect, this implies that some 50,825 of those injured were within the labor-force age groups (15–64). Our estimate of lost production was derived by assuming that each of those who did not require hospitalization missed a half-day of work, while each of those who required hospitalization missed a day of work for each day of hospitalization. We have thus generated a rather conservative estimate of lost production in 1971 due to fire injuries of some $23.9 million.

Overall, we have estimated the economic cost of fire in the

United States in 1971 to be some $3.3 billion. The estimate is summarized in table 5—4. Of course, our concern is not with the economic cost of fire, but rather with that part of this cost that might be attributable to alcohol abuse. What part of the $3.3 billion cost of fire can reasonably be assigned to alcohol abuse? In order to attempt to answer that question, we must look to the rather limited evidence in the literature on the relationship between alcohol abuse and fire.

RESEARCH ON THE RELATIONSHIP BETWEEN FIRE AND ALCOHOL

Alcohol may be related to fire and its consequences in two ways. On the one hand, alcohol abuse may be a contributing cause of fire in the first place. On the other hand, given a fire—whatever its cause—alcohol may well serve to intensify its adverse consequences, because judgment and physical skills are adversely affected even at low levels of blood alcohol content.

Unfortunately, there is but limited evidence on the relationship between alcohol and fire. Alcohol as a probable cause of fire has not been a major concern in fire research. There are, however, three

TABLE 5—4. Estimated Economic Cost of Fire in the United States in 1971

Cost	Estimate (in millions)
Lost production	$ 410.7
Medical treatment	166.2
Property damage	2,743.3
Total economic cost	$3,320.2

Sources: Lost production includes the present value in 1971 of lost future production due to premature death, taken from table 5—2, and the cost of lost production associated with personal injuries, taken from table 5—3.

Medical treatment costs are taken from table 5—3.

Property damage costs are from National Fire Protection Association, "Fires and Fire Losses Classified, 1971," *Fire Journal*, vol. 66 (September 1972), p. 67.

studies of fire fatalities and one study of burn injuries that do provide some evidence on and considerable insight into the relationship between alcohol and the consequences of fire. W. Slater Hollis studied twenty-nine fire deaths of persons aged 16 to 60 that occurred over a period of eight years in Memphis, Tennessee.[5] Hollis found the relationship between blood alcohol content and the number of fire deaths to be quite significant, as reflected in table 5–5. In fact, he concluded that the primary cause of these fire deaths was alcohol consumption. Hollis compared the autopsy results with fire, police, and medical examiner's reports and noted that "alcohol ingestion is the normal accompaniment of fire deaths and the most common attributed primary cause of death."[6] He further stated that

> case after case revealed that fire deaths of children—particularly small children—were attributed to failure by parents aged 16 to 60 to perceive and respond to a fire emergency because of impairment of their sensory, judgment, or physical functions by alcohol consumption.[7]

There are certain problems inherent in Hollis's methodology, and his sample of twenty-nine fire deaths is too small to provide a basis for national projections. Still, his findings do suggest a strong link between alcohol abuse and fire fatalities. At the time of their deaths, at least eighteen of the twenty-nine persons studied by Hollis had a blood alcohol content of .05 or higher.

A second study that provides some evidence of the relationship between alcohol abuse and fire fatalities was conducted by Schmidt

TABLE 5–5. Fire Deaths of Persons Aged 16–60 in Memphis, Tennessee, Over an Eight-Year Period

Blood Alcohol Content	Number of Deaths
.00	5
.01–.04	0
.05–.09	2
.10–.19	4
.20 and over	12
Positive but unknown	6
Total	29

Source: W. S. Hollis, "Drinking: Its Part in Fire Deaths," *Fire Journal*, vol. 67 (May 1973). The source of Hollis's data was records from the Medical Examiner's Office of the State of Tennessee.

and deLint in Ontario, Canada. They undertook a follow-up study of some 6,658 persons who had a history of frequent heavy drinking and had been treated in an alcoholic treatment center. Their primary concern was to compare the mortality experience of alcohol abusers with that of the general population in order to assess the excess mortality attributable to alcohol abuse. Over a period of fourteen years they recorded some 738 deaths among alcohol abusers, which represented a considerable excess mortality. Indeed, the overall relative mortality rate of alcohol abusers was 2.13.[8] One of the highest relative mortality rates of alcohol abusers, 9.70, was found for death by fire.[9] Schmidt and deLint concluded that the proportion of fire deaths in Ontario in 1969 that could be attributed to alcoholism was some 42.75 percent.

Again, the number of fire deaths studied here was very small: in all, eighty-eight persons between the ages of 20 and 69 perished in fires in Ontario in 1969. Of these, thirteen were from the alcoholic sample group. Still, the methodology employed by Schmidt and deLint was very reliable, and the excess mortality manifested by alcohol abusers in the case of fire was statistically very significant. We consider that this study provides reliable empirical evidence of a relationship between alcohol abuse and fire fatalities.

The largest sample of fire deaths yet studied in order to examine the role of alcohol in fire casualties was collected in Maryland as part of a major fire research project. The Applied Physics Laboratory of Johns Hopkins University has initiated a "Fire Problems Program" in conjunction with several state and local agencies in order to study various aspects of fire. As part of their research effort, they studied some 101 fire fatalities that occurred in Maryland over the period October 1971 through May 1973.[10]

The findings of the Johns Hopkins study serve to provide evidence on and insight into the relationships between alcohol and fire and between alcohol and the consequences of fire. First, it was found that smoking was the major ignition source in approximately one-half of the fires studied, and that "alcohol was present in approximately 60% of the 'smoking' fires. In fact, approximately 50% of the 'smoking' fire victims had a level of alcohol of 0.1 gram per 100 ml."[11] Second, they concluded that "alcohol was a major contributor to impeding escape in approximately 30% of the cases."[12]

The results of the Johns Hopkins study serve to provide empirical evidence consonant with the considered speculation that alcohol is related to the consequences of fire in the two ways we mentioned earlier. On the one hand, alcohol abuse is a contributing factor in causing fires in some instances: among the 89 fires studied, alcohol appeared to have been a contributing factor in at least 27 to 30 percent. On the other hand, alcohol serves to impede escape from a fire and thereby intensifies its consequences. In the 101 fire fatalities studied, alcohol was a major contributing factor in impeding the escape of at least 30 persons.

Thus, the limited research conducted to date does suggest a relationship between alcohol and fire. The three studies cited each report a relationship between alcohol and fire fatalities. But the empirical evidence is extremely limited. In the three studies reported in the literature, there were a total of only 143 fire deaths.

There is, finally, a recent study of burn injuries which provides some evidence and insight into the relationship between alcohol and personal injuries.[13] MacArthur and Moore undertook a study of 155 adult major burn cases requiring in-hospital treatment. Their primary concern was to ascertain what factors predisposed certain persons to burn injury. An extensive review of each case was undertaken to determine what factors, if any, might have altered the person's perception of or response to the challenge of heat or the presence of flame and, hence, contributed to the nature or extent of injury. They found that alcohol was the most significant predisposing factor: in fact, 16.8 percent of all burn injury patients studied were under the immediate or long-term influence of alcohol.[14]

These several studies are useful for our present purposes; they provide insight into the relationship between alcohol and fire and some limited empirical evidence of the relationship between alcohol and the consequences of fire. But they serve to remind us that the whole area is indeed underresearched. What is needed is more concentrated research into the relationship between alcohol and fire. The studies cited are not necessarily representative. Their authors made no such claim for them, nor do we. Unfortunately, they represent all we have to work with.

THE ECONOMIC COST OF FIRE THAT MIGHT BE ATTRIBUTABLE TO ALCOHOL ABUSE

At this point we turn to the question of primary concern for our present purposes. What is the economic cost of fire that might be attributable to alcohol abuse? We have estimated the economic cost of fire in 1971 to be some $3.3 billion. What part of this cost is due to alcohol abuse?

An argument could be made that the appropriate answer is no answer. Certainly the state of knowledge concerning the relationship between fire and alcohol abuse is exceedingly limited. The empirical evidence available in the literature is derived from a small number of studies involving relatively small samples. In most instances, the necessary data for an estimate can be derived from but a single observation that may not be at all representative. Perhaps the most compelling reason to avoid attempting an estimate is the knowledge that, unfortunately, no matter how elaborate the disclaimers and qualifications, once a specific numerical estimate is generated it will tend to take on a life of its own.

Still, some evidence is available. Although the information, evidence, and knowledge concerning fires is both more limited and less revealing than we would prefer, the question is whether or not a less than perfectly reliable answer is preferable to no answer. Our judgment is that it is.

In order to generate a tentative estimate of the economic cost of fire that might be attributable to alcohol abuse, we have simply assigned to alcohol abuse that proportion of the total economic cost of fire in each category that the limited evidence available in the literature suggests might be reasonable. Our tentative estimate, as summarized in table 2—6, is some $377.7 million.

Our estimate of the present value in 1971 of lost production due to premature death caused by fire is some $386.8 million. We have chosen as the proportion of lost production that might be assigned to alcohol abuse that implied by the data reported in the Johns Hopkins study, for a number of reasons. First, that study was based on the largest sample. Second, the methodology of that study was more consistent with our intention of assigning economic cost to alcohol abuse. It will be recalled that in the Johns Hopkins study it was found that alcohol was a major contributor in impeding escape in approximately 30 percent of the fire deaths studied. Finally, the 30 percent proportion implied by that study is the lowest of the three and, hence, provides the most conservative estimate that can be derived from available evidence.

If alcohol impeded escape in 30 percent of the 6,776 fire deaths in 1971 the number of premature deaths due to alcohol abuse would

TABLE 5—6. A Tentative Estimate of the Economic Cost of Fire in 1971 That Might Be Attributable to Alcohol Abuse

Type of Cost	Estimated Cost of Fire (in millions)	Proportion That Might Be Attributable to Alcohol Abuse	Tentative Estimate of Economic Cost Due to Alcohol Abuse (in millions)
Present value in 1971 of lost future production due to premature death	$ 386.8	47.8%	$184.9
Medical treatment of personal injuries	166.2	16.8	27.9
Lost production due to personal injury	23.9	16.8	4.0
Property damage			
Building fires	2,266.0	7.1	160.9
Nonbuilding fires	477.3	0	0
Total	$3,320.2		$377.7

Sources: Estimated cost of fire is from table 5–4. For the proportions that might be attributable to alcohol abuse, see text.

have been 2,033. Unfortunately, we were not able to obtain an age distribution for fire deaths in which alcohol served to impede escape. Given the age distribution of alcohol abusers, however, it seems reasonable to conclude that fire deaths among alcohol abusers were concentrated in the 15—64 age group. If the 2,033 premature deaths due to alcohol abuse are assumed to have occurred among those aged 15 to 64, they would represent something on the order of 63.2 percent of all fire deaths in that age group, and would account for some 47.8 percent of the present value in 1971 of lost future production due to premature death caused by fire.

The economic cost of personal injuries requiring medical attention included both the cost of medical treatment for the 107,000 injured persons and the lost production of the some 50,825 injured persons within the labor-force age group (15—64). The proportion of these costs that might be attributable to alcohol abuse is taken to be 16.8 percent, on the basis of the finding in the MacArthur and Moore study that that proportion of all burn injury patients studied were under the immediate or long-term influence of alcohol.

The economic cost of property damage due to fire has been estimated by the National Fire Protection Association. Of the some

$2.7 billion of property damaged in fires in 1971, $2.3 billion involved building fires. Although there is no empirical evidence of the extent to which alcohol can be linked causally to fires in the aggregate, there is some evidence on the relationship between alcohol and smoking as the primary cause of ignition. Moreover, the percentage of building fires in which smoking was the primary cause of ignition is known. Thus, the proportion of the cost of property damaged in building fires that might be attributable to alcohol abuse can be derived from available data. In fact, smoking was identified as the cause of fire in 11.9 percent of all building fires in 1971.[15] This fact, given the finding in the Johns Hopkins study that alcohol was present in 60 percent of fires caused by smoking, provides the basis for our 7.1 percent estimate of the proportion of building fires property damage that might be attributable to alcohol abuse.

Our estimate of the economic cost of fire that might be attributable to alcohol abuse must be taken as a tentative one; the state of knowledge and the available data are such that it must be interpreted with care. We have made the best estimate possible and have attempted to generate a relatively conservative one, but the problems involved in it should not go without note.

First and foremost, of course, is the problem of limited knowledge and limited data. In addition, there is the problem of alcohol abusers inflicting costs on nonabusers, and vice versa. If, for example, an alcohol abuser causes a fire that results in the death of a nonabuser, that death should be assigned to alcohol abuse. Similarly, if the property of an alcohol abuser is damaged in a fire that was caused by a nonabuser, the cost of that damage should not be assigned to alcohol abuse. It is possible, then, to assign costs to the wrong group. On balance, however, given our method of assigning costs, it seems reasonable to conclude that the net effect of any errors in this regard would be to understate the total cost of fire attributed to alcohol abuse. Thus, for example, we assigned the costs of premature death to alcohol abuse on the basis of the proportion of cases in which alcohol was found to be a major contributor to impeding escape. Nonabuser deaths were not assigned to alcohol abuse, and abuser deaths were not assigned, whatever the cause of the fire, unless alcohol served to impede escape and thereby was a primary cause of death. As a further example, in the case of property damage, an assignment was made to alcohol abuse only for those building fires in which smoking was known to be the primary cause of ignition. No assignment was made for the almost 90 percent of building fires that did not involve smoking as a primary cause or for any nonbuilding fires.

Finally, we should note the distinct potential problem of double-counting lost production and medical treatment costs. These costs are appropriately included in the estimated economic cost of fire that might be attributable to alcohol abuse, but they have undoubtedly been included in part in our general estimates of lost production and medical costs for the economy as a whole. Thus, for example, premature death in fire is an instance of the excess mortality of alcohol abusers. Of course, the assignment of fire fatalities to alcohol abuse was based on alcohol impeding escape rather than on the drinking history or drinking problems of the individuals who died. Clearly, not all fire casualties that occur after drinking involve alcoholics or alcohol abusers in the more traditional sense. The costs associated with occasional drinkers are included in the fire context, but not in the lost production context. The same general qualification applies in the case of medical costs. Property damage costs, of course, have not been counted elsewhere.

Actually, we do have a basis for assessing the extent of double counting in the case of lost production due to premature death. It will be recalled that 795 premature deaths in accidental fires were included in chapter 2 in the estimate of lost production due to the excess mortality of heavy drinkers. In effect, some $91.8 million of the economic cost of fire has already been counted in chapter 2. Hence, double counting is considerably more significant in the case of fire than it was in the case of motor vehicle accidents. The double-counted $91.8 million amounts to almost 50 percent of the lost future production due to premature death included in the economic cost of fire attributed to alcohol abuse. This amount should certainly be subtracted from the total estimated economic cost of alcohol abuse. A similar adjustment will be made to allow for double counting in the cases of other lost production and medical care costs.

What conclusion can be drawn from the apparent extent of double couting? On the one hand, of course, there is the distinct possibility that our choice of the proportion of fire fatalities to assign to alcohol abuse was too conservative. We did take the lowest reported proportion of fatalities in which alcohol served to impede escape. On the other hand, there is the distinct possibility that occasional drinkers, even occasional heavy drinkers, do not run the same risk in the case of fire that they do in the case of motor vehicle accidents. Given the nature of the probabilities involved, this seems quite plausible.

NOTES

1. National Fire Protection Association, "Fires and Fire Losses Classified, 1971," *Fire Journal*, vol. 66 (September 1972), p. 67.

2. According to the National Fire Protection Association (NFPA), there were some 11,850 fire deaths in 1971, including 6,558 deaths that occurred in residential fires (*Ibid.*, p. 65). The difference between the number of deaths according to the NFPA and the figure given by the National Center for Health Statistics (see table 5–1) is accounted for by differences in definition. Thus, for example, most of the difference is due to the fact that the NFPA counts death from fire burns in motor vehicle accidents as fire deaths, while the NCHS counts them as motor vehicle accident deaths.

3. Thus, for example, one of the authors has a three-year-old daughter. The present value of her expected lifetime earnings discounted at 6 percent is on the order of $35,000. She is certainly worth more than that to him.

4. U.S. Department of Health, Education, and Welfare, *Flammable Fabrics: Third Annual Report to the President and the Congress*, Fiscal Year 1971, DHEW Publication (FDA) 72–7013 (Washington, D.C.: U.S. Government Printing Office, 1972), p. 71.

5. W. S. Hollis, "Drinking: Its Part in Fire Deaths," *Fire Journal*, vol. 67 (May 1973), pp. 10–11, 13.

6. Ibid., pp. 10–11.

7. Ibid., p. 11.

8. W. Schmidt and J. deLint, "The Mortality of Alcoholic People," *Alcohol Health and Research World*, DHEW Publication No. (NIH) 74–652 (Washington, D.C.: U.S. Government Printing Office, 1973), pp. 16–20. The relative mortality rate is simply the mortality rate of alcohol abusers relative to that of the general population.

9. Ibid., p. 17.

10. The Johns Hopkins University, Applied Physics Laboratory, Fire Problems Program, *Annual Summary Report: July 1, 1972–June 30, 1973* (Silver Spring, Md., August 1973).

11. Ibid., p. 38.

12. Ibid.

13. J. D. MacArthur and F. D. Moore, "Epidemiology of Burns: The Burn-Prone Patient," *Journal of the American Medical Association*, vol. 231, no. 3 (January 20, 1975), pp. 259–63.

14. Ibid., p. 261.

15. Personal communication with Mr. Ottoson, National Fire Protection Association, Boston, Mass.

CHAPTER SIX

ALCOHOL AND THE ECONOMIC COST OF CRIME

INTRODUCTION

Perhaps a discussion of crime and its consequences should start with a dramatic citation of a particularly violent act. Or perhaps a more subtle reference might be made to the exorbitant damage caused by malicious vandals. In fact, one could open virtually any major metropolitan newspaper more or less at random and find a sufficiently startling reference to crime and its consequences.

Crime and antisocial behavior are not, of course, new social phenomena. And public conern about crime and its consequences has undoubtedly existed for as long as crime has existed. There is, however, evidence of a heightened concern in recent years about the problem of crime. As crime rates have increased, and particularly as the rates of violent crimes have increased, the general public has come to view crime as constituting more and more of a problem. This concern clearly reflects a response to the perception of the real social cost of crime. Indeed, it is probably the case that the fear of violence dominates the perception of the real cost of crime. In this context, it is of some significance that the most publicized recent crime-control legislation is commonly referred to as the "Safe Streets Act."

The total number of criminal acts that occur is not known. Much crime goes unreported for a variety of reasons. The Federal Bureau of Investigation does collect data on important offenses as reported to law enforcement agencies and publishes an Index of Crime composed of seven categories of important offenses each year. A summary of crime in the United States in 1971 as reflected in the FBI Index of Crime is outlined in table 6–1.

Of course, many of the real social costs of crime defy quantification. What is the value to be placed on fear for personal safety? How are pain and suffering inflicted by aggravated assault to be measured? How can one assess the anxiety and stigma associated with rape? Although these costs may remain unquantified, they are nonetheless real, and they may well be among the more socially significant costs of crime.

On the other hand, some of the adverse consequences of crime do lend themselves to quantification. A subset of the total economic costs of crime can be estimated, and such estimates represent useful information. Among the adverse consequences of crime certain opportunity costs can be identified and estimated in the form of production that does not occur or in the form of alternatives foregone. In effect, then, the problem of measuring the economic cost of crime is not different in kind from that of measuring the economic costs of fire and motor vehicle accidents.

Our primary concern, of course, is not with the economic cost of crime *in toto*, but rather with that part of the cost that might be assigned to alcohol abuse. As in the previous chapter, we must cope with a two-dimensional problem. The amount of information available to assess the economic cost of crime is, at best, incomplete; and,

TABLE 6–1. A Summary of Crime in the United States in 1971

Offense	Number of Offenses Reported	Crime Rate*	Percentage Increase in Crime Rate, 1960–71
Violent crime:			
Murder and nonnegligent manslaughter	17,630	8.5	70.0
Forcible rape	41,890	20.3	113.7
Robbery	385,910	187.1	212.4
Aggravated assault	364,600	176.8	107.8
Property crime:			
Burglary	2,368,400	1,148.3	128.7
Larceny $50 and over	1,875,200	909.2	221.4
Auto theft	941,600	456.5	151.2

*Crime rate per 100,000 population.
Source: U.S. Department of Justice, Federal Bureau of Investigation, *Uniform Crime Reports for the United States–1971* (Washington, D.C.: U.S. Government Printing Office, 1972), table 2, p. 61.

the state of knowledge concerning the relationship between alcohol abuse and crime is inadequate.

Given the same problems, then, we have adopted the same strategy. We shall ask the same questions and again seek answers in the available literature. Some empirical evidence is available that will allow us to generate estimates of some of the economic costs of crime. These will of necessity be incomplete and will thus represent an understatement of the economic cost of crime.

The inadequate state of knowledge concerning the relationship between alcohol abuse and crime means that any estimate of the economic cost of crime that might be attributable to alcohol abuse will be at best tentative. Still, some evidence is available, and it again seems more appropriate to attempt to generate a tentative estimate identified as such than to ignore the economic cost of crime that may be associated with alcohol abuse.

THE COST OF CRIME

The first comprehensive study of the cost of crime in the United States was completed forty-five years ago by the Wickersham Commission.[1] The study was comprehensive in terms of its conceptual framework, but its empirical success was frustrated by a lack of data. The most recent attempt to assess the economic cost of crime was undertaken for 1965 by the President's Commission on Law Enforcement and Administration of Justice and published in 1967.[2]

Ironically, the 1965 study was also constrained empirically by a lack of data. In fact, the commission noted that

> except in the area of statistics concerning the cost of the criminal justice system . . . the lack of knowledge about which the Wickersham Commission complained 30 years ago is almost as great today.[3]

The commission was able to collect limited information and did generate a somewhat incomplete estimate of the economic impact of crime, as summarized in table 6–2. These estimates are useful for our current purposes, but when one considers the broader implications of the empirical evidence, one should not lose sight of the commission's conclusion that "the amount of information available about [the] economic impact of crime is grossly inadequate."[4]

Actually, given the nature of our interest, these estimates are rather more useful for our purposes than the commission's disclaimer might at first lead one to suppose. The less reliable estimates are in categories that are of limited concern to us, and the problems with the data are such that we know the net direction of error to be toward understatement of the costs we seek to include in an estimate of the economic cost of crime.

The less reliable estimates in table 6–2 are those for property crime. Fortunately, the lack of reliability in these estimates need not directly concern us. It should be obvious that since we are concerned with estimating the economic cost of crime in terms of social opportunity cost, we can ignore the estimated net property loss in the case of property crimes. In a very real sense, property crime

TABLE 6–2. A Summary of the Economic Cost of Crime in the United States in 1965, by Type of Crime

Offense	Number of Offenses Reported	Estimated Cost* (in millions)
Violent Crime:		
Willful homicide	9,850	$750.0
Forcible rape	22,467	2.0
Aggravated assault	206,661	18.3
Robbery	118,916	10.5
Unreported violent crime	not available	34.2
Total		$815.0
Property Crime:		
Vandalism	121,500†	‡
Robbery	118,916	27.0
Burglary	1,173,201	251.0
Larceny over $50	762,352	196.0
Embezzlement	11,500†	200.0
Auto theft	486,568	140.0
Forgery	not available	64.0
Total		$878.0

*Estimated cost of violent crimes includes only lost production and medical costs associated with injury. Estimated cost of property crimes includes only net property loss.

†Includes arrests only. The total number of offenses is not reported.

‡No reliable estimate of vandalism could be made.

Source: Derived from data in President's Commission on Law Enforcement and Administration of Justice, *Task Force Report: Crime and Its Impact—An Assessment* (Washington, D.C.: U.S. Government Printing Office, 1967), chapter 3.

144

The Economic Cost of Alcohol Abuse

simply results in a transfer of property from certain members of society to certain other members of society; in the aggregate, society suffers no loss of property.[5] In this sense, property crime, although not to be condoned, is not unlike approved social mechanisms designed to effect transfers between members of society, such as unemployment compensation, welfare, and social security.

Rather, what we seek to include in an estimate of the economic cost of crime are the real losses to society in terms of social opportunity cost. The real opportunity costs are more likely to result from crimes of violence, whose consequences are manifested in loss of life, personal injuries, and property damage. When crime results in loss of life or serious injury, society clearly suffers in the form of lost production. When a criminal inflicts personal injury, society must forego alternatives in order to provide medical care for the victim. And, of course, such acts as malicious vandalism clearly make society worse off in opportunity-cost terms. Thus our concern is actually limited to the violent-crime section of table 6–2, with the single exception, from the property-crime section, of vandalism.

There are two major problems associated with estimating the costs of violent crime. First, there is the issue of crime being underreported. Certain types of violent crime, most notably forcible rape, are, for a variety of reasons, underreported. To the extent that offenses occurred that were not reported, the cost estimates in table 6–2 are understated. Second, the estimates in table 6–2 include only the cost of lost production due to death and serious injury, and medical costs necessary to treat persons injured during the commission of a violent crime. They do not take into account less tangible costs, such as fear, anxiety, stigma, and pain and suffering, that are often among the most significant consequences of these crimes. These estimates, then, are clearly understated; but they are as a result comparable to those generated in previous chapters. We have consistently chosen conservative estimates and not counted less tangible items. It would seem, therefore, that the estimates in table 6–2 can serve our present purposes.

In fact, the estimated $750 million cost of willful homicide in 1965 was generated by the commission by computing the present value in 1965 of the expected lifetime earnings of the 9,850 victims of homicide in 1965. We have estimated the cost of lost production due to the premature death of the 18,787 homicide victims in 1971 at some $2.2 billion.[6] The estimate, derived from expected lifetime earnings discounted at 6 percent, is outlined in table 6–3.[7] These

TABLE 6–3. Estimated Present Value in 1971 of Lost Future
Production Due to Premature Death Caused by Homicide in 1971

Age Group	Number of Deaths	Present Value in 1971 of Lost Future Production (in millions)
0–4	482	$ 20.4
5–14	388	28.5
15–24	4,693	618.4
25–44	8,334	1,191.4
45–64	3,863	302.8
65 and over	981	9.5
Not stated	46	5.1
Total	18,787	$2,176.1

Sources: Deaths by age are from U.S. Department of Health, Education, and Welfare, National Center for Health Statistics, *Vital Statistics of
the U.S.: 1971,* vol. II–*Mortality,* part A (Washington, D.C.: U.S. Government Printing Office, 1975).

Present value in 1971 of lost future production is derived from earnings
data discounted at 6 percent in B. S. Cooper and W. Brody, "1972
Lifetime Earnings by Age, Sex, Race, and Education Level," Research and
Statistics Note No. 14 (Washington, D.C.: Office of Research and Statistics, Social Security Administration, September 30, 1975).

lives, of course, have a value beyond that of the implied lost production, but even this part of the total value is a significant economic
cost.

The commission's estimate of the cost of other violent crime in
1965 was some $65 million. This amount included both the costs
necessary to treat the injuries incurred during the commission of
violent crimes and the costs of lost production due to serious
personal injury. Medical costs comprised approximately 70 percent of
the total. The commission's estimates were based on limited evidence
that some injury occurs in as much as two-thirds of all reported
Index crimes and that injury sufficiently serious to require hospitalization occurs in one-sixth to one-fifth of such crimes.[8] Using the
commission's 1965 estimates as a base, we have estimated the cost of
reported violent crime other than homicide in 1971 to be some
$98.9 million.

We have chosen not to attempt to estimate the cost of unreported crime for several reasons. First, although there is evidence
that much violent crime, for a variety of reasons, goes unreported,
there is no real basis for estimating the number of unreported
offenses. Second, although we might have extrapolated the commis-

sion's 1965 cost estimate for unreported crimes, there is the distinct possibility that the proportion of unreported crime has changed over time. Certainly the dramatic increase in the number of offenses reported could well derive in part from an increase in the proportion of offenses reported. Finally, it is more consistent with our intention of generating conservative estimates not to include a relatively unreliable estimate of the cost of unreported crime.

Overall, we have estimated the economic cost of violent crime in the United States in 1971 to be some $2.3 billion. Our estimate is summarized in table 6–4. We have included unreported violent crime and vandalism in the table, but no specific cost estimate has been made in either case. Hence, the total estimate is incomplete and understated. The estimate is also understated to the extent that no account is taken of the intangible costs of crime. Our figure of $2.3 billion is thus a rather conservative estimate of the economic cost of crime in 1971.

What part of this cost can reasonably be assigned to alcohol abuse? In order to attempt to answer that question, we must look to the rather limited evidence in the literature on the relationship between alcohol abuse and crime.

RESEARCH ON THE RELATIONSHIP BETWEEN CRIME AND ALCOHOL ABUSE

In recent years, there has been increased concern about and awareness of the problem of alcohol abuse among serious criminal offenders. Kenneth Eaton, former Deputy Director of the National Institute of Alcohol Abuse and Alcoholism, has stated that

> up to half of the Nation's serious criminal offenders have problems with alcohol . . . and [they] may account for as much as 8 percent of the nine million alcoholic persons in the country.[9]

Although this statement has dramatic value, its informational value for our purposes is rather limited. To know the number of criminals who are alcohol abusers, or even the number of alcohol abusers who are criminals, is not to know the role of alcohol in the commission of a crime. A person's alcohol problem may or may not be related to any criminal act he or she commits. The state of knowledge is such

TABLE 6–4. Estimated Economic Cost of Violent Crime in the United States in 1971

Offense	Number of Offenses	Estimated Cost (in millions)
Homicide	18,787	$2,176.1
Forcible rape	41,890	5.2
Robbery	385,910	48.2
Aggravated assault	364,600	45.5
Unreported violent crime	Not known	Not estimated
Vandalism	Not known	Not estimated
Total		$2,275.0

Sources: The estimated cost of homicide is from table 6–3. Estimated costs for other violent crimes were derived by applying the data on injury and hospitalization from President's Commission on Law Enforcement and Administration of Justice, *Task Force Report: Crime and Its Impact—An Assessment* (Washington, D.C.: U.S. Government Printing Office, 1967), chapter 3, to the number of offenses reported for 1971 in U.S. Department of Justice, Federal Bureau of Investigation, *Uniform Crime Reports for the United States–1971* (Washington, D.C.: U.S. Government Printing Office, 1972). Medical costs were inflated by the medical care component of the Consumer Price Index, and earnings were inflated by a wage index.

that we do not know the role of alcohol in crime. Existing research is simply inadequate to assess the extent to which the costs of crime may be due to alcohol abuse.

Still, there is increasing circumstantial evidence linking alcohol to certain violent crimes. An extensive review of available research relating alcohol to particular violent crimes has revealed a significant relationship in the cases of criminal homicide, assault, forcible rape, and other sex offenses. However, there is a need for more precise documentation of the association between alcohol and specific crimes. Controlled studies are rare. Existing studies are deficient in that they lack baseline data against which to compare cases in which alcohol is involved in violent crimes. As the National Commission on Causes and Prevention of Violence concluded in this context,

> it is not known how many other drinkers do not become involved in violent behavior, or how often the same person may be drinking but not engage in violence.[10]

Several researchers have looked at perpetrators of specific crimes and identified the proportion of those drinking immediately before or at the time of the offense. Thus, there is empirical evidence of the extent to which alcohol and crime coexist. In effect, several studies provide specific evidence of an association between alcohol and crime. But certain critical questions remain unanswered. Would the crime have been committed in the absence of alcohol consumption? What is the net role of alcohol abuse in violent crime? The state of knowledge and available research is not sufficient to answer these questions. We are constrained by the lack of specific knowledge concerning the net impact of alcohol on human behavior. We can observe a relationship between alcohol and crime, but we can not infer causality.

Still, an estimate of the relationship between alcohol and certain crimes constitutes useful information. As the staff report of the National Commission on Causes and Prevention of Violence states,

> No drug, narcotic, or alcohol beverage presently known will by itself lead to violence. Nevertheless, these substances may through misuse or abuse facilitate behavior which may result in violence to persons or property.[11]

A number of specific studies reported in the literature have found a significant association between alcohol and homicide. Wolfgang's study is the one most often cited.[12] He analyzed data collected by the Philadelphia Police Department between 1948 and 1952 and found that among homicide cases involving 621 offenders and 588 victims, 64 percent involved alcohol ingestion by at least one of the parties. Alcohol also affected the manner of inflicting death. Seventy-two percent of 228 stabbings, 55 percent of 194 shootings, 69 percent of 128 beatings, and 45 percent of 38 other slayings involved alcohol. Wolfgang did not record the precise amount of alcohol present; he noted only its presence or absence. Although it would not be appropriate to take the mere presence of alcohol as evidence of alcohol abuse, the Wolfgang data are indicative of a significant relationship between alcohol and homicide.

The relative order of magnitude of the relationship between alcohol and homicide found by Wolfgang is consistent with those found in two studies of homicide victims. In his study of Baltimore data,[13] Fisher found that 69 percent of criminal-homicide victims had been drinking. In a study that included not only noting the presence of alcohol, but also taking its specific measurement, Cleveland found that 44 percent of a sample of homicide victims had a blood alcohol content greater than .15.[14] This evidence concerning victims is a further indication of a relationship between alcohol and homicide.

The most specific empirical evidence linking alcohol abuse to homicide on the offender side is provided in a study by Lloyd Shupe.[15] Shupe undertook a ten-year study in Columbus, Ohio, that involved a chemical analysis of the alcohol content of the trapped urine of all persons over 18 years of age arrested during or immediately following the alleged commission of a specific felony. Among the thirty persons arrested for murder, 67 percent had a blood alcohol concentration greater than .10.

On balance, although the empirical evidence is certainly limited and the studies done to date are far from definitive, the available data consistently indicate a significant relationship between alcohol and homicide. In fact, in those instances in which the blood alcohol content was measured, a level that would generally indicate alcohol abuse was found for 44 percent of victims in one study and 67 percent of offenders in another study. It seems reasonable to conclude that there is an association between alcohol and homicide, and it may be fair to speculate that alcohol is a contributing factor in homicide.

A significant association with alcohol has also been found for aggravated assault. In an early study, Banay found assault to be the leading crime among inebriates incarcerated in Sing Sing prison between 1938 and 1940.[16] A number of studies in recent years have identified associations between alcohol and assault that are indicative of a significant relationship. Pittman and Handy, for example, undertook a study of patterns in aggravated assault cases in St. Louis. [17] They found alcohol present in 24 percent of the offenders and 25 percent of the victims. In a similar study undertaken in Montreal, Tardif found alcohol present in 37 percent of the offenders and 25 percent of the victims.[18] Finally, the District of Columbia Crime Commission found that 35 percent of 121 offenders apprehended and identified and 46 percent of their victims had been drinking prior to a case of assault.[19] Although these cases perhaps have limited generalizability, their results are consistent. It would appear that aggravated assault is more likely to occur when alcohol is disproportionately present.

Studies of forcible rape and other sex offenses have also found a relationship between these violent crimes and alcohol. Lloyd Shupe, for example, found that 45 percent of rape cases involved persons with a blood alcohol content of .10 or higher.[20] Amir did an extensive study of 646 cases of forcible rape investigated by the Philadelphia Police Department from 1958 to 1960.[21] He found that alcohol played a role in one-third of these rape cases: in 3 percent of cases offenders only had been drinking; in 10 percent victims only, and in 21 percent both offender and victim. Thus, in 24 percent of all rape cases the offender had been drinking. Each of the 19 cases in which alcohol was present in the offender only involved the use of force.

Thus, in the case of forcible rape as with other violent crimes, there appears to be a significant relationship between the crime and alcohol. In the cases studied, something on the order of 24 to 45 percent of the crimes committed involved alcohol. Again, the evidence, though limited, is consistent.

There is also some empirical evidence of a relationship between alcohol and the sexual molesting of children. McCaghy, for example, undertook a study of 158 men convicted of sexually molesting a child under 14 years of age.[22] Fifty of the convicted molesters, 32 percent, admitted their guilt and implicated alcohol as a cause. Nau's findings, in a study undertaken in Germany, were similar.[23] Although the empirical evidence obtained in a German study is not necessarily applicable to this country, Nau's findings are of some interest. He observed 55 child abusers (29 women) at the Forensic Psychiatric Division of the Institute für Gerichtliche and Soziale Medicin at the Free University in Berlin and a sample of 50 child abusers (22 women) apprehended by the local police in 1965. Fifty-seven percent of the male child abusers and 42 percent of the females were found to be alcoholics. Furthermore, 44 percent of the men and 23 percent of the women were under the influence of alcohol at the time of committing their offense. Nau noted that alcohol had an excitative effect, leading to brutal actions by 85 percent of the males and 55 percent of the females.

The relationship between alcohol and violence in the sexual molesting of children is further documented in a study guide published by the Sex Information and Education Council.[24] They note that

> violence, either heterosexual or homosexual, is most often limited to men who have histories of individual deterioration, commonly marked by alcoholism or, among adolescent males, histories of mental deficiency. What is being suggested is not that the alcoholic or mentally deficient become sex offenders, but that, when these attributes occur in combination with sex-offense behavior, there is greater potential for violence.[25]

Some of the extensive research that has been done at the Kinsey Institute for Sex Research provides additional insight into the relationship between alcohol and sex offenses. Gebhard and his colleagues reported many of the results of sex research at the Kinsey Institute that are relevant to our current concern in a work entitled *Sex Offenders: An Analysis of Types*, which, among other things, explored the role of alcohol in crimes involving various sex offenses.[26] They undertook a study that included 1,356 white males convicted of sex offenses. Overall, sex offenders were found to have been drunk in 21 percent of all cases. An additional 8 percent had been drinking but were not determined to have been drunk. In 8 percent of the cases the researchers were not able to determine whether or not alcohol had been involved.

Gebhard and his colleagues also analyzed the relationship between alcohol and several specific types of sex offenses. The relationship was most significant in cases categorized as heterosexual aggression against children. Some two-thirds of all offenders in such cases were drunk; an additional 10 percent had been drinking prior to the offense. Heterosexual aggression against adult women, the category that includes forcible rape, was the category with the second most significant alcohol relationship. Thirty-nine percent of all offenders in this category were drunk, and an additional 15 percent had been drinking prior to the offense. The authors' analysis of the relationship between alcohol and sex offenses led them to conclude that there was a relationship and that

> there is a clear picture of drunkenness being a greater factor in more aberrant crimes such as those involving children or the use of force.[27]

We started this section by citing the undocumented statement of a government official that up to half of the country's serious criminal offenders have problems with alcohol. An extensive review of the literature does reveal specific empirical evidence more or less consistent with that statement. A significant relationship between alcohol and the several types of violent crime was found in study after study. In the case of homicide, for example, the presence of alcohol was found in an exceedingly significant proportion of the cases studied: indeed, in at least one study that measured blood alcohol content, a level of BAC that would generally be considered to constitute alcohol abuse was found in some 67 percent of offenders. There is certainly an association between alcohol and homicide, and it may be that alcohol is a contributing factor in homicide.

The empirical evidence suggests that aggravated assault is more likely to occur when alcohol is disproportionately present. In separate studies, alcohol was found to be present in 24 to 37 percent of offenders. Alcohol presence was also found in 25 to 46 percent of the victims in the assault cases studied.

The several studies of forcible rape and other sex offenses imply a significant relationship between these crimes and alcohol. In fact, among the studies of forcible rape, the lowest proportion of cases in which alcohol was found to be present in offenders was some 24 percent. In the most extensive research study available on sex crimes, the study at the Kinsey Institute reported by Gebhard and his colleagues, sex offenders were found to have been drunk in 21 percent of all cases.

On the whole, although the empirical evidence must be interpreted with some care, it is certainly indicative of a significant relationship between alcohol and crime. Still, one should be careful about drawing inferences. There is need for more precise documentation of the association between alcohol and specific crimes. Controlled studies are critical, and they are rare in this field. Although the empirical evidence is consistent and significant, it is nonetheless of limited value.

ECONOMIC COST OF CRIME THAT IS ASSOCIATED WITH ALCOHOL

The state of knowledge is inadequate to assess the extent to which the association between alcohol and crime is indicative of a contributing, let alone causal, role for alcohol. The circumstantial evidence that alcohol and crime are related is overwhelming, but does alcohol cause crime? Is some part of the cost of crime due to alcohol abuse? Probably, but we have no real basis for assigning a specific part of the cost of crime to alcohol abuse. In fact, we can generate an estimate of the cost of crime that is associated with alcohol, but not an estimate of the cost of crime that is due to alcohol abuse.

Some might ask why we seem to be treating alcohol and the cost of crime in a different manner from the way we treated alcohol and the cost of other things such as fire and motor vehicle accidents. In fact, it might seem that the problems inherent in the fire and crime contexts are similar. Fire was an underresearched area and the evidence was exceedingly limited; yet we undertook to estimate the economic cost of fire that might be assigned to alcohol abuse. Is the difference one of degree? Is it only that crime is more underresearched than fire, so that the evidence in the case of crime is even more limited than it was in the case of fire?

No! In fact, there is a real difference. It is not that the evidence is more limited, but rather that the evidence is less revealing. Take the case of the economic cost of lost production due to premature death, for example. In the case of fire deaths, we assigned premature deaths to alcohol abuse on the basis of the proportion of cases in which alcohol was found to be a major contributor to impeding escape. The evidence was limited, but it was revealing. In effect, we were able to assign fire deaths because there was evidence that alcohol served to impede escape and thereby was a primary cause of death. In the case of homicide, on the other hand, the evidence does not suggest any basis for assigning premature deaths. Two-thirds of all persons who commit homicide may well be alcohol abusers at the time of their offense, but there is nothing in the empirical evidence that suggests the proportion of homicide deaths that would not have occurred in the absence of alcohol. We might well speculate that alcohol abuse is a contributing factor in homicide and other violent crime—it undoubtedly is in some proportion of cases—but available evidence and knowledge are not sufficient to assign specific proportions to alcohol abuse.

Thus, the estimate outlined in table 6–5 is not an estimate of the economic cost of crime that might be due to alcohol abuse. Rather, it is an estimate of the economic cost of crime in which alcohol is associated with the crime. Given the estimate of the economic cost of crime from the previous section, we have estimated the cost of crime in which alcohol is associated by applying a proportion of offenses in which alcohol was associated with the given crime, on the basis of the empirical evidence in the available literature. In each instance, we have tried to select a proportion that is for offenders and, where possible, where the presence of alcohol was determined by measurement to be in the alcohol-abuse range of blood alcohol content. Thus, the 67 percent estimate for homicide is from the Shupe study and represents the proportion of offenders arrested who had a blood alcohol content of greater than .10. An alternative might have been the 64 percent of all homicide cases studied by Wolfgang that involved alcohol. The difference in the two proportions is rather insignificant.

The 24 percent estimate for forcible rape is from the extensive study by Amir and represents the proportion of all rape cases in

TABLE 6–5. Estimated Economic Cost in 1971 of Violent Crime in Which Alcohol Was Associated with the Crime

Offense	Estimated Cost of Crime (in millions)	Proportion of Offenses in Which Alcohol Is Associated	Estimated Cost of Crime in Which Alcohol Is Associated (in millions)
Homicide	$2,176.1	67%	$1,451.5
Forcible rape	5.2	24	1.2
Robbery	48.2	Not known	0.0
Aggravated assault	45.5	30	13.7
Total	$2,275.0		$1,466.4

Sources: Estimated cost of crime is from table 6–4. For proportion of offenses in which alcohol is associated with the crime, see text.

which it was determined that the offender was drinking. Given the evidence in the literature reviewed, this is a low estimate of the association of alcohol with the crime of forcible rape. Studies that assessed the presence of alcohol in both victim and offender would indicate a higher proportion of rape cases associated with alcohol. Given the nature of our concern, it seems more reasonable to include only cases in which the offender was drinking.

Finally, the 30 percent estimate for aggravated assault represents the midpoint of the range of proportions in which alcohol was found to be present among offenders in the several studies of assault cases.

Of course, even this estimate of the economic cost of crime in which alcohol is associated with the crime is rather conservative. No account has been taken of unreported crime that might be associated with alcohol. Furthermore, no estimate is possible of the undoubtedly considerable property damage done by malicious vandals under the influence of alcohol.

Again, however, the reader is cautioned to interpret the estimate of $1.5 billion as what it is—an estimate of the economic cost of crime in which alcohol is associated with the crime—and not what it is not—an estimate of the economic cost of crime due to alcohol abuse.

NOTES

1. U.S. National Commission on Law Observance and Enforcement, *Report on the Cost of Crime* (Washington, D.C.: U.S. Government Printing Office, 1931).

2. President's Commission on Law Enforcement and Administration of Justice, *Task Force Report: Crime and Its Impact—An Assessment* (Washington, D.C.: U.S. Government Printing Office, 1967), chapter 3.

3. Ibid., p. 42.

4. Ibid., p. 39.

5. There is, of course, an opportunity cost incurred when goods and services such as locks, alarms, and the like must be produced to protect property.

6. According to the FBI Index of Crime, there were 17,630 murders and nonnegligent manslaughter deaths in 1971. U.S. Department of Health, Education and Welfare, National Center for Health Statistics, *Vital Statistics of the United States: 1971*, vol. II—*Mortality*, part A (Washington, D.C.: U.S. Government Printing Office, 1975), however, reports some 18,787 deaths due to homicide. We have taken the figure from the latter source both because it is probably more reliable and because the source provides a breakdown by age and sex that is necessary in order to generate an estimate of the present value of future earnings.

7. The commission's estimate was discounted at 5 percent. We have employed the more conservative discount rate of 6 percent throughout this book.

8. President's Commission on Law Enforcement and Administration of Justice, *Task Force Report,* p. 45. They assumed that the rates of injury and hospitalization for unreported crimes were only one-half those for reported crimes.

9. U.S. National Institute on Alcohol Abuse and Alcoholism, "Alcohol Abuse by Felons 'Target of Concern,'" *Alcohol and Health Notes* (Rockville, Md.: National Clearinghouse for Alcohol Information, October 1973), p. 2.

10. U.S. National Commission on Causes and Prevention of Violence, *Crimes of Violence* (staff report), vol. 12 (Washington, D.C.: U.S. Government Printing Office, 1969), p. 642.

11. Ibid., p. 683.

12. M. E. Wolfgang, *Patterns in Criminal Homicide* (New York: John Wiley and Sons, 1966).

13. R. S. Fisher, "Symposium on Compulsory Use of Chemical Tests for Alcohol Intoxication," *Maryland State Medical Journal*, vol. 3 (1954), pp. 291–2.

14. F. P. Cleveland, "Problems in Homicide Investigation, IV: Relationship of Alcohol to the Home," *Journal of Medicine*, Cincinnati, vol. 36 (1955), pp. 28–30.

15. Lloyd Shupe, "Alcohol and Crime: A Study of Urine Alcohol Concentration Found in 882 Persons Arrested during or Immediately after Committing a Felony," *Journal of Criminal Law, Criminology, and Police Science*, vol. 44 (1954).

16. R. S. Banay, "Alcoholism and Crime," *Quarterly Journal of Studies on Alcohol*, vol. 2 (1941–42), pp. 686–716.

17. D. Pittman and W. Handy, "Patterns in Criminal Aggravated Assault," *Journal of Criminal Law, Criminology, and Police Science*, vol. 55, no. 4 (December 1964).

18. G. Tardif, "La Criminalité de Violence" (Master's thesis, University of Montreal, 1966), cited in U.S. National Commission on Causes and Prevention of Violence, *Crimes of Violence*, p. 645.

19. Report of the President's Commission on Crime in the District of Columbia (Washington: U.S. Government Printing Office, 1966), cited in U.S. National Commission on Causes and Prevention of Violence, *Crimes of Violence*, p. 644.

20. L. Shupe, *Report on Alcohol*, American Business Men's Research Foundation, Illinois (fall 1971).

21. M. Amir, "Alcohol and Forcible Rape," *British Journal of Addiction*, vol. 62 (1967), pp. 219–32, cited in U.S. National Commission on Causes and Prevention of Violence, *Crimes of Violence*, p. 644.

22. C. H. McCaghy, "Drinking and Deviance Disavowal: Case of Child Molesters," *Social Problems*, vol. 16 (1968), pp. 45–49.

23. E. Nau, "Kindesmisshandlung," *Monatsschrift fur Kinderheilkunde*, vol. 115 (1967), pp. 192–94.

24. J. H. Gagon and W. M. Simon, *Sexual Encounters between Adults and Children*, Study Guide No. 11 (Sex Information and Education Council of the U.S., 1970).

25. Ibid., p. 10.

26. P. Gebhard, J. Gagon, W. Pomeroy, and C. Christenson, *Sex Offenders: An Analysis of Types* (New York: Harper and Row, 1965).

27. Ibid., p. 762.

CHAPTER SEVEN

THE ECONOMIC COST OF SOCIAL RESPONSES TO ALCOHOL ABUSE

INTRODUCTION

In the last five chapters we have concentrated on the economic costs that derive from alcohol abuse, might be attributable to alcohol abuse, or are associated with alcohol. We have attempted to estimate the value of the lost production, excess health care costs, and costs of motor vehicle accidents due or attributable to alcohol abuse; the costs of fire that might be attributable to alcohol abuse; and the cost of violent crime that is associated with alcohol. In this chapter we turn our attention to costs that arise as a result of some social response to alcohol abuse or the consequences of alcohol abuse. The specific response may be more or less related to alcohol abuse; it may be a direct or indirect response; but the critical question is whether or not economic costs in the form of particular program expenditures are higher because of alcohol abuse.

A number of programs have come into being as a direct response to alcoholism and alcohol abuse. The federal government, for example, sponsors a number of programs of research, treatment, prevention, and training in the alcoholism field. As alcoholism has increasingly come to be viewed within our society as a disease, the social response has included programs that divert some part of society's scarce resources from alternative uses. Such a response implies real economic cost, which should be assigned to alcohol abuse.

Other examples that could be cited involve less direct or less obvious responses to alcohol abuse. Consider public expenditures for highway safety or fire protection, for example. These expenditures represent society's response to the threats of traffic accidents and fire. In previous chapters, we have seen the extent to which alcohol abuse increases the risk of motor vehicle accidents and intensifies the consequences of fire. Indeed, alcohol abuse is disproportionately associated with more severe types of accidents and fires. In the absence of alcohol abuse, society could either spend less on fire protection and highway safety or, presumably, get more for its current level of expenditures. Hence, although the social expenditure in this case may not be a direct response to alcohol abuse, the level of the response is affected by alcohol abuse. The extra resources which society has to divert to highway safety and fire protection because of alcohol abuse represent an economic cost that should be assigned to alcohol abuse.

Even the indirect social responses to alcohol abuse are rather easy to identify, although not necessarily easy to quantify. It is in the nature of a social system to respond to antisocial behavior and adverse circumstances with contervailing mechanisms. Hence, more often than not, the social responses to alcohol abuse can be traced by reflecting directly on the real social losses occasioned by alcohol abuse in the first instance.

Thus, alcohol abuse often has an adverse impact on productivity and results in lost production. Quite apart from the magnitude of the economic cost of lost production is the question of how the burden of that cost is shared. Economic losses in the form of lost production usually result in lost income. In the absence of any social response to this loss, individual alcohol abusers and their families would bear the burden of the loss. It is important to recognize, however, that society in general has been unwilling to ignore the plight of particularly low-income families and individuals; rather, the social welfare system has evolved as a response to such misfortune. The social welfare system does not, of course, exist because of alcohol abuse, but some part of the client load and some part of the concomitant cost of the system does represent a response to alcohol abuse as one kind of personal and family misfortune. If alcohol abuse did not exist, then society could either spend less on its social welfare system or provide more services to those whose misfortunes were not associated with alcohol abuse.

Further, alcohol abuse often has an adverse impact on health. The extra health care costs due to alcohol abuse have been estimated to constitute a significant proportion of the total health care costs in our society. We have already noted that as alcoholism has increasingly come to be viewed within our society as a disease, the social response has been to develop programs to prevent, treat, and control the disease. Whatever the cost of these programs, they should be assigned to alcohol abuse.

We have noted the fact that alcohol abuse increases the risk and intensifies the consequences of traffic accidents and fires. The social response to traffic accidents and fires involves diverting resources to highway safety and fire protection. Some part of the total cost of highway safety and fire protection should be assigned to alcohol abuse.

Finally, alcohol abuse often involves antisocial behavior that results in social losses. We have seen the extent to which alcohol is associated with violent crime, for example. The social system includes a criminal justice system component, and some part of that component's total cost should be attributed to alcohol abuse, since some part of the total social response represented by the criminal justice system is a response to the antisocial behavior associated with alcohol abuse.

In the next few sections, we shall attempt to generate estimates of the economic costs of programs and activities that represent social responses to alcohol abuse or its consequences.

ALCOHOL AND THE SOCIAL WELFARE SYSTEM

There is a rather extensive social welfare system in our society. In large part, the social welfare system that has evolved in this country reflects the extent to which our society has been unwilling to ignore the plight of the particularly disadvantaged. But the nature of the system, and what many see as its relative inefficiencies, also reflects the extent to which the system has evolved from a series of specific social responses to particular social phenomena. Thus, for example, most public aid is provided through a number of categorical assistance programs. Our society does not have a general income-maintenance program for those with particularly low income, but rather a number of specific programs for persons in specific categories. To understand our social welfare system and its evolution over time, one must, we think, reflect on it as representing a set of social responses

to the plight of particular components of our society—the unemployed, the aged, the mentally retarded, the blind, the disabled, poor
children, and so forth. But whatever the origin and evolution of our
social welfare system, it represents a significant component of our
economy.

Total social welfare expenditures in 1971, for example,
amounted to $254.9 billion and represented 24.2 percent of the
gross national product in that year.[1] Social welfare expenditures
include both public and private expenditures for income maintenance, welfare and other services, health, and education. The
public expenditures, of course, dominate and amount to over 70
percent of the total.

Among the components of social welfare expenditures, income
maintenance and welfare and other services amount to over 40
percent of the total and over 50 percent of the public expenditures.
These are the programs most specifically designed to transfer income
to the relatively disadvantaged among our society. Of course, some
significant part of the health and education expenditures, particularly in the public sector, are also designed to transfer real income in
kind[2] to the disadvantaged.

In fact, most social welfare expenditures involve cash transfer
payments and are not real costs to society in the sense of opportunity cost. Some members of society give up real income in order to
provide transfer payments, and some other members of society
derive the benefits from those payments, but society in the aggregate
neither gains nor loses as a consequence of the transfers. In effect,
transfer payments represent a reallocation of resources rather than a
loss of resources. But some of the expenditures on social welfare
programs are not in the form of transfer payments. Some part of the
total expenditure does reflect the real cost of providing specific
social services and administering social welfare programs. The provision of services and the administration of programs do involve the
use of scarce resources and therefore represent real opportunity
costs.

Our present concern is not with social welfare programs per se, or
even with the real opportunity costs associated with such programs.
Rather, our concern is with the extent to which the level of social
welfare programs is affected by alcohol abuse. The social welfare
system does not exist because of alcohol abuse, but some part of the
client load and some part of the real cost of the social welfare system
does represent a response to alcohol abuse. In chapter 2, we saw the

significant extent to which alcohol abuse unfavorably affects earnings and the extent to which households that include alcohol abusers
are disproportionately represented among the lower-income groups.
Thus, for example, while only 5.5 percent of nonabuser households
had incomes below $4,000 in 1968, 15.8 percent of abuser house-
holds had incomes below that level.[3] These relatively low-income
households are those most likely to be eligible for welfare programs
and to be receiving transfer payments and social services. Quite apart
from the actual transfer payments, if alcohol abuse did not exist,
then society could either spend less on its social welfare system or
provide more services to non-alcohol-related cases. What, then, is the
real cost of the social welfare system that might be assigned to
alcohol abuse?

   In order to answer that question, we need two estimates. First,
we need an estimate of the real cost of the social welfare system, or
rather of those components of the system that involve transfer
payments that are likely to include a significant response specifically
to alcohol abuse. Those components of the system would seem to
be: (a) unemployment compensation programs; (b) workmen's compensation programs; (c) public assistance programs providing income
maintenance; (d) special income-maintenance programs, such as
emergency relief, food stamp programs, and the like; and (e) other
special welfare and social services programs. Second, we need an
estimate of the proportion of the client load of these programs that
might reasonably be associated with alcohol abuse.

   An estimate of the real cost of those components of the social
welfare system that probably are most relevant in the context of
alcohol abuse is given in table 7–1. In the aggregate, these five
programs expended some $33.6 billion.[4] Of the total, approximately
90 percent was in the form of transfer payments and, hence, did not
represent a real cost to society. The remaining 10 percent, or some
$3.5 billion, represented the real opportunity cost of these programs
in terms of the resources utilized to provide social services and
administer the programs.[5]

   An estimate of the economic cost of these social welfare programs attributable to alcohol abuse can be obtained on the basis of
certain simple and reasonable assumptions suggested by the literature
reviewed and by the analysis completed in previous chapters. What
we need, in essence, is an estimate of the proportion of the administrative cost of each program that is likely to be associated with
alcohol abuse. We have actually made three estimates—one for unem-

TABLE 7−1. Estimated Cost of Certain Components of the Social Welfare System in 1971 (in millions)

Program	Transfer Payments	Social Services and Administrative Expenses	Total Actual Expenditures
Unemployment	$ 6,673.9	$ 456.3	$ 7,130.2
Workmen's compensation	2,437.3	166.7	2,604.0
Public assistance	10,271.5	2,103.0	12,374.5
Other public aid	3,456.5	236.3	3,692.8
Welfare and other social services	7,339.8	501.9	7,841.7
Total	$30,179.0	$3,464.2	$33,643.2

Source: Derived from data in A. M. Skolnik and S. R. Dales, "Social Welfare Expenditures, 1971–72," *Social Security Bulletin,* vol. 35 (December 1972), pp. 3–17.

ployment programs, one for workmen's compensation programs, and one for general poverty-related income-maintenance programs.

Our estimate of the excess unemployment burden associated with alcohol abuse is based on general estimates of the proportion of alcohol abusers in the labor force and the excess unemployment rate of alcoholics as estimated by Holtmann. In general, estimates of the proportion of alcohol abusers in the labor force range from 4 to 8 percent; we have used the lower figure to be conservative. Holtmann has estimated the excess unemployment rate of alcoholics to be on the order of 25 percent.[6] Given that the general unemployment rate in 1971 was 5.9 percent of the labor force, we have estimated the proportion of unemployment due to alcohol abuse at some 18.2 percent. In essence, excess unemployment is derived in the same way as excess mortality was derived in chapter 2: thus, excess unemployment is equal to the actual level of unemployment less the level of unemployment that would have obtained if alcohol abusers had had the same unemployment rate as nonabusers.[7]

Our estimate of the excess burden for general poverty-related income-maintenance programs was derived in essentially the same way. The estimate was based on the distribution of household incomes summarized in table 2−1. We have assumed that, in general, households in the lowest two income classes represent the overall poverty load. It will be recalled that 15.8 percent of abuser households were in the lowest two income classes. Given that among all households some 7.4 percent were in the lowest two income classes, we have estimated the proportion of the poverty load due to alcohol abuse at some 24.2 percent. In effect, the excess poverty load is equal to the actual poverty load, represented by households in the lowest two income classes, less the poverty load that would have obtained if abuser households had had the same poverty rate as nonabuser households.

Finally, we have estimated the proportion of workmen's compensation due to alcohol abuse to be on the order of 11.4 percent. Workmen's compensation, of course, covers injuries sustained in accidents on the job. To the best of our knowledge, there are no estimates of the extent to which alcohol abusers are involved in job-related accidents, although the general impression is certainly that they have more than their share. In general, we have found alcohol abusers to have a higher risk of accidents. In the case of motor vehicle accidents, for example, alcohol abusers have been found to have a higher accident rate than nonabusers, with their rate increasing with the relative seriousness of the accident. In fact, the extra proportion of motor vehicle accidents resulting in personal injury that were due to alcohol abuse was estimated in chapter 4 to be some 11.4 percent. A similar relationship was found between alcohol abuse and accidental burn injuries. Some 16.8 percent of accidental burn injuries were attributed to alcohol abuse in chapter 5. Although the nature of the fire burn data do not provide the basis for estimating the excess proportion due to alcohol abuse, it would seem to be consistent with the excess proportion of motor vehicle accidents due to alcohol abuse that resulted in personal injuries. We have taken this figure (11.4 percent) as an arbitrary but probably reasonable approximation of the excess proportion of workmen's compensation due to alcohol abuse.

By applying these estimates of the excess proportions of unemployment, workmen's compensation, and general poverty-related income-maintenance programs due to alcohol abuse to the administrative cost of the several programs, we can estimate the economic cost of these social welfare programs that can be attributed to alcohol abuse. Our estimate of some $789.6 million is given in table 7–2.

ALCOHOL PROGRAM COSTS

Although general social welfare programs may constitute an indirect response to alcohol abuse, a number of programs have come

TABLE 7-2. Estimated Economic Cost of Certain Components of the Social Welfare System in 1971 Attributable to Alcohol Abuse

Program	Estimated Administrative Cost (in millions)	Proportion Associated with Alcohol Abuse	Estimated Economic Cost Attributable to Alcohol Abuse (in millions)
Unemployment	$ 456.3	18.2%	$ 83.0
Workmen's compensation	166.7	11.4	19.0
Public assistance	2,103.0	24.2	508.9
Other public aid	236.3	24.2	57.2
Welfare and other social services	501.9	24.2	121.5
Total	$3,464.2		$789.6

Sources: Estimated administrative cost is from table 7-1. For proportions associated with alcohol abuse, see text.

into being as a direct and specific response to alcoholism and alcohol abuse. As our society has increasingly come to view alcoholism as a disease, the social response has included more and more programs involving research, treatment, rehabilitation, prevention, and training in the field of alcohol abuse. In assessing the economic cost of alcohol abuse, it is certainly appropriate to include the real costs of these programs, which represent a specific social response to alcohol abuse.

In 1971, the federal budget included some $70 million specifically earmarked for alcohol programs under the Comprehensive Alcohol Abuse Act of 1970.[8] In addition, considerable sums were expended by the federal government on programs authorized under different legislation. Furthermore, a significant amount was expended on alcohol programs by state and local governments. Finally, several alcohol programs are sponsored in the private sector. Alcoholics Anonymous is perhaps the best-known private organization, but such other groups as the National Council on Alcoholism expend rather significant amounts on alcohol programs throughout the United States.

Indeed, programs designed for the prevention of alcoholism and for the treatment and rehabilitation of alcohol abusers are fragmented, relatively uncoordinated, and often duplicative. As a consequence, it is rather unclear who is spending what for whom. There is no practical way to ascertain the exact total expenditures on alcohol programs. In the federal budget, for example, expenditures on alcohol programs are spread throughout the budgets of several agencies. A review of the fiscal 1971 budget revealed alcohol-program expenditures by the departments of Health, Education, and Welfare, Transportation, Labor, and Justice, as well as by the Veterans Administration, the Postal Service, and the Office of Economic Opportunity. Overall, the federal budget in 1971 included in excess of $125 million in line items specifically designated for alcohol programs. In addition, although no specific line items for alcohol-program expenditures appeared in their 1971 budgets, there were indications that such expenditures were also made by the departments of Defense and Housing and Urban Development.

Government expenditures below the federal level on alcohol programs are even more difficult to ascertain, since there is no single governmental budget to review, as there is in the case of the federal government. On the basis of the amounts budgeted at the state level for state alcohol-program agencies and treatment in state-supported institutions, it is estimated that state expenditures for alcohol programs in 1971 were in excess of $200 million.

Even if we had a single budgetary source of estimates for alcohol-program expenditures, it is unlikely that they would reflect the total expenditure on such programs. Funds allocated under other program designations are often used to treat alcohol abusers. This is undoubtedly the case, for example, with respect to medical vendor payments under several programs that number alcohol abusers among their client load—the Medicaid program being a case in point.

In order to provide some insight into the relative order of magnitude of alcohol-program expenditures, we have tried to estimate the cost of alcohol treatment, rehabilitation, research, and training programs in 1971. These estimates are summarized in table 7–3.

As the data in table 7–3 suggest, the vast majority of expenditures in alcohol programs are for treatment and rehabilitation. Over 90 percent of all alcohol-program expenditures represent vendor payments to health care institutions on behalf of alcohol abusers. Thus, most of the real cost involved in alcohol-program expenditures has already been counted among the health care costs of alcohol abuse and alcoholism, which were considered in chapter 3. Actually, given that there is no practical way to ascertain the total actual expenditures on alcohol programs, it is a fortuitous coincidence that most such expenditures have in fact been included elsewhere in our estimate of the economic cost of alcohol abuse.

Still, there is some proportion of the expenditures on alcohol programs that represents a real cost to society and has not been counted in any other context. Expenditures on research and training are specific social responses to alcohol abuse that represent a real cost to society and as such should be included in the aggregate economic cost of alcohol abuse. In 1971, they amounted to $15.8 million. Moreover, although that part of the total expenditures for alcohol programs that went for treatment and rehabilitation will be reflected in health care costs, the administrative cost of those programs is a real cost to society that should be included as an alcohol-program cost per se. On the assumption that the cost of administering alcohol programs is similar to that of administering public assistance programs, it seems reasonable to estimate the administrative cost of alcohol programs at 6.4 percent, or $41.2 million. Hence, that part of the economic cost in 1971 of alcohol programs representing a direct social response to alcohol abuse that has not been included elsewhere was on the order of $57 million.

TABLE 7—3. Estimated Expenditures on Alcohol Treatment, Rehabilitation, Research, and Training in 1971, by Type of Provider

Provider	Total Expenditures (in millions)
Treatment and rehabilitation:	
State and county mental institutions	$185.0
Private mental institutions	4.8
Veterans Administration hospitals	166.5
General hospitals—psychiatric services	237.7
Community mental health centers	38.5
Halfway houses for alcoholics	11.3
Total	$643.8
Research:	
Department of Health, Education, and Welfare	6.6
Department of Transportation	7.4
Total	$ 14.0
Training:	
Department of Health, Education, and Welfare	1.8
Total expenditures	$659.6

Source: Derived from data reported in the following publications: U.S. Department of Health, Education, and Welfare, National Institute of Mental Health, *Utilization of Mental Health Facilities by Persons Diagnosed with Alcohol Disorders*, DHEW Publication No. (HSM) 73-9114 (Washington, D.C.: U.S. Government Printing Office, 1972); U.S. Department of Health, Education, and Welfare, National Institute of Mental Health, *Halfway Houses Serving the Mentally Ill and Alcoholics, 1969–70*, DHEW Publication No. (HSM) 72-9049 (Washington, D.C.: U.S. Government Printing Office, 1971); M. S. Cannon, *Alcoholism Halfway Houses—General Characteristics*, Statistical Note 73 (Rockville, Md.: Health Services and Mental Health Administration, National Institute of Mental Health, 1973); *Hospital Statistics, 1971* (Chicago: American Hospital Association, 1972); M. E. Chafetz and H. W. Demone, Jr., "Programs to Control Alcoholism," *American Handbook of Psychiatry*, vol. 2 (February 1974); *The Budget of the United States Government, Fiscal Year 1971* (Washington, D.C.: U.S. Government Printing Office, 1970); and *Special Analyses, Budget of the United States Government, Fiscal Year 1971* (Washington, D.C.: U.S. Government Printing Office, 1970).

HIGHWAY SAFETY AND FIRE PROTECTION

Public expenditures for highway safety and fire protection are of a significant order. In 1971, approximately $480 million was spent in the United States on highway safety and some $2.3 billion on fire protection.[9] These expenditures represent the social response to the threats of traffic accidents and fires. The question of current concern is, what part of this response might reasonably be attributed to alcohol abuse?

The extent to which alcohol abuse increases the risk and consequences of both traffic accidents and fires has been delineated in previous chapters. There would seem to be little doubt that some part of the total cost of highway safety and fire protection should be assigned to alcohol abuse. In the absence of alcohol abuse, society could either spend less on these items or, presumably, get more for its current level of expenditure. But what is the appropriate proportion?

The theoretical basis of this chapter is the argument that various economic costs arise because of specific social responses to alcohol abuse. The critical question in the current context is, just what is society responding to when it allocates resources to highway safety and fire protection? Is society responding to the general threat of accidents? Is the response proportional to the number of incidents? Maybe so, but it is more likely that society's response is to the more extreme cases—carnage on the highway and the fires that result in catastrophe.

In short, it seems reasonable to ask whether society's expenditures on highway safety are reflective of the 16 million-plus accidents that occurred in 1971, or whether the 55 thousand fatalities had a more than proportionate impact on the total response. Would legislators have voted approximately $480 million for highway safety if society's perspective on traffic accidents were dominated by a few million dented fenders, more or less? It seems unlikely. More probably, our outlook (and our response) is determined by highway fatalities and serious personal injuries.

The same is undoubtedly the case with respect to fire. In fact, not only is the social response in the case of the threat of fire likely to be more than proportionately influenced by fires that result in death, but the response is probably influenced considerably by the relatively unlikely threat of conflagration.

Indeed, one might speculate that the significant difference in the orders of magnitude of society's expenditures for highway safety and fire protection is explained in some part by the fact that there is no traffic-accident counterpart to conflagration. Alternatively, one might speculate that the level of the social response has some impact on the outcome—society spends much more on fire protection and the social losses due to fire are considerably less.[10]

The question of what society is responding to when it allocates resources to highway safety and fire protection is critical in the current context because the answer to the question suggests the proportion of total expenditures that should be assigned to alcohol abuse. In the case of traffic accidents, for example, the proportion of all accidents attributable to alcohol abuse was 6.8 percent. But the proportion of accidents attributable to alcohol abuse was higher for more serious accidents. In fact, the proportion attributable to alcohol abuse was 11.4 percent for accidents resulting in personal injury and 40.8 percent for fatal accidents.[11] If the social response is proportional to the number of accidents, then 6.8 percent of highway safety expenditures might appropriately be assigned to alcohol abuse. On the other hand, if the social response is more than proportionately determined by extreme cases such as fatal accidents, then a considerably higher proportion should be assigned to alcohol abuse.

In fact, it seems reasonable to assume that the social response is proportional to the social loss. The reason that the social response to extreme cases appears more than proportionate is that more extreme cases involve a higher social loss. Society values a human life more highly than an automobile, so society responds to the loss of life more than to property damage. Hence, an appropriate allocation of highway safety expenditures to alcohol abuse would seem to be the proportion of the social loss occasioned by traffic accidents that is attributable to alcohol abuse.

The proportion of the estimated economic cost of traffic accidents attributed to alcohol abuse is a conservative estimate of the proportion of the social loss occasioned by traffic accidents attributable to alcohol abuse. It will be recalled that the economic cost understates the real social loss, because certain losses are less tangible and do not lend themselves to quantification or precise estimation. Such real losses as lost household production, family anguish, pain and suffering, anxiety, and the like are excluded from our estimate of the economic cost of traffic accidents. Since the excluded social losses are more likely to occur in connection with the more serious accidents, a higher proportion of which are attributable to alcohol abuse, the proportion of the estimated economic cost attributed to alcohol abuse is a conservative estimate of the proportion of real social loss sustained because of it.

Since the proportion of the estimated economic cost of motor vehicle accidents attributed to alcohol abuse was 15.5 percent,[12] it seems appropriate to attribute some $74 million of highway safety expenditures as a social response to alcohol abuse.

The same logic would seem to apply in the context of fire. Given that the proportion of the estimated economic cost of fire attributed to alcohol abuse was 11.4 percent,[13] it seems appropriate to attribute some $262 million of fire protection expenditures as a social response to alcohol abuse.

ALCOHOL AND THE CRIMINAL JUSTICE SYSTEM

Just as the social welfare system is designed to respond to particularly adverse economic circumstances, the criminal justice system is designed to respond to extreme antisocial behavior. The concern of this section is the cost of alcohol abuse implicit in the components of the criminal justice system—the police, the courts, and correctional institutions. This is a valid concern, since alcohol abuse often results in antisocial behavior and some part of the overall social response represented by the criminal justice system must be viewed as a response to antisocial behavior associated with alcohol abuse. In 1971, some $10.4 billion was expended within the criminal justice system.[14] What part of that sum involved crimes that were associated with alcohol abuse?

A reasonably straightforward approach to answering this question would be to reflect on the activities of the police, the courts, and correctional institutions to determine what proportion of the total activity of each was involved with coping with crime and antisocial behavior that was associated with alcohol. Useful data are provided by the President's Commission on Law Enforcement and Administration of Justice, which undertook an analysis of the FBI Index crimes for 1965 and computed the cost of each index crime to the several components of the criminal justice system. Their estimates are outlined in table 7—4. We have used the commission's data to derive estimates of the cost to the criminal justice system in 1971 of several types of crime.

Our estimates are based on a number of assumptions that should be made explicit. First, we have assumed that the commission's estimates for 1965 are valid. Second, we have assumed that the proportionate costs per type of crime for the seven offenses they included were the same in 1971 as they were in 1965. This assumption seems reasonable given that the two years were only six years apart and that an analysis of arrests, reported by the FBI in *Uniform Crime Reports for the United States*, indicates that the proportions of arrests by type of crime were similar for the two years.

TABLE 7–4. Estimated Cost of the Criminal Justice System in 1965, by Type of Crime (in millions)

Type of Crime	Cost of			Total, Criminal Justice System
	Police	Courts	Corrections	
Index crimes:				
Homicide	$ 4.2	$ 3.8	$ 34.0	$ 41.9
Forcible rape	8.2	4.0	8.8	21.0
Robbery	61.6	23.5	61.7	146.8
Aggravated assault	101.9	22.6	64.2	188.7
Burglary	588.8	98.1	130.9	817.8
Larceny over $50	382.5	45.3	75.5	503.3
Auto theft	252.9	83.0	41.5	377.5
Total	$1,400.1	$280.3	$ 416.6	$2,097.0
Non-Index crimes and other activities	1,391.9	467.7	616.4	2,476.0
Grand total	$2,792.0	$748.0	$1,033.0	$4,573.0

Source: Derived from data in U.S. President's Commission on Law Enforcement and Administration of Justice, *The Challenge of Crime in a Free Society* (New York: E. P. Dutton and Co., 1968).

Third, in order to estimate costs for certain non-Index crimes of particular concern, we have assumed that their cost per crime was the same as the cost per crime of certain similar Index crimes. Specifically, we have assumed that the cost per arrest for assaults generally is equal to the cost per arrest for aggravated assaults; and that the cost per arrest for other sex offenses is equal to the cost per arrest for forcible rape.

Finally, in order to include the cost of certain offenses that are clearly alcohol-related, we have assumed the cost per arrest for the offenses of driving under the influence and drunkenness to be $60. This estimate is based on fairly reliable, albeit limited, data. Thus, for example, in a fairly comprehensive time and motion study completed in Phoenix in 1971, the average cost incurred by the police and courts in apprehension and hearings per typical public inebriate case was $22.50.[15] Incarceration costs averaged just over $6 per day in 1971, and an average jail sentence of six days seems a reasonable estimate for these offenses.[16] These estimates are outlined in column 2 of table 7–5 and provide a basis for estimating the cost to the criminal justice system of coping with offenses associated with alcohol.

TABLE 7–5. Estimated Cost of Alcohol-Related Crime to the Criminal Justice System in 1971

Offense	Number of Arrests	Criminal Justice System Costs (in millions)	Proportion of Offenses Associated with Alcohol	Estimated Cost of Offenses Associated with Alcohol (in millions)
Homicide	20,780	$ 95.7	67%	$ 64.1
Forcible rape	20,120	47.8	24	11.5
Other sex offenses	61,300	145.6	29	42.2
Robbery	113,360	334.9		
Aggravated assault	172,490	430.6	30	129.2
Other assaults	377,000	941.1	30	282.3
Burglary	395,500	1866.0		
Larceny	828,200	1148.3		
Auto theft	157,100	861.2		
Forgery, fraud, etc.*	289,300			
Vice†	958,900			
Driving under the influence	644,100	38.6	100	38.6
Drunkenness	1,804,900	108.3	100	108.3
Disorderly conduct	750,000			
Vagrancy	91,600			
Vandalism	155,300			
All other offenses	1,799,800			
Total	8,639,750			$676.2
Police protection and other nonarrest activities				
Grand total		$10,434.0		$676.2

*Includes forgery, counterfeiting, fraud, embezzlement, and the buying, receiving, or possession of stolen property.

†Includes prostitution and commercialized vice, narcotics, and gambling and liquor law violations.

Sources: Arrest data are from U.S. Department of Justice, Federal Bureau of Investigation, Uniform Crime Reports for the United States–1971 (Washington, D.C.: U.S. Government Printing Office, 1972), table 23, p. 115.

Aggregate criminal justice system costs for 1971 are from U.S. Bureau of the Census, Statistical Abstract of the United States: 1973 (Washington, D.C.: U.S. Government Printing Office, 1973), table 250, p. 155.

Criminal justice system costs by offense were derived from data in table 7–4; see text.

For proportion of offenses associated with alcohol, see text and chapter 6.

Given the cost of each type of offense to the criminal justice system, all that remains is to estimate the proportion of each cost that available evidence indicates might be associated with alcohol. In the case of homicide, forcible rape, other sex offenses, aggravated assault, and other assault, we have estimated the proportion of offenses associated with alcohol on the basis of the empirical evidence cited in chapter 6. In two instances, the proportion of offenses associated with alcohol is 100 percent—driving under the influence and drunkenness are clearly alcohol-associated offenses by definition. Together, these seven offenses represented an estimated cost to the criminal justice system in 1971 of crime associated with alcohol of some $676.2 million. Although this is a significant sum, it represents only approximately 6.5 percent of the cost of the criminal justice system and may understate the extent of the economic cost of the criminal justice system that represents a social response to alcohol abuse.

In the case of several other crimes the proportion of offenses associated with alcohol is likely to be positive and significant—disorderly conduct, vagrancy, and vandalism, for example, are often associated with alcohol—but there is no empirical evidence upon which to base a specific estimate of the proportion. Moreover, it is quite likely that a considerable proportion of general police protection that is not related to the apprehension of criminals represents a social response to alcohol abuse. Expenditures on police protection clearly represent a social response to the threat of violence. Given the disproportionate association between violent crimes and alcohol, it seems quite reasonable to argue that perhaps an equally disproportionate part of the expenditures for police protection represents a social response to alcohol abuse. In effect, as in the case of expenditures for fire protection and highway safety, it would seem that the social response is proportional to the perception of real social cost. If we knew the proportion of the real social cost of crime or even of the economic cost of crime that might be attributable to alcohol abuse, we would have a basis for estimating that part of the cost of police protection that represents a social response to alcohol abuse.

Whatever the validity of the theoretical argument, however, given the nature of the data and the lack of knowledge concerning the role of alcohol in crime, we shall have to settle for the estimate of $676.2 million as the economic cost to the criminal justice system of coping with crimes that are associated with alcohol.

THE ECONOMIC COST OF SOCIAL RESPONSES TO ALCOHOL ABUSE

We have now come full circle. In the five previous chapters, we concentrated on the economic costs that derive from alcohol abuse. In this chapter, we have been concerned with the social responses to alcohol abuse. There is, in fact, a certain social symmetry to the cost and the response. Alcohol abuse adversely affects productivity, its economic cost manifested in lost production and lower earnings. But the social system is designed to provide a mechanism for some part of the burden of that cost to be shared. That mechanism, the social welfare system, involves additional economic costs.

As alcoholism is increasingly viewed as a disease, and the real costs of the disease are manifested as health care costs, society responds with specific programs designed to treat, prevent, and research the disease. These programs involve expenditures on health care for alcohol abusers, and in large part represent another social mechanism for transferring part of the burden of alcohol abuse. But in order to provide for such a transfer, society incurs additional economic costs within the alcohol programs.

Alcohol abuse increases the risk and intensifies the consequences of motor vehicle accidents and fires. Economic costs are manifested in the form of premature death, personal injuries, and property damage. Society responds to the real social costs of motor vehicle accidents and fires by expending considerable sums on highway safety and fire protection. This is a rational response, but it involves a real economic cost.

Finally, alcohol abuse results in antisocial behavior. Alcohol is associated with crime, especially violent crime. But the social system includes a criminal justice mechanism to cope with antisocial behavior, and society responds to increased violence by increasing the magnitude, and hence the economic cost, of the criminal justice system.

Thus, to the extent that alcohol abuse exists, there will be a social response. That social response will involve economic costs, and they must be included in any estimate of the total economic cost of alcohol abuse. In 1971, the economic cost of the social responses to alcohol abuse, as summarized in table 7–6, amounted to some $1.9 billion. If alcohol abuse had not existed in 1971, society would have been able to divert the resources represented by this $1.9 billion to alternative uses.

TABLE 7–6. Estimated Economic
Cost in 1971 of Social Responses to
Alcohol Abuse

Response	Cost (in millions)
Social welfare system	$ 789.6
Alcohol programs	57.0
Highway safety	74.0
Fire protection	262.0
Criminal justice system	676.2
Total	$1,858.8

Still, one should not assume that society could have saved $1.9 billion by not responding to alcohol abuse in 1971. At any point in time, the total economic cost of alcohol abuse may well be lower as a consequence of the social responses to it. To the extent that these social responses succeed in their intended purpose, the economic costs of alcohol abuse in other contexts will be lower. In effect, the cost of social responses to alcohol abuse in 1971 may well have represented a social bargain, but they were part of the total economic cost of alcohol abuse and must be included therein.

NOTES

1. A. M. Skolnik and S. R. Dales, "Social Welfare Expenditures, 1971–72," *Social Security Bulletin*, vol. 35 (December 1972), pp. 3–17.

2. That is, real goods and services are transferred, and hence real income *in kind* is transferred.

3. See table 2–1.

4. Total expenditures were actually more, but we have excluded expenditures on medical services, since medical care costs under social welfare programs were implicitly included in the estimated cost of health care services (see chapter 3).

5. Social services and administrative expenses were reported separately for the public assistance program, and administrative expenses amounted to 6.4 percent of total expenditures. The social services and administrative expenses of the other four programs were estimated at 6.4 percent of total expenditures. This amounts to assuming that administrative expenses are the same for the other programs as they are for public assistance, and that no real cost is incurred for social services. This will obviously tend to understate the real cost and, hence, yield a conservative estimate.

6. A. G. Holtmann, Jr., "The Value of Human Resources and Alcoholism," (unpublished Ph.D. dissertation, Washington University, St. Louis, 1963), p. 53. Holtmann's estimate was based on several studies reported in B. Chodorkoff, H. Krystal, J. Nunn, and R. Wittenberg, "Employment Characteristics of Hospitalized Alcoholics," *Quarterly Journal of Studies on Alcohol*, vol. 22 (1961), pp. 106–10.

7. In effect, the appropriate calculation is:

$$EU = \dot{u}L - \dot{n}L, \text{ with } \dot{n}L = \dot{u}L\,[1 - k(A/L)]\,/(N/L),$$

where: EU = excess unemployment
$\dot{u}$ = unemployment rate of the entire labor force
$\dot{n}$ = unemployment rate of nonabusers
$\dot{a}$ = unemployment rate of abusers
k = relative unemployment rate of abusers $(k = \dot{a}/\dot{u})$
A = abusers in the labor force
N = nonabusers in the labor force
L = labor force $(L = A + N)$

8. The extent to which the social response to alcohol abuse has been increasing in recent years is perhaps reflected in the fact that the NIAAA budget for fiscal 1975 was $146 million.

9. U.S. Department of Transportation, National Highway Traffic Safety Administration, *Safety '71: A Report on Activities under the National Traffic and Motor Vehicle Safety Act*, vol. 2 (Washington, D.C.: U.S. Government Printing Office, 1972), appendix C, table 3, p. 7; and U.S. Bureau of the Census, *Statistical Abstract of the United States: 1973* (Washington, D.C.: U.S. Government Printing Office, 1973), table 668, p. 419.

10. The two alternatives, of course, are not mutually exclusive.

11. See table 4–10.

12. The estimated economic cost of motor vehicle accidents was $30.5 billion; the estimated cost attributed to alcohol abuse was $4.7 billion. See table 4–11.

13. The estimated economic cost of fire was $3.3 billion; the estimated cost attributed to alcohol abuse was $377.7 million. See table 5–6.

14. U.S. Bureau of the Census, *Statistical Abstract of the United States: 1973*, table 250, p. 155.

15. D. M. Overcash, [Special Report] for City of Phoenix, Advisory Committee on Drug Abuse Control, 1971.

16. San Francisco Committee on Crime, "Report on Non-Victim Crime in San Francisco" (June 1971), for example, reports an average jail sentence for drunkenness offenders to be 27.5 days. Of course there is no national standard for length of jail sentence, and not all arrests result in jail sentences. A 6-day average sentence is somewhat arbitrary, but it seems reasonable and perhaps conservative.

CHAPTER EIGHT

SUMMARY AND CONCLUSIONS

THE GENERAL PROBLEM

We set out to estimate the economic cost of alcohol abuse and alcoholism. Conceptually, the problem was straightforward. The alcohol literature and a little analysis allowed us to identify the major contexts within which alcohol abuse might be expected to result in opportunity costs to society. Unfortunately, although the major sources of economic cost were easily enough delineated, previous research within these areas had not, in general, succeeded in isolating the net effect that might be attributed to alcohol abuse alone.

Hence, although the conceptual aspect of the problem was straightforward, the empirical aspect of the problem was not. Part of the problem that we had to cope with was simply a lack of knowledge. Much is known about alcohol and the consequences of its abuse, but much more scientific work remains to be done before any claim can be made concerning the effects of alcohol abuse on health and behavior and the subsequent impact such effects have upon the individual and upon society.

The other part of the empirical problem was a lack of data. In particular, there is a lack of data specific to alcohol abuse and the consequences of alcohol abuse. Indeed, there is a surprising lack of agreement among experts in the field as to just how alcoholism or alcohol abuse should be defined. Earlier work in the field tended to be concerned with "alcoholism," but the exact meaning of the term often varied from expert to expert. In fact, the term "alcohol abuse" seems to have evolved in part because of the lack of agreement over the earlier term. In recent years, much of the more useful research has tended to concentrate rather on so-called "problems" associated with drinking practices.

THE PREVALENCE ISSUE

A related issue in the alcohol field concerns the question of the prevalence of alcohol abuse. The prevailing estimate of the number of alcohol abusers and alcoholics is some 9 million. Actually, when one tries to document this estimate, one concludes that it is nothing more than oral tradition. Apparently, someone once said that there were 9 million alcoholics, he was quoted, the quotation was cited, the citation was referenced, and so forth. Indeed, when one reflects on the lack of agreement as to the definition of alcohol abuse, one can understand the prevalence dilemma. If there is no general agreement as to what alcoholism *is*, there is no basis for determining how many have it.

Actually, in the context of estimating the economic cost of alcohol abuse, this is not the problem that it might at first seem. Since our concern is with measuring the opportunity costs of alcohol abuse and its consequences in several contexts, the fact that what constitutes alcohol abuse may vary across the several contexts is not a problem. Rather, what we need to know in each instance is the extent of alcohol abuse as it is relevant in that context. Thus, "alcohol abuse" is a generic term that can be taken to cover the spectrum of contexts within which the abuse of alcohol in some form is manifested in adverse consequences that result in economic costs to society. Concentration on a single prevalence rate is in fact counterproductive and may well have caused previous attempts to estimate the economic cost of alcohol abuse to go astray.

Thus, for example, is occasional heavy drinking alcohol abuse? The answer would seem to depend on the consequences. If a person is an occasional heavy drinker who confines his drinking to nonwork periods, such that it has no adverse impact on his productivity, then in the context of lost production it is not abuse. On the other hand, if the occasional heavy drinker chooses to operate a motor vehicle while under the influence of alcohol, then his drinking can have rather dramatic adverse consequences, and would most certainly be classified, in that context, as alcohol abuse. What constitutes alcohol abuse, then, may vary with the circumstances and the consequences, and the prevalence rates will necessarily vary as well.

THE COSTS OF LOST PRODUCTION

Lost production is synonomous with foregone output or opportunity cost and is perhaps the most obvious economic cost conceptually. Alcohol abuse can unfavorably affect productivity in a number of ways. It may lead to unemployment, absenteeism, and tardiness. Moreover, the worker with alcohol problems is often less productive on the job. In addition, he may have an adverse impact on fellow workers or complementary factors of production, such as capital equipment.

The works of Cahalan and his colleagues on American drinking practices seemingly constitute a breakthrough in determining who might be classified as an abuser for purposes of measuring the economic cost of alcohol abuse in the context of lost production. They have identified a group of drinkers that apparently have difficulty functioning in society. If these drinkers are having difficulty in their general social roles, problems in their work roles are to be expected. The degree of their work problems could be measured by comparing their incomes with those of otherwise similar persons who are not drinkers having such problems.

Using data provided by the Social Research Group of the School of Public Health, University of California at Berkeley, we were able to estimate the difference in income between households that included a male abuser and households that did not. After making an adjustment to allow for differences in earnings between abusers and nonabusers that would be due to sociocultural/economic factors such as age, education, family structure, and the like, we estimated that households with an alcohol-abusing male between the ages of 21 and 59 present had lower earnings in the aggregate on the order of $11.4 billion. This was the estimated economic cost in 1971 of lost production due to alcohol abuse.

Some reasonable estimates were available of the cost to the army in 1971 of lost production due to alcohol abuse. We used these estimates to estimate the economic cost of lost production to the entire military in 1971 at some $361 million.

We also estimated the present value in 1971 of future production lost because of premature death in 1971 due to alcohol abuse. There is a considerable literature on the relationship between alcohol and mortality. Indeed, there are almost too many estimates of the relative mortality rate of alcohol abusers—such estimates range, in the literature, from just over 1.0 to well in excess of 3.0. The problem, of course, lies in part in how the population at risk is defined. In fact, excess mortality is apparently concentrated among those who are frequent heavy drinkers. Although specific to the some 5 percent of the population who are frequent heavy drinkers, excess mortality due to alcohol abuse is significant and accounted for something on the order of 6.5 to 7 percent of all deaths in 1971 among males in the productive years between 20 and 64. We have estimated the present value in 1971 of their lost future production to be some $3.1 billion.

Hence, we were able to estimate lost market production among males in the civilian labor force, aged 21–59; lost production among military personnel; and the present value in 1971 of lost future market production among males aged 20–64 who died prematurely in 1971. Because of insufficient data and lack of knowledge, we were not able to estimate lost market production among males under 21 and over 59; lost market production of women; the present value in 1971 of lost future production among those who died prematurely in 1971 who were not males aged 20–64; and, perhaps most significantly, lost nonmarket production.

On balance, our estimate of the economic cost of lost production due to alcohol abuse is both conservative and incomplete. In sum, we have estimated the cost of lost production at some $14.9 billion, which represents a lower limit to the economic cost of lost production due to alcohol abuse.

HEALTH CARE COSTS

Economic cost is manifested in ways other than lost production. It is necessary to produce certain goods and services to cope with the consequences of alcohol abuse; hence, society must forego the alternative goods and services that could have been produced if alcohol abuse had not generated such consequences. The most obvious and perhaps most significant example of this kind of cost involves the extra health care that must be produced to treat the disease of alcoholism and the diseases exacerbated by alcohol abuse.

The available cause-specific excess mortality data certainly suggest that alcohol abuse affects health care costs across a rather broad spectrum of diseases. Excess mortality is particularly high for alcoholism and cirrhosis of the liver, the diseases usually associated with alcohol abuse. But significant excess mortality rates also obtain for several other causes, including heart disease, certain cancers, pneumonia, and stomach and duodenal ulcer. Given the pattern of excess mortality, one would expect considerable excess morbidity as well. Excess morbidity would be expected to result in economic cost in the form of extra health care costs.

Total national health expenditures in 1971 amounted to over $80 billion, almost $70 billion of which represented expenditures by and for the adult population. The question of concern is what part of that total represented extra health care costs due to alcohol abuse.

Certain estimates were available in direct or indirect form in the literature. The available literature suggests a rather significant excess utilization of health care services by alcohol abusers and alcoholics, particularly of hospital services. Unfortunately, the literature did not provide much evidence on nonhospital health care services. In addition, the NIAAA provided us with hospitalization data for some 17,000 Alcohol Treatment Center patients. In part because available data provided no real basis for estimating the cost of most nonhospital services, and in part because the estimates of extra hospital care costs implied by available data were so significant, a special survey was undertaken to provide some independent information on the proportionate use of health care services by alcohol abusers and alcoholics.

The special survey was limited, given time and budget constraints, and was not intended to be exhaustive or definitive. It did, however, serve two intended purposes. It provided a check of sorts on the relative orders of magnitude of the estimates previously available; and it covered a broader spectrum of health care services utilization and consequently allowed us to estimate the extra cost due to alcohol abuse for more specific types of health services.

In effect, information was marshalled from three separate sources in order to estimate the cost of health care due to alcohol abuse. The confidence one might have in any estimate derived from any one of the sources might not be particularly high; but a comparison of the relative orders of magnitude of the separate estimates based on each of the three sources suggests a certain credibility in the aggregate. The extent to which the three sources provide estimates which tend to reenforce each other certainly raises the level of confidence in the final estimate.

The information marshalled to estimate the cost of health care due to alcohol abuse also provides a rough check on the prevalence of alcohol abuse. Thus, for example, the experts estimated that approximately 25 percent of all general-hospital days were accounted for by alcohol abusers. Now, since we know that there were some 242 million patient-days in general hospitals in 1971, the implication is that alcohol abusers used 60.5 million of these days. The experts also estimated that alcohol abusers used 8.6 days per abuser per year. Hence, the implied number of alcohol abusers is just over 7 million.

We have estimated national health care expenditures due to alcohol abuse and alcoholism in 1971 to have been between $6 and $11.7 billion. Our best single estimate of the economic cost of health services due to alcohol abuse and alcoholism is $8.3 billion, somewhat below the midpoint of the range.

Excess mortality due to alcohol abuse was estimated to account for almost 7 percent of all male deaths in 1971. Excess morbidity due to alcohol abuse has been estimated to have accounted for 10.2 percent of all health care expenditures in that year. The two estimates certainly seem consistent and reasonable in relation to each other.

MOTOR VEHICLE ACCIDENTS

It has been well documented that alcohol can have an adverse effect on drivers. In fact, studies indicate that vision, coordination, judgment, and concentration begin to deteriorate at rather low levels of blood alcohol content. Hence, to the extent that alcohol has a deleterious effect on task performance among those who drive under its influence, it tends to increase the risk of motor vehicle accidents and to intensify the consequences of accidents that do occur. Thus, alcohol abuse in the context of motor vehicle accidents involves driving under the influence and does account for a significant part of the economic cost of motor vehicle accidents that is manifested in loss of life, personal injuries, and property damage.

The selection of a .05 percent blood alcohol content as indicative of alcohol abuse in the context of motor vehicle accidents has considerable empirical justification. An extensive review of the literature suggested that an immediate blood alcohol content of .05 percent or higher at the time of a motor vehicle accident can be taken as a measure of alcohol abuse.

The availability of studies that included a population-at-risk control group provided us with a basis for estimating the proportion of accidents that might be attributable to alcohol abuse. After adjusting for the obvious fact that alcohol abusers would have motor vehicle accidents even if they were not abusers, we estimated that abusers are involved in an extra 6.8 percent of all accidents. In addition, the proportion of accidents attributable to alcohol abuse tends to increase dramatically with the seriousness of the accident.

The National Highway Traffic Safety Administration of the United States Department of Transportation completed a comprehensive study of motor vehicle accidents in 1971 and estimated the economic cost of such accidents to be some $46 billion. Even when adjusted to exclude less tangible items and to incorporate a more conservative discount rate, the cost was on the order of $30 billion. We have estimated the economic cost in 1971 of motor vehicle accidents attributable to alcohol abuse at some $4.7 billion.

Included in the economic cost of motor vehicle accidents attributed to alcohol abuse are some $239 million in medical care costs and $3.0 billion in lost production costs, including $2.1 billion as the present value in 1971 of future production lost because of premature death. Since separate estimates of lost production and medical care costs due to alcohol abuse were made for the economy as a whole, there is the distinct possibility of some double counting. However, the definition of alcohol abuse in the context of motor vehicle accidents was based on the immediate blood alcohol content at the time of the accident rather than on the chronic drinking history or drinking problems of the individuals involved. Clearly, not all accidents that occur after drinking involve alcoholics or alcohol abusers in the more traditional sense of those terms. The costs associated with occasional drinking are included in the motor vehicle context, but not in the lost production or medical care contexts. Thus, although some double counting has occurred, it is not very significant.

In fact, it was determined that only some $41.3 million was double counted in the case of lost future production due to premature death. This amounts to less than 2 percent of the lost future production included in the economic cost of motor vehicle accidents due to alcohol abuse. This amount should, of course, be subtracted from the total estimated economic cost of alcohol abuse. A similar adjustment can be made to allow for double counting in the cases of other lost production and medical care costs.

FIRE

Fires are similar to motor vehicle accidents in many respects. The economic costs of fire are similar in kind to those of other types of accidents, involving adverse consequences manifested as loss of life, personal injuries, and property damage. Our concern was not with the economic cost of fire per se, but rather with that part of this cost that might reasonably be attributed to alcohol abuse. In effect, we sought answers to the same questions in the context of fire that we asked in the context of motor vehicle accidents. Conceptually, the problem is the same. Unfortunately, however, we found the whole area of fire to be surprisingly underresearched.

Alcohol may be related to fire and the consequences of fire in two ways. On the one hand, alcohol abuse may be a contributing cause of fire in the first place. On the other hand, given a fire—whatever its cause—alcohol may well serve to intensify its consequences, because judgment and physical skills are adversely affected even at low levels of blood alcohol content.

There is limited but consistent evidence that alcohol is a major contributor in impeding escape and therefore a cause of fire fatalities. There is also extremely limited evidence that a significant proportion of burn injuries can be attributed to alcohol abuse. Finally, although there is no empirical evidence of the extent to which alcohol can be linked causally to fires in the aggregate, there is some reasonable evidence of a relationship between alcohol and smoking as the primary cause of ignition.

We have estimated the economic cost of fire in 1971 to be some $3.3 billion. We have also generated a tentative estimate of the economic cost of fire due to alcohol abuse of some $378 million. We consider the estimate tentative because of the limited knowledge and the limited data. It does seem to us more appropriate to generate a tentative estimate, identified as such, than to ignore the economic cost of fire that might be due to alcohol abuse.

Included in the economic cost of fire due to alcohol abuse is some $27.9 million in medical care costs and $189 million in lost production, $185 million of which represents the present value in 1971 of lost future production due to premature death. Since separate estimates of lost production and medical care costs due to alcohol abuse were made in the aggregate, an adjustment is in order to take account of potential double counting.

The assignment of fire fatalities to alcohol abuse was based on alcohol impeding escape rather than on the chronic drinking history or drinking problems of the individuals who died. Clearly, not all fire casualties that occur after drinking involve alcoholics or alcohol abusers in the more traditional sense. The costs associated with occasional drinking are included in the fire context, but not in the lost production or medical care contexts. Property damage costs, of course, have not been counted elsewhere.

Still, double counting is considerably more significant in the case of fire than in the case of motor vehicle accidents. In fact, it was determined that some $91.8 million was double-counted in the case of lost future production due to premature death. This amounts to almost 50 percent of the lost future production included in the estimated economic cost of fire due to alcohol abuse. This double-counted amount should certainly be subtracted from the total estimated economic cost of alcohol abuse. A similar adjustment should be made to allow for double counting in the cases of other lost production and medical care costs.

What conclusion can be drawn from the apparent extent of double counting? On the one hand, of course, there is the distinct possibility that our estimates of the proportion of fire fatalities assignable to alcohol abuse were too conservative. We did take the lowest reported proportion of fatalities in which alcohol served to impede escape. Proportions twice as high have been reported. On the other hand, there is the distinct possibility that occasional drinkers, even occasional heavy drinkers, do not run the same risk in the case of fire that they do in the case of motor vehicle accidents. Given the nature of the probabilities involved, this seems to us quite plausible.

CRIME

In recent years, there has been increased concern about and awareness of the problem of alcohol abuse in the context of crime, particularly with respect to serious offenders, but available evidence and knowledge are insufficient to ascertain the extent to which alcohol abuse results in crime.

There is increasing circumstantial evidence linking alcohol to certain kinds of violent crime. An extensive review of available research has revealed a significant relationship in the cases of criminal homicide, assault, and forcible rape and other sex offenses. However, there is a need for more precise documentation of the association between alcohol and specific crimes. Controlled studies are rare.

Existing studies are deficient in that they lack baseline data against which to compare cases in which alcohol is involved in violent crimes.

On balance, although the empirical evidence must be interpreted with some care, it is certainly indicative of a significant relationship between alcohol and crime. In the case of homocide, for example, the presence of alcohol was determined in an exceedingly significant proportion of cases studied. In at least one study that measured blood alcohol content, a level that would generally be considered to constitute alcohol abuse was found in some 67 percent of offenders. The empirical evidence suggests that aggravated assault is more likely to occur in an environment in which alcohol is disproportionately present. In separate studies of assault, the presence of alcohol was determined for between 24 and 37 percent of all offenders. The same relationship is found for forcible rape crimes and other sex offenses. In the most extensive research yet done on sex crimes, a study at the Kinsey Institute, sex offenders were determined to have been drunk in 21 percent of all cases.

Still, the state of knowledge is inadequate to assess the extent to which the association between alcohol and crime is indicative of a contributing, let alone causal, role. We know that alcohol and crime are related; but does alcohol cause crime? Is some part of the cost of crime due to alcohol abuse? Probably, but we have no real basis for assigning a specific part of the cost of crime to alcohol abuse. We can generate an estimate of that part of the cost of crime that is associated with alcohol, but not an estimate of that part of the cost that is due to alcohol abuse.

We have estimated the economic cost of violent crime in 1971 to be on the order of $2.3 billion. Since there is no empirical basis for estimating the portion of this cost due to alcohol abuse, we have settled for an estimate of the cost of crime that is *associated* with alcohol of some $1.5 billion.

SOCIAL RESPONSES TO ALCOHOL ABUSE

There is a certain social symmetry to the economic cost of alcohol abuse and the social response to that cost. Alcohol abuse adversely affects productivity and the economic cost is manifested in lost production and lower earnings. But the social system includes a social welfare system designed to transfer some of the burden of that cost. That system, in turn, carries its own, additional economic cost.

As alcoholism is increasingly viewed as a disease, and the real costs are manifested as health care costs, society responds with specific programs to treat, prevent, and research the disease. These programs involve expenditures on health care for alcohol abusers, and in large part represent still another social mechanism for transferring part of the burden of alcohol abuse. But in order to effect such a transfer, society incurs additional economic costs within these programs.

Alcohol abuse increases the risk and intensifies the consequences of motor vehicle accidents and fires. Economic costs are manifested in loss of life, personal injuries, and property damage. Society responds to these real social costs by expending considerable sums on highway safety and fire protection. The response is quite rational, but it involves a real economic cost.

Finally, alcohol abuse results in antisocial behavior. Alcohol is associated with crime, especially violent crime. The social system includes a criminal justice component to cope with antisocial behavior, and society responds to increased violence by increasing the magnitude, and hence the economic cost, of the criminal justice system.

To the extent that alcohol abuse occurs, there will be a social response to alcohol abuse. The social response will involve economic costs, and they have to be included in the estimate of the total economic cost of alcohol abuse.

We have estimated that the economic cost of social responses to alcohol abuse in 1971 was on the order of $1.9 billion. If alcohol abuse did not exist, society could have diverted the resources represented by this $1.9 billion to alternative uses. Of course, given that alcohol abuse did exist, one should not assume that society could have saved $1.9 billion by not responding to it. In fact, the total economic cost of alcohol abuse may well have been lower as a consequence of the social responses to it. Clearly, to the extent that the social responses served their intended purpose, the economic cost of such responses may well have represented a social bargain.

THE ECONOMIC COST OF ALCOHOL ABUSE AND ITS IMPLICATIONS FOR SOCIAL POLICY

Our summary of the estimated economic cost due to alcohol abuse and associated with alcohol is presented in table 8–1. We

TABLE 8–1. Estimated Economic Cost of Alcohol Abuse in 1971

Economic Cost		Estimated Cost (in millions)
Economic cost due to alcohol abuse		
Lost production:		
Lost market production in 1971	$11,427.7	
Lost military production in 1971	360.8	
Present value in 1971 of lost future production due to excess mortality in 1971	3,080.7	$14,869.2
Health care costs		8,293.0
Motor vehicle accident losses:		
Total	4,729.0	
Less double-counted items:		
Lost production in 1971	16.4	
Lost future production	41.3	
Health care costs	4.7	
	62.4	4,666.6
Fire losses:		
Total	377.7	
Less double-counted items:		
Lost production in 1971	2.0	
Lost future production	91.8	
Health care costs	13.9	
	107.7	270.0
Social responses:		
Social welfare system	789.6	
Alcohol programs	57.0	
Highway safety	74.0	
Fire protection	262.0	
Criminal justice system	146.9	1,329.5
Total economic cost due to alcohol abuse		$29,428.3
Economic cost associated with alcohol		
Violent crime		1,466.4
Criminal justice system		529.3
Total economic cost associated with alcohol		$ 1,995.7
Total economic cost due to alcohol abuse and associated with alcohol		$31,424.0

have estimated the economic cost due to alcohol abuse to be some $29.4 billion. This amount includes the costs of lost production, health care costs, and the costs of motor vehicle accidents and fire net of double-counted lost production and health care costs resulting from alcohol abuse. Our estimate also includes the economic cost of social responses in the form of the social welfare system, alcohol programs, and expenditures for highway safety and fire protection, and the cost to the criminal justice system of coping with drunkenness and driving under the influence.

In addition, we have estimated the economic cost associated with alcohol to be on the order of $2.0 billion. This amount includes the cost of violent crime associated with alcohol, and the cost to the criminal justice system of coping with such violent crime as is associated with alcohol.

Taken together, the economic cost due to alcohol abuse and associated with alcohol amounted to some $31.4 billion in 1971. Alcohol abuse does indeed have a significant economic impact on society.

The economic cost of lost production is the most significant. In fact, the analysis outlined in chapter 2 has served to provide new insight as to the scope and magnitude of lost production due to alcohol abuse. The income distribution data utilized in our analysis are "new" in the sense that they have not been widely circulated prior to this time. They indeed provide insight as to the difference in earnings and income between abusers and nonabusers.

Of course, the correlation between alcohol abuse and low income has been known for some time, but more often than not the information was dismissed from analytical consideration because other factors known to influence income were obscuring the relationship between alcohol abuse and income. When gross differences in income between abusers and nonabusers were used as an approximation to lost production, there was of necessity considerable uncertainty as to the extent of overstatement, and the estimate was consequently less reliable and of limited usefulness. We have adjusted the gross difference to allow for differences in earnings between abusers and nonabusers that may be due to sociocultural/economic factors such as age, education, family structure, and the like. Hence, our estimate is more likely to represent the net difference due to alcohol abuse and is considerably less uncertain.

Our estimate of the economic cost of lost production is incomplete and conservative. It does not include certain lost market production, and, most notably, it does not include lost production in the nonmarket sector. Thus, it can be taken as a lower limit to the extent of lost production due to alcohol abuse.

The analysis of excess mortality in chapter 2 also provides certain new insight into this rather significant consequence of alcohol abuse. We were rather fortunate to have decided to undertake our analysis at a time when new survey data concerning the relationship between alcohol and mortality were available. In the past, of course, there has been no lack of estimates of the excess mortality rate of alcohol abusers. The key to understanding excess mortality, however, and certainly the key to estimating the present value of lost future production associated with premature death due to alcohol abuse, lies in choosing the appropriate prevalence rate for alcohol abuse. Excess mortality is concentrated among those who are frequent heavy drinkers.

In fact, in this context, a general conclusion that we have drawn is that there is no single prevalence rate for alcohol abuse that will serve in all cases. The prevalence of alcohol abuse depends on the context and the consequences. In the case of lost production, those who drink with high consequences are alcohol abusers. In the case of excess mortality, heavy frequent drinkers are alcohol abusers.

Health care costs due to alcohol abuse are second in significance only to the costs of lost production. Indeed, when we first estimated health care costs on the basis of evidence available in the relevant literature, we were concerned at how high the estimates were. We did not have a high degree of confidence in them. Our degree of confidence in our own estimate of health care costs due to alcohol abuse derives in large part from the fact that several similar estimates of health care costs were generated on the basis of evidence from different, presumably independent sources.

Moreover, a comparison of the excess mortality due to alcohol abuse and the excess morbidity of abusers implied by health care costs tends to reinforce our health care cost estimates. Heavy frequent drinkers are alcohol abusers in the case of excess mortality; they undoubtedly represent the most significant proportion of alcohol abusers in the case of health care costs as well. Excess mortality among frequent heavy drinkers accounts for almost 7 percent of all deaths, while excess morbidity among frequent heavy drinkers *and* other alcohol abusers accounts for approximately 10 percent of all health care costs.

Next in order of significance (i.e., magnitude) is the economic cost of motor vehicle accidents. Our analysis suggests that alcohol abuse in the context of traffic accidents must be defined quite differently than in virtually all other contexts. Occasional rather than chronic alcohol abusers dominate the costs of motor vehicle accidents. In fact, the extent of double counting in the case of traffic accident costs is indicative of the significance of this implication of our analysis. Less than 2 percent of the motor vehicle accident fatalities due to alcohol abuse were accounted for in the excess mortality of frequent heavy drinkers. Alcohol abuse is of paramount concern in the context of highway safety, but if the problem is to be coped with, attention must be directed not at alcohol abuse in the more traditional sense, but rather at alcohol abuse as it is relevant to motor vehicle accidents.

The contrast between traffic accidents and fires in this context is striking. It would appear that fire is particularly hazardous for chronic alcohol abusers. Almost 40 percent of fire fatalities due to alcohol abuse were accounted for in the excess mortality of frequent heavy drinkers.

A significant policy implication can perhaps be drawn from this comparison, especially in light of the contrasting social expenditures on these two problems. In view of the orders of magnitude of the economic costs involved, society spends disproportionately more on fire protection than on highway safety. Alternatively, one could speculate that the social response to fire has succeeded in its intended purpose: i.e., fire costs are considerably lower because of fire protection expenditures. Whatever the case, given the level of social costs incurred in motor vehicle accidents due to alcohol abuse, an increased level of highway safety expenditures directed specifically at alcohol abuse would seem to be a reasonable subject for public policy consideration. The apparent relative success of the speed-limit policy induced by the recent energy shortage would seem to auger well for highway policy directed at alcohol abuse.

Perhaps the most obvious policy implication that can be drawn from our analysis is the need to gather additional information and seek new knowledge. We have noted before that economic analysis alone is not sufficient to determine the cost of alcohol abuse. Economic analysis is only a tool, and its application is limited by what is known about the social and economic behavior of people with alcohol problems. At present, the necessary process of integrating knowledge and data from alcohol research, health sciences research, behavioral science, economics, and other social sciences is just beginning. Indeed, we could argue that although the economic cost of alcohol abuse as estimated seems to indicate the areas of appropriate policy concern, the specific directions of sound social policy would be more sharply delineated by further research into several specific areas.

Thus, we know that lost production due to alcohol abuse is a prime candidate for policy concern. But too little is known about the process of alcohol abuse to know which programs will be most effective in rehabilitating alcohol abusers and in preventing alcohol abuse in the first place. The policy implications of our analysis are that, on the one hand, lost production is a sufficiently significant economic cost of alcohol abuse to warrant public-policy efforts, but that, on the other hand, the level of knowledge is such that considerable effort should be directed toward research that will serve to direct those policy efforts into the channels that have the greatest potential for success.

In the context of health care costs, there is the distinct possibility that a more efficient allocation of health resources could be affected if the decision makers in the health care system were aware of the extent to which their activities are directed toward alcohol abusers and especially toward the diseases exacerbated by alcohol abuse. There is also the clear policy implication that research into the relationship between alcohol abuse and certain diseases is appropriate. Quite apart from the benefits that would accrue to alcohol abusers, such research has the potential for saving resources for alternative uses equivalent to approximately 10 percent of the nation's total health care expenditures that currently must be diverted to cope with the consequence of the excess morbidity of alcohol abusers.

Some might argue that the research into the relationship between motor vehicle accidents and alcohol abuse has not involved national samples and does not warrant generalizations to the nation as a whole. Although this is so, the evidence would appear sufficiently reliable and significant to warrant policy directed at controlling alcohol abuse in the context of motor vehicle accidents. We do not argue against further research into the relationship between alcohol abuse and traffic accidents; rather, we would argue that the potential benefits would be greater in the case of research into how best to reduce driving after drinking.

Fire and crime, as noted, are both surprisingly underresearched. Perhaps the area most in need of research is the role of alcohol in crime. One could hardly argue aginst the policy relevance of research into the extent to which alcohol abuse contributes to violent crime.

We have been constrained in our application of the tool of

economic analysis by the available knowledge and the available data. All of our cost estimates were intentionally biased in a conservative direction. And some of the real costs of alcohol abuse defy quantification. In most instances, then, our estimates are both conservative and incomplete, and they can therefore be taken as lower limits of the economic cost of alcohol abuse. There is a very real sense in which such lower limits or bounded estimates have real operational significance. In some cases, only specific, complete, accurate information will do. In most cases, however, it is useful to know that something is "at least equal to . . ." If one were preparing a laboratory experiment, one might need to know the exact temperature. But if one were trying to decide whether or not to add antifreeze to a car radiator, one would be content with knowing whether the temperature were above or below 32 degrees. Although this seems intuitively obvious to us, there are apparently many who question the value of incomplete information.

There are those, even in positions that involve decision making, who seriously ask the question "Does incomplete information have any value?" To this question, we would answer, yes, definitely. We do not live in a certain world. Individuals and social policy makers must continuously make decisions in the face of uncertainty. It would be a wonderful world indeed if complete information were available each time an important, or even trivial, decision had to be made. But it would also be a world foreign to any who have ever been involved in a decision-making process. In the face of uncertainty, some information is clearly often better than no information, and incomplete information is usually better than no information.

We set out to estimate the economic cost of alcohol abuse and alcoholism. Conceptually, the problem was straightforward. It amounted to finding answers to three questions: Who? What? How much? First, there was the question of just how many individuals are afflicted by alcoholism or alcohol abuse. Second, there was the question of just what impact alcohol abuse has upon the afflicted individual and upon others. Third, there was the issue of measuring or quantifying the real economic costs associated with the actual consequences of alcohol abuse.

Although the problem was conceptually straightforward, empirically it was not. We knew at the outset that the major problem that we would have to contend with was simply a lack of knowledge. Much is known about alcohol and the consequences of its abuse, but much scientific work remains to be done before any claim can be made concerning the effects of alcohol abuse on health and behavior and the subsequent impact such effects have upon the individual and upon society. We were aware of the fact that estimating the economic cost of alcohol abuse would be difficult—that it would require a careful, considered, systematic analysis. We knew also that the end result would be a set of figures that, though hopefully better and more useful than previous estimates, would at best represent a conservative and incomplete estimate of the economic cost of alcohol abuse. Still, we undertook the task because it seemed to be well worth the effort.

Now that we have finished, we are rather pleased with the results of our efforts. We have generated a set of estimates that should have more policy significance than just the shock value of large numbers. It does indeed seem that the task was worth the effort. But, of course, it is not for us to judge. We leave it to the reader to judge the value of our efforts.

INDEX

Index

197